Hiking
COLORADO'S GEOLOGY

D0124318

RALPH LEE HOPKINS
LINDY BIRKEL HOPKINS

THE
MOUNTAINEERS

To all of Colorado's geologists past and present,
in whose footsteps we have followed.

Published by
The Mountaineers
1001 SW Klickitat Way, Suite 201
Seattle, WA 98134

First printing 2000, second printing 2002, third printing 2004

Published simultaneously in Great Britain by Cordee, 3a DeMontfort Street, Leicester, England, LE1 7HD

Manufactured in the United States of America

Managing Editor: Kathleen Cubley
Editor: Kathy Walker
Series cover designer: Watson Graphics
Series book designer: Ani Rucki
Layout by Jennifer LaRock Shontz
Maps by Moore Creative Design
All photographs by Ralph Lee Hopkins

Cover photograph: *Golden light at dawn, Chasm Lake below Longs Peak, Rocky Mountain National Park*
Frontispiece: *Cascades over Colorado's Precambrian basement, Columbine Falls, Rocky Mountain National Park*

Library of Congress Cataloging-in-Publication Data

Hopkins, Ralph Lee.
    Hiking Colorado's geology / Ralph Lee Hopkins and Lindy Birkel
Hopkins. — 1st ed.
        p.   cm.
Includes bibliographical references and index.
    ISBN 0-89886-708-8 (pbk.)
1. Hiking—Colorado—Guidebooks. 2. Geology—Colorado—Guidebooks.
3. Colorado—Guidebooks. I. Hopkins, Lindy Birkel, 1959– II. Title.
    GV199.42.C6 H66 2000
    557.88—dc21
                                                    99-050995

Printed on recycled paper

Contents

PART 3. THE HIGH PLAINS 207
CHAPTER 11. COLORADO'S HIGH PLAINS 208

Glossary 223

Appendices

Index 238

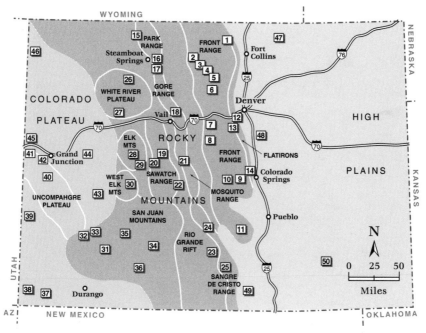

Colorado geology hikes

TABLE 1

Highlights of Colorado's Geologic Time Scale

Major events that shaped the landscape. For chronological order, read from the bottom up.

MILLIONS OF YEARS	GEOLOGIC TIME	GEOLOGIC EVENTS
.008–1.8	Pleistocene	*Ice Age* glaciers sculpt Rocky Mountains into U-shaped valleys, cirques, and jagged peaks.
25–present	Oligocene to Holocene	Several surges of renewed uplift; most recent uplift beginning 10 million years ago elevates the Rocky Mountains, Great Plains, and Colorado Plateau to modern-day heights. Enlivened rivers deepen valleys and carve canyons.
30–present	Oligocene to Holocene	*Rio Grand Rift:* faulting downdrops Arkansas and San Luis Valleys along Sawatch and Sangre de Cristo uplifts.
35–22	Oligocene to Miocene	Major volcanic activity: San Juan and West Elk Mountains, Never Summer Mountains and Rabbit Ears Range, Thirtynine Mile Volcanic Field, Spanish Peaks.
45–35	Eocene	*Rocky Mountain Surface:* erosion strips sedimentary layers from uplifts, exposing basement rocks and flattening mountain tops.
70–45	Cretaceous to Eocene	Laramide Orogeny: major mountain building uplifts Precambrian basement and warps overlying sedimentary layers.
100–70	Cretaceous	*Cretaceous Seaway* floods Colorado depositing marine, shoreline, and stream sediments. Dinosaurs disappear at the end of the Cretaceous.
248–145	Triassic to Jurassic	Ancestral Rockies flattened by erosion; winds pile sand into Wingate, Navajo, and Entrada dune fields; dinosaurs leave footprints and bones in Morrison Formation river channels.
325–248	Pennsylvanian to Permian	*Ancestral Rocky Mountains;* basement uplifts form Uncompahgre and Front Range Highlands, separated by a deep valley called the *Central Colorado Trough;* mountains erode, depositing thick aprons of sediment along the flanks of the uplifts; thick salt accumulates in the Paradox Basin.
544–320	Cambrian to Mississippian	Colorado intermittently below sea level; marine sediments blanket region with layers of sandstone, limestone, and shale.
1,000–544	Precambrian	Erosion bevels ancient mountains into flattened surface that becomes Colorado's *basement rock.*
1,400–1,000	Precambrian	*Granitic* intrusions; Pikes Peak Granite and pegmatite dikes (1,000); Silver Plume Granite of Longs Peak and Mount Evans batholith (1,400).
1,700	Precambrian	*Continental accretion* assembles Colorado; major mountain building forms metamorphic basement rocks (gneiss and schist); intrusion of the Boulder Creek Granite.

GEOLOGIC TIME (in millions of years)				Development of Plants and Animals
Eon	Era	Period	Epoch	
Phanerozoic	CENOZOIC	QUATERNARY	Holocene — 0.008	Humans develop
			Pleistocene — 1.8 —	Ice Ages
		TERTIARY	Pliocene — 5.3 —	"Age of Mammals"
			Miocene — 23.8 —	
			Oligocene — 33.7 —	
			Eocene — 55.5 —	
			Paleocene — 65.0 —	
	MESOZOIC	CRETACEOUS — 145	"Age of Reptiles"	Extinctions of dinosaurs and many other species
		JURASSIC — 213		First flowering plants First birds
		TRIASSIC — 248		Dinosaurs dominant
	PALEOZOIC	PERMIAN — 286	"Age of Amphibians"	Extinctions of trilobites and many other marine animals
		PENNSYLVANIAN — 325		First reptiles Coal swamps
		MISSISSIPPIAN — 360		Amphibians abundant
		DEVONIAN — 410	"Age of Fishes"	First insect fossils Fishes dominant
		SILURIAN — 440		First land plants
		ORDOVICIAN — 505	"Age of Invertebrates"	First fishes Trilobites dominant
		CAMBRIAN — 544		First organisms with shells
Proterozoic	2500	PRECAMBRIAN (Makes up about 85% of the geologic time scale)		First multi-celled organisms
Archean	3800			First one-celled organisms
Hadean	4500			Age of oldest rocks

Geologic time scale

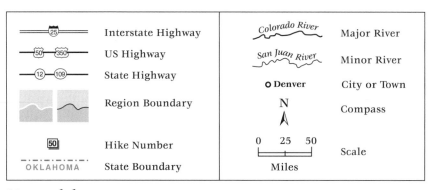

═══25═══	Interstate Highway	*Colorado River*	Major River	
─50── ──350─	US Highway	*San Juan River*	Minor River	
─12── ──109─	State Highway	o **Denver**	City or Town	
	Region Boundary	**N** ⋀	Compass	
50	Hike Number	0 25 50	Scale	
OKLAHOMA	State Boundary	Miles		

Map symbols

Acknowledgments

Without the helpful suggestions and encouragement of friends and colleagues, writing a book such as this one would not be possible, nor would it be as much fun. We only wish we could have included more of the great hikes that were suggested to us.

First, a special thank you to R. Scott Babcock, for suggesting that we tackle this project, and to Jane Forsyth and Deb Olsen, for taking time to help us with our book proposal while looking for rocks and polar bears in Spitsbergen. Our thanks to Bob Martin, John Wray, Jonathan Cooley, Deb Harris, Russ Hopkins, Don Usner, and everyone who offered possible hikes for the book. Our heart-felt thanks to all the geologists who took the time and care to read the manuscript: to Steve Cumella who, for his dedication to Colorado and geology, suffered through not one but two drafts; to Jonathan Cooley for his ideas, distractions, and hospitality in Fruita; to Bob Strong for his love of the trail and dedication to detail; to Bill Hood for generously contributing his time and breadth of knowledge; and to Stan Beus who somehow found the time while marooned on Hawaii. Thanks also to the fine people at Mountaineers Books whose flexibility, patience, and efficiency contributed greatly to our writing experience, and to Kathy Walker for her attention to detail and suggestions for improving the manuscript. And finally, thank you to our colleagues at Lindblad Special Expeditions for the time off from our travels and their understanding about the commitment it took to finish this book.

The authors take full responsibility for any errors or omissions of geologic facts, dates, and other information. We welcome suggestions for improving the next edition.

Preface: How to Use this Book

Hiking Colorado's Geology is an invitation to experience first hand your own journey through the ancient landscapes and tumultuous events that have shaped and "rocked" Colorado throughout its geologic history.

Many of the geology hikes included here are short, easy, and accessible; others are longer, more strenuous, and remote. Although it is not possible to include all of Colorado's many different geologic attractions within one book, we hope the mix of hikes will give you a good overview of how the region took shape and will spark your interest in further geologic exploration.

We have attempted to make this book useful for everyone interested in Colorado's geology, whether novice or experienced. The book's introduction and the chapter introductions provide basic information as background for each hike. For geologic beginners especially, we highly recommend reading these introductions before going ahead with your selected hike. Important geologic terms and concepts are shown in *italics* where they are discussed in the text and are listed in the glossary at the back of the book. The geologic time scale and table 1, Highlights of Colorado's Geologic Time Scale, at the front of the book may also be helpful. We have also included a reading list if you are interested in a more in-depth overview of Colorado's geology and geology in general (see appendix A, Recommended Reading). In addition, appendix B lists key references for each hike, should you want to pursue anything in greater detail than we could provide here.

The hikes described in this book include many of Colorado's most popular trails. Be sure to inquire about local conditions and regulations when planning your trip. Keep in mind that all trails within wilderness areas, national parks, and national monuments are off-limits to bicycles and other forms of mechanized travel. Dogs are also prohibited in many areas. Please do all you can to minimize impact on the land so that those who follow your footsteps will find little or no trace of your visit.

We offer *Hiking Colorado's Geology* with the hopes that it will be a source of enjoyment and discovery for every fan of Colorado's incomparable landscape.

Balanced rock in the Wheeler Geologic Area, San Juan Mountains

Introduction

Colorado is located at the crossroads of three of the continent's most distinctive geologic landscapes. From the sculpted layers of the Colorado Plateau on the west to the open reach of the High Plains on the east, some of the continent's most substantial mountains rise up to form the Colorado Rockies. Although the Rocky Mountains extend from Canada down into New Mexico, Colorado is deservedly called the Rocky Mountain State. All of the Rockies' loftiest peaks, the renowned "fourteeners," stand within its borders, their dominance accentuated by the plain and plateau landscapes that flank them.

But Colorado was not always as we see it today. If you could rewind time nearly 2 billion years and could step into a fast-forward replay of Colorado's geologic history, you would first rise to mountain highs and then stumble in erosion until regaining firm footing on a flat plain, only to rise up and then fall flat again, and again. A tropical sea would then wash overhead, submerging you in warm currents and incubating the planet's first shelled organisms at your feet. Before long, the seas would ebb and you would lift skyward once again, only to stumble down to the flats yet again. Then you would walk angled into the wind, pelted with flying sand off a vast system of dunes restlessly shifting across the region. Later, you would slink under cover in muddy swamps, staying out of sight of predatory dinosaurs. Then, perhaps looking over your shoulder, you would have a moment to bask along a sandy seashore. Before long, mountains would lift you up once more and would again crumble beneath your feet. Molten *lava* would flow around your ankles, and at other times, *volcanic rocks* would spew from mountains, burying you in ash. In the final frames, you would rise to the top of today's Rockies, then cool off as ice formed around you. You would repeatedly freeze and thaw as *glaciers* advanced and retreated over you, carving mountain peaks and contouring them into the shapes that would bring you into the present day.

Exploring the geology of present-day Colorado is like experiencing part of this journey through time. Today's landscape is a collection of fragments that read like a highlight film of the past 2 billion years. This book invites you to explore Colorado from this perspective of how events in the past

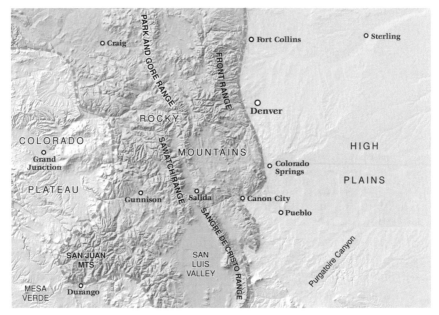

Landforms of Colorado

have culminated in the three dramatically different geologic landscapes of Colorado today.

COLORADO'S GEOLOGIC LANDSCAPES

All of the forces in Colorado's tumultuous past have contributed to modern Colorado. Today, it is a juxtaposition of three different and complex landscapes, and yet, over millions of years, these too will eventually transform. Fortunately, their duration will be much longer than the life of this book. It is therefore safe, for our purposes, to approach the geologic exploration of Colorado by discussing the three definable provinces present today—the Rocky Mountains, the Colorado Plateau, and the High Plains.

COLORADO'S ROCKY MOUNTAINS

Past turmoil defines Colorado's Rockies. For nearly 2 billion years, mountains have repeatedly risen and crumbled here, scattering their remains throughout the region. The modern Rockies are a conglomeration of remnants from these events pushed skyward once again. They are the heart of the Southern Rocky Mountains, a province that extends from the Laramie Mountains in Wyoming south to Santa Fe, New Mexico. In the big picture, the Southern Rocky Mountains are just the southern part of the western U.S. Rocky Mountains which stretch from Canada to New Mexico.

14

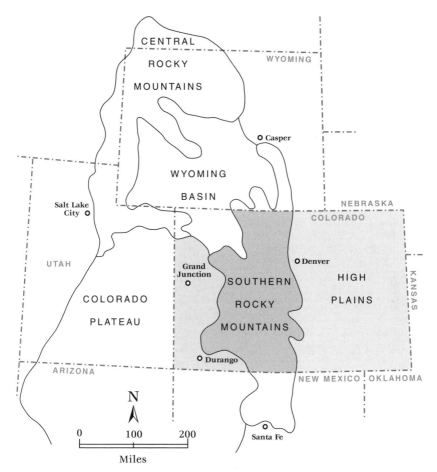

Colorado's geologic provinces

In Wyoming, the Southern Rockies are separated from the Central Rockies by the high desert flatlands of the Wyoming Basin. Within Colorado, the Rockies are the dominant landscape, spanning the state's center from north to south.

THE COLORADO PLATEAU

To the west of the Rockies lies the Colorado Plateau, the land of canyons, mesas, and sculpted rock formations that surrounds the Four Corners region where Colorado, Arizona, New Mexico, and Utah meet. Throughout its history, layers of *sediment* accumulated on the Plateau as climate changes swept the landscape. Despite the upheaval in the Rocky Mountain region immediately to the east, the Plateau was relatively stable. Its layers remain largely stacked in sequence, like a layercake. This scenic

15

Sandstone cliffs at Mesa Verde, Colorado Plateau

landscape is dominated by a labyrinth of canyons cut through these layers by the Colorado River and its tributaries. The region is home to the greatest concentration of national parks and monuments in the United States, including Colorado's Mesa Verde and Black Canyon of the Gunnison National Parks, and Colorado and Dinosaur National Monuments.

THE HIGH PLAINS

The abrupt transition from the plains of eastern Colorado to the imposing mountain front of the Rockies is one of Colorado's most striking features. The flatlands east of the mountains are part of the Great Plains, a broad sweep of land that extends across North America from Texas to Canada. Despite the geologic tumult that built the Rocky Mountains, the Great Plains have remained the continent's stable interior. The central part of this region, from Nebraska and Wyoming south through eastern Colorado to the Texas panhandle, is known as the High Plains. This landscape has uplifted slowly and tilted gently to meet the Rockies a mile above sea level. It is an undulating grassland that shelters a deep record of Colorado's past mountain, sea, and desert landscapes.

WILD ROCKS: THE STORY OF THE LANDSCAPE

Most of Colorado's *rocks* have spent time in the underworld, in the earth's inferno deep below the surface. From there, some rocketed skyward, others oozed through cracks in the crust, or cooled and then pushed to the surface. They then took shape amidst the planet's wind, waves, ice, and rain. Each rock and landform carries its own story within its composition and structure. By knowing a little bit about rocks, you can pick one up on the trail and expand that rock into an entire landscape that once existed or a major event that once occurred.

Simply put, rocks are natural combinations of minerals. Thousands of different minerals exist in nature, but only certain ones are common in rocks, and are called rock-forming minerals. Some of them are simple and familiar, like the grains of quartz sand found along a beach.

Rocks form from minerals in three basic ways that allow them to be classified into three types: *igneous, metamorphic,* and *sedimentary.* Although the minerals forming them may be the same, the three rock types are distinct. Understanding their basic differences is the first step in interpreting the landscape.

TABLE 2

Common Rock Forming Minerals

MINERAL NAME	COLOR	APPEARANCE
Feldspar	White, gray, or pink	Distinct crystal surfaces
Quartz	Colorless to transparent	Glassy, irregular, and chunky
Mica	Gray, black, dark brown	Flat, flaky crystals
Hornblende	Dark green to black	Elongate crystals
Augite	Dark green to black	Elongate, rectangular crystals
Olivine	Pale green	Glassy, small, round
Calcite	White, gray, tan	Sugary crystals

IGNEOUS ROCKS

Igneous rocks are born from fire. They are formed in the wild, smoldering cauldron deep within the earth where minerals are melted into completely liquid molten material called *magma*. Magma, which is less dense than surrounding solid rock, tends to rise, forcing its way toward the surface. As the magma rises, it cools and solidifies, producing a crystalline mixture of minerals called an igneous rock. Many of the mountains in Colorado's Rockies are eroded cores of hard, resistant igneous rocks.

If magma is unable to reach the surface, it cools slowly to form a *pluton*, a name derived from Pluto, the Greek god of the underworld. This slow cooling, which may take place many miles below the surface, allows time for crystals to grow large enough to be seen with the naked eye—one way that plutonic rocks can be identified. Plutonic rocks are also called *intrusive igneous rocks* since they "intrude" into the surrounding rocks. There are many places in Colorado where uplift and erosion have exposed plutonic rocks at the surface. Perhaps best known is Pikes Peak, a pluton that formed about 1 billion years ago and then pushed up through the earth's crust.

Pikes Peak is composed of *granite*, one in a series of intrusive rock types that owe their light color to the dominant minerals *quartz* and *feldspar*. Granite may also be peppered with dark mineral flakes such as *mica* or with black needles of *hornblende*. There are also "hybrid" granites such as *granodiorite* and quartz monzonite that look like granite but contain slightly different blends of minerals. Geologists generally refer to granite and all its similar gradations by using the term *granitic*. While dark and medium-colored plutonic rocks are abundant elsewhere, the most common plutonic rocks in Colorado are granitic.

Magma that travels all the way to the earth's surface before it cools forms *extrusive igneous rocks*, better known as *volcanic rocks*, named after Vulcan, the Greek god of fire. Parts of Colorado have a fiery history. In fact, the San Juan Mountains represent one of Northern America's largest volcanic mountain ranges. Now dormant, San Juan volcanoes erupted between 35 and 22 million years ago, spewing volcanic rocks over a wide area in the southwestern corner of the state.

The magma in explosive volcanoes contains a high concentration of dissolved gas. As though shaken like a soft drink, pressure builds up within this viscous brew and eventually causes it to explode in an eruption that spews out a tremendous cloud of super-heated gas mixed with shattered fragments of rock, minerals, and volcanic glass—rapidly cooled magma in which no crystals have formed. The material created by explosive eruptions is called *pyroclastic*, from the Greek *pyro* meaning "fire" and *clastic* meaning "particle."

Igneous intrusions tell a wild story in the Front Range's Nokhu Crags

Tuff is a volcanic rock formed by the accumulation of pyroclastics. Most of the volcanic glasses in tuff are microscopic fragments of ash. Pumice is volcanic glass laced with a honeycomb network of air pockets, or *vesicles*. Volcanic *breccia* is a pyroclastic rock formed from a mixture of ash and larger volcanic fragments of mostly *andesite* and *rhyolite* that range in size from pebbles up to boulders the size of Volkswagens. Explosive eruptions in the San Juan Mountains and the West Elk Mountains nearby built up thick piles of ash and breccia.

TABLE 3

Common Igneous Rocks

INTRUSIVE/PLUTONIC (COARSE-GRAINED)	COLOR (COMMON MINERALS)	EXTRUSIVE/VOLCANIC (FINE-GRAINED)
Granite	Light-colored, can be pink to red (quartz, feldspar, mica, minor hornblende)	Rhyolite
Granodiorite	Light gray (feldspar, quartz, hornblende, mica, minor augite)	Dacite
Diorite	Medium to dark gray (feldspar, hornblende, mica, augite)	Andesite
Gabbro	Dark gray to greenish black (feldspar, augite, olivine, minor hornblende)	Basalt

In contrast, less pressurized extrusions, such as those that formed Grand Mesa and the Flat Tops of the White River Plateau, simply spill out magma at the surface which then flows as *lava* away from its source under the influence of gravity. Repeated eruptions over a period of time may accumulate to form a thick sequence of layered, solidified lava, such as *basalt*, which caps Grand Mesa and the Flat Tops of the White River Plateau. Since lava cools relatively quickly, there is little time for crystals to grow very large.

Hand sample of granitic rock

In general, extrusive rocks cool much more quickly than intrusive igneous rocks and therefore have smaller crystals. Since crystal formation is a slow process, crystal size is the main distinguishing feature between intrusive and extrusive igneous rocks.

METAMORPHIC ROCKS

Metamorphic rocks also come from the underworld. They are rocks of transformation in which temperature and pressure change their minerals without causing a complete igneous meltdown. The name metamorphic is derived from the Greek *meta* meaning "change" and *morphe* meaning "form."

Colorado's metamorphic rocks are some of the oldest rocks in the state. They formed during major mountain-building events when friction and massive upsurgences of igneous plutons metamorphosed the surrounding rocks with their heat and pressure about 1.7 billion years ago. In these events, *volcanic* and *sedimentary rocks* were transformed into metamorphic *schist* and *gneiss*. These ancient metamorphic rocks, and the igneous plutons that intruded them, are found in the eroded cores of mountain ranges like the Front, Sawatch, Park, and Gore Ranges. They are also exposed where rivers have carved deep canyons down into these oldest layers, in places like the Unaweep Canyon on the Uncompahgre Plateau and the Black Canyon of the Gunnison River.

In the initial stages of the metamorphic process, at relatively low temperatures and pressures, change may be minimal so that features of the original rock (called the parent rock) are still recognizable. With gentle cooking, the existing mineral grains simply enlarge and become fused. In this way, the sedimentary rock *shale* transforms into the metamorphic rock *slate, sandstone* alters into *quartzite,* and *limestone* becomes *marble.*

If temperature and pressure conditions intensify, the minerals grow

TABLE 4

Common Metamorphic Rocks

ROCK NAME	PARENT ROCK	TEXTURE/FEATURES
Quartzite	Sandstone	Interlocking crystals, sugary appearance
Marble	Limestone/dolomite	Fine to coarse interlocking crystals
Slate	Shale/siltstone	Fine-grained, splits into thin sheets
Schist	Shale/siltstone	Visible crystals that are elongate and aligned
Gneiss	Granite, sandstone, or sandstone/shale	Banded, may be folded or contorted

Boulder of banded gneiss, Indian Peaks, Front Range

larger and their alignment becomes more pronounced, which further transforms the rock. For instance, this is what happens when slate is altered to schist, a metamorphic rock in which shiny *mica* minerals all align in the same direction. If conditions further intensify, the minerals may segregate into light and dark bands to form the metamorphic rock gneiss (pronounced "nice"). In gneiss, dark layers of platy or elongate minerals such as mica and hornblende alternate with layers of light-colored quartz and feldspar. During intense heat and pressure, the mineral banding in schist and gneiss may become deformed, often bent, folded, and swirled into complex patterns like ribbons of multi-colored taffy. Massively deformed metamorphic rocks such as these, called banded gneiss, compose many of Colorado's mountains.

If temperature and pressure conditions reach extremes, partial melting of the parent rock can occur, producing pockets of magma. The resulting rock, called *migmatite,* is a mixture of igneous and metamorphic rocks and is the most deformed and confusing looking of all. If conditions further intensify, the rocks completely melt and the resulting magma is recycled back into igneous rock. Thus, they come full circle and the cycle can begin again.

SEDIMENTARY ROCKS
While igneous and metamorphic rocks are undoubtedly brewing beneath Colorado's surface, there are no smoking guns, no visible signs of their

TABLE 5

Common Sedimentary Rocks

ROCK NAME	GRAIN SIZE	FEATURES
Shale/mudstone and siltstone	Clay and silt	Thin bedded, mud cracks, forms slopes
Sandstone	Sand	Mostly quartz, cross-beds, forms ridges and cliffs
Arkose sandstone	Sand	Contains feldspar
Conglomerate	Pebbles, cobbles, boulders	Thick bedded, contains rounded rock fragments
Limestone	Crystalline	Fizzes in acid, may contain fossils; forms cliffs
Gypsum/halite	Crystalline	Soft, friable; interlocking network of crystals

Sandstone cliffs at Colorado National Monument

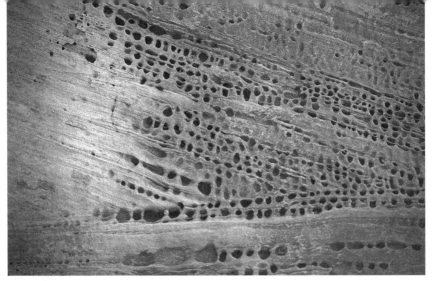

Artistic patterns of erosion in cross-bedded boulder of Wingate Sandstone, Dolores River Canyon

action today in the Colorado landscape. In contrast, *sedimentary rock* action is on display daily. The formation of sedimentary rocks can begin with the thud of a rock dislodging from an outcrop, the abrasive whirl of a sandy gust, or the slide of ball-bearing pebbles underfoot.

Most of Colorado's sedimentary rocks begin as fragments of eroded rock. Gravity, wind, water, and ice may then carry them to places where they accumulate, and ultimately, they may be buried by succeeding layers of deposition. Stacked sediments may become consolidated or lithified into clastic sedimentary rocks, the most common type of sedimentary rock found in Colorado. In the erosional stage that leads to formation of clastic sedimentary rocks, the grains, called *sediment*, are often sorted into distinct size ranges. As each layer is buried by newer material, the sediment is compacted and cemented together. The smallest clay-sized particles form *shale* or *mudstone*, silt-sized grains become *siltstone,* sand-sized grains become *sandstone,* and gravel forms *conglomerate.*

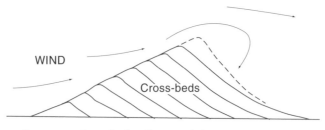

Cross - section of migrating sand dune

Cross-beds form as dune crests advance downwind

24

In addition to clastic sedimentary rocks, there are two other types of sedimentary rocks. Chemical sedimentary rocks form when sediment crystallizes directly from water, such as when seawater evaporates to form the minerals halite (table salt) and gypsum, the soft mineral used in sheetrock. Chemical sedimentary rocks are not common in Colorado, although they do occur in the Central Colorado Trough and Paradox Basin where gypsum and salt deposits accumulated during the evaporation of ancient seaways.

Organic sedimentary rocks, the third type, form by accumulation of the remains of organisms, such as the fossil shells which compose *limestone* or the plant remains that compress into coal. Limestone is an important type of organic sedimentary rock in Colorado. The Leadville Limestone found on the flanks of the Sawatch and Mosquito Ranges, and in the Colorado River canyons near Glenwood Springs, is particularly prominent. The Leadville Limestone, deposited in a warm, tropical ocean more than 300 million years ago, contains fossil shells that are visible in the rock. The fossil remains in limestones are made of the mineral *calcite*, which is manufactured biologically by organisms to create their shells or skeletons.

With the exception of the Elk Mountains and their famous red sedimentary layers, most of Colorado's mountains are primarily eroded cores of igneous and metamorphic rocks. In contrast, the Colorado Plateau and High Plains are sedimentary landscapes where, over the eons, layer after layer of sedimentary rocks have stacked like the layers of a birthday cake. Since both of these landscapes are relatively stable, the oldest horizontal layers, called *strata*, are still found at the bottom of their stacks.

SEDIMENTARY STRUCTURES

Occasionally, during the deposition of sediments, a geologic process may leave a fingerprint, a distinctive pattern within a sedimentary layer. These features, called sedimentary structures, are frozen in place when other layers are deposited on top of them, preserving their form. For example, *ripplemarks* are created when wind or currents leave their mark in sand or silt along shorelines or in dune environments. *Cross-beds* are parallel, sloped layers that form by the advancing crests of wind-blown dunes or submerged water-transported sediments. Mudcracks are formed as sediment dries out, such as in a lakebed, tidal flat, or riverbed.

Eventually, sedimentary structures may become exposed by erosion, revealing features of the ancient environment where their sediments accumulated. For example, giant cross-bed patterns in the Wingate Sandstone along the Dolores River on the Colorado Plateau record the passage of huge Sahara-like sand dunes about 200 million years ago.

GEOLOGIC STRUCTURES—FAULTS, FOLDS, AND FRACTURES

Colorado's rocks reveal the effects of a restless earth. Throughout geologic time, the constant motion of the earth's surface causes stress in the rocks. This motion is caused by a process called *plate tectonics* (described in the next section). The stress builds until major adjustments take place to relieve the pressure, translating it into movement such as the uplift of entire mountain ranges, like the Rocky Mountains. Much of the time, however, the effects of stress are more subtle, perhaps only warping the rocks, like the gently tilted sedimentary layers of the Colorado Plateau and High Plains.

Within Colorado, the earth has assumed every possible posture to relieve its stress. It has reclined, inclined, bent over backward, decurved, recurved, twisted, bent, and broken. These movements create definable geologic features that can be read simply by looking at the landscape.

If the rock layers buckle or bend without breaking, a fold is created. The simplest type of fold is a *monocline,* in which the rock layers change from horizontal to steeply inclined and back to horizontal again, like a rug draped across a step. Good examples of monoclines are found on the Colorado Plateau where sedimentary layers are draped across steps in the underlying Precambrian *igneous* and *metamorphic* rocks.

If the rocks are squeezed or compressed, rock layers can form upward domelike folds called *anticlines* or downwarped folds called *synclines.* Many of the uplifts that occurred in the Rocky Mountains were originally anticlines that rose through the earth's surface like emerging mushrooms.

Often when rocks are folded, they break along *fractures* (also called joints). Fractures are important in

Ripplemarks in Dakota Sandstone, Dinosaur Ridge near Denver

26

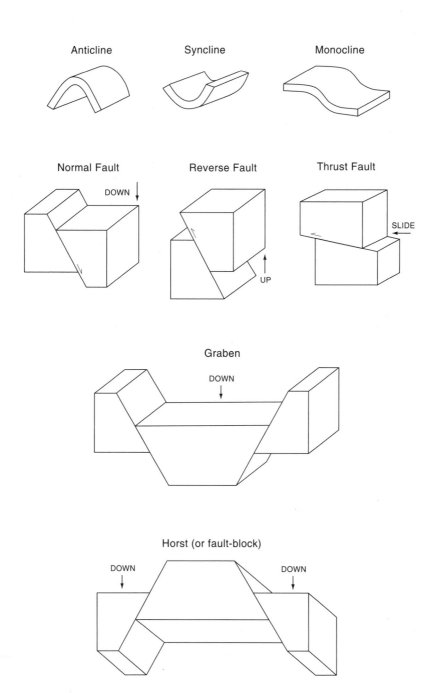

Anticline   Syncline   Monocline

Normal Fault   Reverse Fault   Thrust Fault

DOWN

UP

SLIDE

Graben

DOWN

Horst (or fault-block)

DOWN   DOWN

Major types of faults and folds

27

Monocline in the San Juan Mountains

the formation of different landforms because breaks in the rock provide zones of weakness that can be directly attacked by weathering and erosion. The formation of cliffs, arches, canyons, and other landform features is typically influenced by the orientation of fractures.

If the rocks on either side of a fracture move past one another—up, down, or sideways—the break in the rock is called a *fault*. Faults are considered "normal" if one side simply drops down relative to the other. "Reverse" faults result when one side is pushed up relative to another. Normal faults are typically produced by extension, or pulling apart the land. Sometimes a large block of rock bounded by normal faults on either side will drop down, creating a *graben*, the German word for "grave." The San Luis Valley is Colorado's biggest example of a graben.

In another case, if a block bounded by normal faults is uplifted, it becomes a *fault-block* mountain range called a *horst* (the opposite of a graben). The Sangre de Cristo Range, which is bounded by the San Luis Valley on the west and the Wet Valley on the east, is an example of a fault-block mountain range. The amount of movement on the west-bounding normal fault, called the Sangre de Cristo Fault, has been more than 20,000 feet, a vertical distance of nearly 4 miles!

Reverse faults typically occur when the land is squeezed under impact. One type of structure called a faulted anticline forms when a block of rock squeezes up from below, bending the overlying rocks upward along reverse faults at the margins of the uplift. Many of Colorado's mountain ranges are faulted anticlines where the uplifted rock core (typically igneous and metamorphic rocks) tilts the sedimentary layers along the flanks of the uplift.

A *thrust fault* is a special kind of reverse fault in which the break in the rocks along which movement is occurring is at a very low angle or almost horizontal. In this instance, rocks above the fault slide over the top of rocks beneath the fault. The Elk Mountains around Aspen formed this way.

Examples of these geologic structures can occur on any scale, from small outcrops to major features extending for dozens of miles. They are important indications of the history of movements that rocks have undergone through geologic time.

PLATE TECTONICS—CONTINENTS ON THE MOVE

Unlike pie crust, the earth's crust is not bound to its heated center. It is more like crackers laid on top of a boiling pot of split pea soup. Large pieces of earth's crust move across the viscous interior, shifting positions and colliding with one another. These movements are the underlying force in the creation of Colorado's landscape.

Geologists have determined that the earth's surface is divided into about a dozen giant slabs of rock called *plates*. Some plates bear *granitic* continents, such as the North American Plate, where Colorado is located. Other plates carry islands and basaltic ocean floor, such as the Pacific Plate, which is largely submerged beneath the Pacific Ocean. *Plate tectonics* is the science that describes how these plates move around the globe over time, an idea that was first called continental drift. The moving plates carry the continents, shifting them around on the surface of the earth.

The constant wandering of crustal plates is driven by the radioactive heat engine of the earth's interior. The plates, which are rigid sections of rock, ride around on top of a hot, dense rock in the upper part of the earth's mantle that is soft and flows like plastic. Relative to the size of the earth, the patchwork of moving plates that covers the earth is very thin. The earth's mantle can be compared to the boiling soup, where convection currents rise to the surface, begin to cool, and then sink down to where they are reheated, only to rise again. Convection cells in the mantle drive the motion of the plates on the earth's surface.

Much of the geologic action at the earth's surface such as earthquakes, volcanoes, and mountain building takes place at the boundaries between

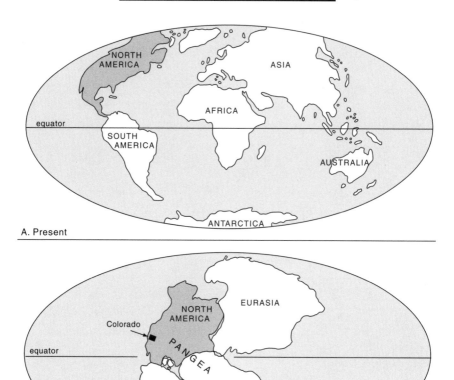

A. Present

B. 200 million years ago

Continents on the move

plates. California's San Andreas Fault is perhaps the most modern-day plate boundary. Along the San Andreas Fault, the Pacific Plate is moving toward the northwest past the North American Plate at a rate of about 2 inches per year. As these plates slide past each other, stress created in the rocks shifts the land, occasionally grinding hard enough to be felt as an earthquake. At the current rate of movement, in about 18.5 million years, Los Angeles, which is on the Pacific Plate, will have moved far enough north to be opposite San Francisco on the North American Plate.

Another type of plate motion occurs along the Pacific Northwest coast of North America, where the Juan de Fuca Plate is pushing beneath the North American Plate. When plates come together like this, one plate is forced beneath the other, a process known as *subduction*. As the Juan de Fuca Plate descends into the hot mantle, it partially melts. The melted rock

30

then rises back to the surface and erupts explosively into the overriding North American Plate. This action fuels the fire for the active volcanoes in the Cascade Range such as Mount St. Helens. Subduction is one way the earth recycles its crust—although it melts into pea soup, heading to the bottom of the pot, it does rise again.

A third type of plate interaction occurs when two plates move away from each other and new material from the mantle rises to the surface as magma. When this action takes place in the middle of the ocean, the process is called sea-floor spreading and the upwelling magma emerges as deep-sea lava that creates new ocean floor. If the plates are moving away from each other on land, the process is called *rifting*. During rifting, the continental crust is stretched and thinned. This extension breaks the crust along normal faults, and a rift valley forms as a central graben drops down. The faults may act as pathways for upwelling magma and thus allow basalt lava to flow out along the margins of the rift valley. The Arkansas and San Luis Valleys in Colorado are examples of rift valleys that have formed along the *Rio Grande Rift,* which extends from central Colorado south into New Mexico.

If rifting continues, the continental crust may pull completely apart, down-dropping the rift below sea level and eventually causing it to flood with seawater. Perhaps it will someday be possible to sail a boat from the Gulf of Mexico up the Rio Grande Valley to Leadville, Colorado.

Plate tectonic events have had a profound effect on Colorado's rocks. Geologists now recognize that the continental margin of western North America is a mosaic of crustal fragments that have been added onto the west coast by a process called *continental accretion.* Nearly 2 billion years ago, the plate fragments may have begun rafting onto an ancient continent whose southern margin was where Wyoming is today. This was Colorado's beginning, the time when its oldest rocks were formed and when the tectonic events were inititated that would erect mountains on its landscape many times over the succeeding years.

PREPARING TO HIKE THE GEOLOGY

Hiking the geology of Colorado does not require any expensive or fancy equipment. Simply using this book and adding a few special items to your backpack will prepare you to "geologize" in the field.

WHAT TO BRING

Since most of Colorado is at fairly high elevation, the temperature and weather conditions can change drastically. In fact, in the Rocky Mountains, it can snow any month of the year! As you prepare to hike in Colorado, ask

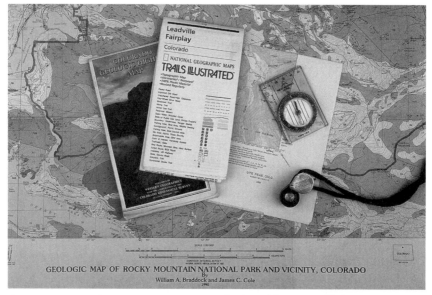

GEOLOGIC MAP OF ROCKY MOUNTAIN NATIONAL PARK AND VICINITY, COLORADO
By
William A. Braddock and James C. Cole
1990

An assortment of maps, a compass, and a hand lens are all that is needed to "hike the geology."

yourself, What do I need to survive the worst conditions I might possibly encounter?

Start with the basics, including sturdy boots, appropriate clothing, food and water, a hat, sunscreen, raingear (both jacket and pants), and a backpack or waistpack to carry things. Also, be sure to carry the Ten Essentials: (1) flashlight with extra batteries, (2) map, (3) compass, (4) extra food, (5) extra clothing (something warm), (6) sunglasses, (7) first-aid kit, (8) pocket knife, (9) waterproof matches, and (10) candle or firestarter.

For exploring the geology, a few other items are wise to bring: (1) a small magnifying glass or *hand lens* to examine rocks up close, (2) a waterproof notebook and pencil to record observations and questions for later investigation (you always think you will remember, but write it down anyway!), (3) and a felt-tip waterproof pen for marking rock samples you may wish to collect (but remember that collecting is prohibited in the parks, monuments, and preserves described in this book).

TOPOGRAPHIC AND GEOLOGIC MAPS

Geologists love maps. Perhaps you already have the bug. If you do, welcome to map paradise.

The description for each hike in this book lists the topographic maps useful for that specific hike. Topographic maps, or "topo maps" for short, provide basic information about elevation, the nature of the landscape (steep or flat), place names, and trail locations. When you are out on the trail, it's good practice to know your location on your topo map at all times. It's also a good idea to protect it from getting wet with a zip-lock bag.

Rocks come alive when you examine them up close with a hand lens.

The parallel lines (contour lines) on topographic maps connect points of equal elevation, like rings around a bathtub. The lines are spaced by elevation gain, so the closer the lines, the steeper the terrain. Standard topographic maps are provided by the U.S. Geological Survey (USGS). The most useful and easily readable format is the USGS 7.5-minute quadrangle map because it has the largest scale. In certain cases, you may need several quadrangle maps to cover a single hike. An alternative style of topographic map is published by National Geographic Maps Trails Illustrated Series (to order, call 1-800-962-1643). These useful waterproof maps cover many of the popular hiking destinations in Colorado. Both types of topo maps are available at stores that sell outdoor gear and are on file at many university libraries.

Geologic maps are another type of map entirely. They are works of art (and science!). By using different colors for each rock formation or group of formations, geologists have plotted a dizzying spectrum of patterns that represent the rocks that are exposed at the surface and form the landscape. Standardized symbols show features such as *faults* and folds, and each geologic map has its own legend that lists and describes all the rocks and symbols. The USGS has published a number of geologic maps that cover Colorado, from the wall-sized state map to smaller quadrangle maps. Geologic maps can be ordered from the USGS and are also on file at many university libraries. A list of geologic maps for the hikes in this book is provided in appendix C, Geologic Maps.

A NOTE ABOUT SAFETY

Safety is an important concern in all outdoor activities. No guidebook can alert you to every hazard or anticipate the limitations of every reader. Therefore, the descriptions of roads, trails, routes, and natural features in this book are not representations that a particular place or excursion will be safe for your party. When you follow any of the routes described in this book, you assume responsibility for your own safety. Under normal conditions, such excursions require the usual attention to traffic, road and trail conditions, weather, terrain, the capabilities of your party, and other factors. Keeping informed on current conditions and exercising common sense are the keys to a safe, enjoyable outing.

The Mountaineers

▶ *The jagged skyline of the Sneffels Range, San Juan Mountains*

Part 1
COLORADO'S ROCKY MOUNTAINS

The Rocky Mountains are about as permanent as wind-blown dunes when viewed in the vast scale of geologic time. Over the past 2 billion years, mountains have risen in the Colorado region and then eroded away again many times. Many pieces of the geologic story are missing as significant rocks have washed away or were buried by younger rock layers or by vegetation. Even so, trails in the Rocky Mountains wind through enough clues to give great insight into the ups and downs of Colorado's tumultuous geologic history.

At the top of Mount Elbert, the highest peak in the Rockies (14,433 feet), lies 1.7 billion-year-old metamorphic rock, some of the oldest rock in Colorado. These ancient rocks are part of Colorado's basement—the Precambrian foundation that underlies the state. How did Colorado's basement end up on top?

This is not the first time the basement has risen to great heights in the Colorado region. It is *plate tectonics,* world-class movements of the earth's crust, that have impacted Colorado enough to build mountains again and again (see Plate Tectonics—Continents on the Move). Each time this happens, weathering and erosion crumble the mountains back down. Today's Rockies are currently under this siege. Erosion persistently modifies their silhouettes, etching them subtly earthward.

The first mountains emerged in this region about 1.7 billion years ago during the Precambrian, when slabs of the earth's crust accreted onto the continent about where Wyoming is today. This is when Colorado's basement formed. Repeated impact along the growing plate boundary folded, faulted, and uplifted the landscape, erecting a great mountain range in the area that would later become Colorado. A long period of weathering and erosion followed, eventually wearing down the mountains to a gentle landscape of low hills and shallow valleys.

Metamorphic *basement rocks* hint that such mountains may have uplifted and declined many times during the Precambrian. Colorado's metamorphic basement reads like a chronicle of repeated mountain-building events, even though no debris from these mountains can be found today. Each mountain-building event appears to have contorted the metamorphic basement rock, adding its own signature twists and turns. Now that the basement has uplifted into view, the Precambrian record is revealed in the rocks.

After many periods of rise and fall, the once-mountainous landscape was flooded by a shallow sea during the early Paleozoic era, about 500 million years ago. The basement was bathed in marine sediments for almost 200 million years. The seas ebbed during the Pennsylvanian, about 300 million years ago, as the North American Plate collided and bonded with other plates to begin the formation of one giant continent called *Pangea*. Collisions squeezed the Colorado region, causing the *Ancestral Rocky Mountains* to push up through the surface under the impact. The result was two separate mountain ranges that, despite their name, bear no resemblance to the modern Rocky Mountains.

COLORADO'S BASEMENT ROCKS

Colorado's oldest rocks are its basement, the geologic foundation of the state. They have ridden up and down with the landscape for nearly 2 billion years. Today, more than 85 percent of the *basement rocks* are buried beneath younger rocks. They are exposed only where erosion has bared them, such as along the crests of major mountain ranges and in some of the deeper canyons.

The Colorado Basement Province adhered itself to the much older core of North America in repeated collisions of *continental accretion*. As segments of the earth's crust crashed into the ancient rocks of the

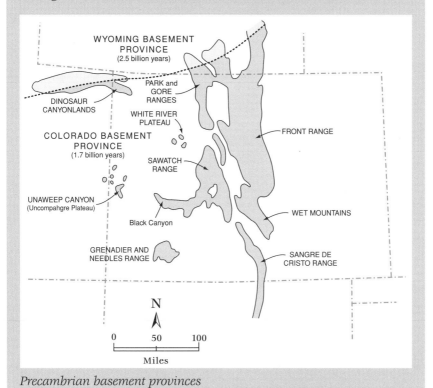

Precambrian basement provinces

37

Wyoming Basement Province, *volcanic* and *sedimentary rocks* were deeply buried under a massive mountain range that formed during the collisions. Deep burial and subsequent igneous intrusions metamorphosed the volcanic and sedimentary rocks into *gneiss* and *schist* beginning about 1.7 billion years ago. These contorted, deformed rocks are the oldest and most widespread basement rocks in Colorado.

Accretion continued and igneous *plutons* intruded the basement several more times during the Precambrian in clustered events around 1.4 and 1 billion years ago. These large *batholiths* and smaller plutons of mostly *granitic* rocks further deformed the *metamorphic rocks* and became part of the basement.

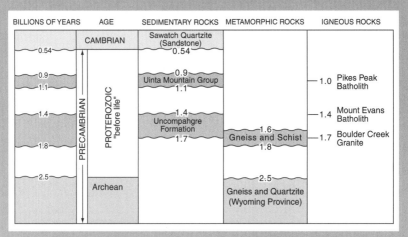

Colorado's basement rocks: chart of major Precambrian rock units

As the mountainous landscape waned under the force of erosion, Precambrian sediment drained from the mountains and accumulated in thick piles in places where the metamorphic basement down-dropped between faults. Today, these *sediments* (now altered to *quartzite*) are known as the Uncompahgre Formation and the Uinta Mountain Group. Because of their origins in the Precambrian, these metamorphosed sedimentary rocks are also considered part of the basement.

It took almost 1 billion years for Colorado to lay this foundation. It still forms the footing of much of the state, visible in deep canyons. But, it is also the state's backbone, the resistant rock visible at the top of the Rockies.

The rise of the Ancestral Rockies continued into the Permian, lifting ancient basement rocks and the younger marine *sedimentary rock* that covered them. As ice, rain, and wind battered the new peaks, the sedimentary layers were stripped off and swept into rivers that poured down the mountains, creating thick piles of rubble and debris. The positions of these former mountains are now marked by areas where the older sedimentary layers that once covered the basement are missing and red *sandstones* and *conglomerates*, or younger *strata*, rest directly on basement rocks.

Near the end of the Permian, even the basement rocks that crowned the once lofty peaks of the Ancestral Rockies were reduced to a series of low hills. By this time, all the world's continents had joined together to form the supercontinent Pangea. The gigantic landmass had a major influence on world climate which became dominated by arid and semi-arid conditions. Wind-blown dunes of sand began to sweep across the eroded Colorado landscape. These dunes were part of a vast desert that covered much of the Rocky Mountain states during the Permian.

At the beginning of the Mesozoic era, about 245 million years ago, relatively dry climatic conditions persisted in western Pangea where Colorado was located. Rivers meandered across a dunescape where dinosaurs flourished.

About 150 million years ago, in the late Jurassic, the Atlantic Ocean floor began to crack open, initiating an episode of sea-floor spreading that still pushes North America westward away from the Eurasian Plate. The North American continent began to override a slab of oceanic crust called the Farallon Plate along its west coast. The Farallon Plate slid beneath the North American continent. This movement initiated major volcanic activity, continental accretion, and mountain building along the western coast of North America.

About 100 million years ago, during the Cretaceous, seas flooded the interior of the North American continent as it subsided under the heavy load of the mountains constructed to the west. Colorado was located east of the mountains, along the western shore of the inland *Cretaceous Seaway* that stretched from the Gulf of Mexico to the Arctic Ocean. During this time, sea levels fluctuated worldwide as ocean basins changed shape alongside shifting tectonic plates. When the seas made their final retreat about 70 million years ago, *sediments* as thick as 2 miles covered the eroded basement stumps of the Ancestral Rocky Mountain uplifts.

This set the stage for the *Laramide Orogeny*, a major mountain-building event that helped define the present-day Colorado Rockies about 70 million years ago. As continental accretion continued along North America's west coast and as the Atlantic Ocean continued to spread, Colorado's basement became squeezed, pushing up the precursors to the modern Rockies and forming mountains in roughly the same places they stand today.

By about 35 million years ago, the Laramide mountains were deeply eroded and reduced to a series of low, isolated mountains largely buried in their own debris. This flattened landscape is now referred to as the *Rocky Mountain Surface,* and although the mountains have risen again, the flattened surface still marks portions of the modern skyline.

THE LARAMIDE OROGENY

The *Laramide Orogeny* was not Colorado's most recent mountain-building event but it was the event that defined where the Rockies are today. It began in late Cretaceous time, about 70 million years ago, amidst the stubble of the Ancestral Rockies and the thick layers of sediment piled on top of them.

The origins of this event, though probably triggered by *continental accretion* and *subduction* on the continent's west coast, remain a mystery. The emergence of the Rockies so far inland from the plate boundary is a geologic anomaly. Geologists speculate that about 70 million years ago, the pace of Atlantic sea-floor spreading may have

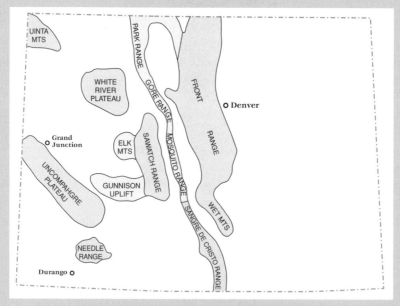

Laramide uplifts in Colorado

quickened, accelerating the rate of subduction of the Pacific sea floor beneath North America. This may have flattened the angle of subduction, causing the Pacific Plate to impinge on Colorado's *basement rocks*. The rocks squeezed like an accordion, sending some blocks skyward to become mountains.

Laramide uplifts are oriented generally north–south in Colorado. They are separated by downwarped areas that filled with sediment eroded off the crests of the uplifts. As the *sedimentary rocks* that once draped over the mountains were removed, the resistant Precambrian

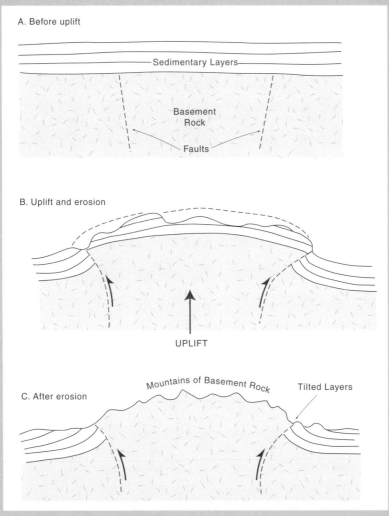

A. Before uplift

Sedimentary Layers

Basement Rock

Faults

B. Uplift and erosion

UPLIFT

C. After erosion

Mountains of Basement Rock

Tilted Layers

Basement uplifts during the Laramide Orogeny

basement rocks emerged at the summits. Ultimately, weathering and erosion buried most of these mountains up to their necks in their own rubble. The peaks did not reach their modern heights until the Pliocene, within the last 10 million years, when broad regional uplift erected the modern Rockies along the ancient Laramide mountain blueprint.

An explosive period ensued in the region, spewing volcanic layers in the San Juan and West Elk Mountains. Other active volcanic centers during this time existed in places such as the Never Summer Mountains and the Rabbit Ears Range in northern Colorado. This fiery episode occurred during the Oligocene and Miocene between 35 and 22 million years ago. During this episode, a tremendous volume of volcanic rocks showered the last remnants of the Laramide mountains.

In addition to the volcanic activity at the surface, great masses of *igneous rocks* intruded many ranges during this time. These large *batholiths*, bared by erosion, now protrude in many parts of Colorado including the Sawatch Range, the Elk Mountains, the San Juans, and parts of the Front Range.

During the Oligocene, from about 30 to 26 million years ago, a long network of valleys formed along the crest of Colorado's Rockies, dividing the Sawatch Range from the Mosquito Range and the Sangre de Cristo Range from the San Juan Mountains. This feature is called the *Rio Grande Rift*, a deep gash in Colorado's surface that extends from the upper Arkansas River Valley near Leadville, south through the San Luis Valley into New Mexico.

The final episode in shaping the Colorado Rockies landscape began about 25 million years ago, also during the Oligocene, when the entire Rocky Mountain region was uplifted, including the adjacent Colorado Plateau and High Plains. This broad regional surge uplifted today's mountains even as the Colorado landscape was being stretched apart.

Regional uplift and faulting continued through the Pliocene and into the Pleistocene and may even be continuing to this day. The last major pulse of uplift beginning about 10 million years ago drove the region higher. The Rockies have elevated 6,000 feet or more during the past 10 million years. It was during this time that Colorado's fourteeners were born.

The finishing touches to the Colorado Rockies were applied by a succession of *glaciers* that advanced and retreated in the mountains during the Pleistocene *Ice Age*. Some of the most dramatic features of the alpine

Metamorphic basement rock exposed in Unaweep Canyon, Colorado Plateau

landscape—sharp-edged mountains, ice-carved basins, and U-shaped valleys—were carved by Ice Age glaciers within the past 1.8 million years. The present-day Colorado Rocky Mountain landscape was essentially complete by the end of the last major glaciation, only 12,000 years ago.

Chapter 1
THE FRONT RANGE

To hike in Colorado's Front Range is to come face to face with the power of uplift and the artistry of ice and water. The Front Range marks the boundary where the horizontal High Plains end and the landscape turns abruptly vertical. It is the impressive eastern limit of the *Laramide Orogeny* and the largest of the Laramide mountain-building uplifts. Against the vast undulations of the High Plains, the sky-highness of the Front Range appears regal.

This king of Southern Rockies uplifts is really a collection of mountain

Dusting of snow on Pikes Peak, viewed through the Gateway at Garden of the Gods

ranges that ascended together and, interconnected, extend southward for nearly 200 miles from the Medicine Bow Mountains along the Wyoming border to the Wet Mountains south of Colorado City. Prominent fourteeners crown the skyline, including Pikes Peak near Colorado Springs, Mount Evans west of Denver, and Longs Peak in Rocky Mountain National Park.

Long before these peaks dominated the Front Range, the eastern arm of the Ancestral Rockies towered here as their precursor about 300 million years ago. After the demise of the Ancestral Rockies, the Front Range rode upward in the Laramide elevator as Colorado's roof was raised during the late Cretaceous, 70 million years ago. But, by the close of the Eocene, about 35 million years ago, the roof had crumbled. The mountaintops were beveled off by erosion and surrounded by their own debris, creating a flattened upland landscape called the *Rocky Mountain Surface.*

About 35 million years ago Colorado's volcanic period ignited, sending far-reaching volcanic rock and debris across the landscape. In a little more than 10 million years, the Thirtynine Mile Volcanic Field in the south and the Never Summer Mountains in the north left their mark in *lava,* ash, and *breccia* across the Rocky Mountain Surface.

Then, 25 million years ago, many of the old faults that defined the long-since vanished Laramide mountains reactivated. The Front Range rose again as a broad upwarp, or *anticline,* bounded on the east and west by a series of faults that extended the length of the range. This uplift surged during the past 10 million years to bring the Rockies up to their present-day skyline. As testament to the magnitude of the uplift, the same Precambrian *basement rocks* that stand above 14,000 feet on Longs Peak are buried nearly 2 miles deep beneath Denver!

This renewed uplift also elevated the Rocky Mountain Surface, now recognizable as the flattened and subdued summits along many parts of the Front Range. But most of the uplifts did not remain level. Rivers were unleashed from the new mountain heights, instigating intense canyon-cutting that carved deeply into the skyline in such places as the Royal Gorge, Big Thompson Canyon, and Cache La Poudre Canyon.

This mountain template was completed about 5 million years ago. Then, during the *Ice Age,* between 1.8 million and 12,000 years ago, surges of Pleistocene ice repeatedly engulfed the peaks of the Front Range. Powerful glaciers ground down the flanks of the mountains, carving the U-shaped valleys, alpine *cirques,* and sharp mountain peaks so familiar today.

The resulting grandeur gives the Front Range an air of permanence. But hiking through the high country reveals that rivers and ice continue to exert their erosional force, extending the long legacy of Front Range mountain shaping into the present day.

GLACIAL LANDFORMS

Colorado's Rocky Mountain landscapes were sculpted by frozen fingers of ice. Every major mountain range was changed dramatically by the reach of *glaciers*.

This all happened during the Pleistocene *Ice Age* over the past 1.8 million years. Although many cycles of glaciation may have affected Colorado, evidence remains from only the last two major glacial episodes because these later events wiped the slate clean. The Bull Lake Glaciation began about 300,000 years ago and ended about 130,000 years ago. The other, called the Pinedale Glaciation, began about 30,000 years ago and ended about 15,000 to 12,000 years ago.

Another recent but minor glacial period, called the *Little Ice Age,* began around 700 years ago and ended within the last 200 years. Colorado's small glaciers that still persist on north- and east-facing slopes in the Front Range may be remnants of the Little Ice Age.

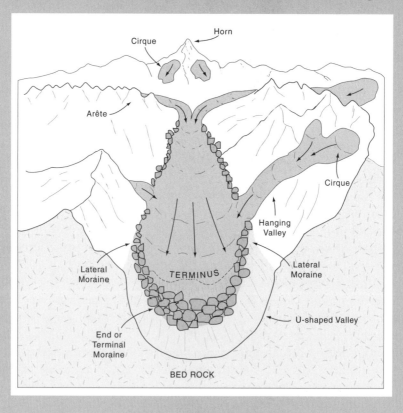

Although no great, single ice sheet edged into Colorado, the Southern Rockies were cloaked in ice during each glacial advance. Up to this time, the Colorado landscape had been characterized by V-shaped stream valleys and steep canyons eroded solely by rivers. The glaciers advanced like superpowered rivers of ice, grinding down the sides of mountains and slowly flowing through major mountain valleys to as low as 8,000 feet.

Glaciers carve the landscape like a scouring conveyor belt rather than a bulldozer. As the ice moves downslope, it both flows internally and slips along its base. As it moves, it picks up boulders and carries them along. It is these rocks, trapped within the ice, that powerfully grind the terrain. Their force is often revealed by *striations*, the scratches and grooves left behind on outcrops that were scraped over by the captured rocks.

The boulders are eventually broken up and dumped into piles of unsorted rocks and debris along the side of the glacier (*lateral moraine*) or at the front of the glacier (*end moraine*). Since each glacial advance wipes the slate clean of all previous advances, end moraines mark the maximum reach of the ice.

As the glaciers advanced and retreated across Colorado, they gouged narrow stream valleys into broad U-shaped valleys. On the sides of mountains, ice etched at tall peaks, creating knife-edged ridges (arêtes) and pyramid-shaped peaks (horns). The heads of valleys were carved into horseshoe-shaped amphitheaters called *cirques* (pronounced "seerks"), and basins were scoured in bedrock creating high mountain lakes called tarns. *Hanging valleys* mark intersections where a smaller tributary glacier met a larger glacier leaving behind a valley that appears to "hang" above the deeper valley floor. These features read like glacial fingerprints on Colorado's mountainous terrain.

The mark of glaciers—striations and smoothed rock surface in the Sangre de Cristo Range

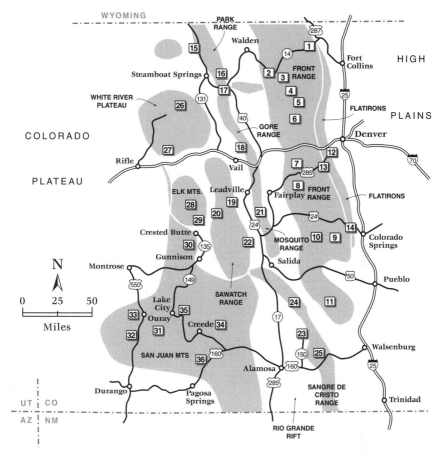

Rocky Mountain geology hikes

Hike
1

GREYROCK MOUNTAIN

MARGIN OF A GRANITIC INTRUSION

Hike to the top of Greyrock, a mountain of Precambrian granite, for a great look at some of the events that formed the Rockies.

DISTANCE ■ 5.6 miles round trip

ELEVATION ■ 5,550 to 7,613 feet

DIFFICULTY ■ Moderate

TOPOGRAPHIC MAPS ■ USGS Poudre Park; Trails Illustrated #101

GEOLOGIC MAP ■ 1

KEY REFERENCE ■ 1

49

PRECAUTIONS ■ Beware of poison ivy along the lower reaches of the trail. Avoid the summit during approaching thunderstorms. The last 0.5 mile to the summit is rocky and steep but not technical. Be sure to watch every step.

FOR INFORMATION ■ Estes-Poudre Ranger District

About the Landscape: This hike explores an ancient intrusion that formed much of the basement core of the northern Front Range. Greyrock is an isolated mountain of *granitic* rock surrounded by the older *metamorphic* rock it intruded 1.4 billion years ago. This hike crosses the margin of the intrusion on its way to the summit of Greyrock Mountain. Spectacular views from Greyrock's rounded summit stretch eastward across the High Plains and westward up Cache La Poudre Canyon toward the crest of the Never Summer and Medicine Bow Mountains.

Trail Guide: To reach the Greyrock Trailhead, drive 10.5 miles north from Fort Collins on US Highway 287 (which is also Colorado Highway 14 along this stretch). Turn left onto Colorado Highway 14 and drive 8.7 miles along the Cache La Poudre River to the Greyrock Trail parking area on the left. The trailhead is located across the road from the parking area and on the other side of a bridge across the river.

From the trailhead, the Greyrock Trail parallels the river heading west, or upstream, for about the first 0.25 mile, then turns north and follows a side drainage. The trail crosses the small creek several times. Large boulders near the crossings have washed down from the surrounding hillsides. These are 1.7 billion-year-old Precambrian metamorphic *basement rocks* of *schist* and *gneiss.* The dark, shiny rocks are mica schist. Look closely to see flat crystals of *mica* within the rock. Veins of lighter-colored igneous *quartz* and *feldspar* fill *fractures* that cut through the schist, revealing an ancient igneous intrusion into the metamorphic "parent" rock.

At about the 0.5-mile point, a sign marks where the Greyrock Trail splits into the Meadow Trail to the left and the Summit Trail to the right. Stay right and follow the Summit Trail for the most direct route to the top of Greyrock Mountain.

For the next 1.7 miles, the trail climbs along a drainage strewn with boulders of schist and gneiss, then switchbacks up to a saddle below Greyrock Mountain. As you climb higher, note the rounded hills a short distance north of the trail. These hills appear much different than the sharp and jagged hillsides that have characterized the scenery along the trail to this point. The change in the landscape is caused by a change in the rocks, from metamorphic to granitic.

The rounded hills, including Greyrock Mountain (not yet in view), are

Exfoliating granitic summit of Greyrock Mountain

part of the Log Cabin Batholith, a granitic intrusion that swelled up through much of the metamorphic basement core of the northern Front Range about 1.4 billion years ago.

The trail continues by climbing right along the margin of the granitic intrusion. In several places, it's possible to see the dark-colored schist in direct contact with the much lighter granitic rock that intruded it. As the trail approaches a saddle toward the top of the hill, it crosses into granitic rock. You have crossed over the place where the molten brew of *magma* welled up into the metamorphic rock. The towering monolith of Greyrock Mountain is now in view ahead. From here to the summit, the rocks underfoot are granitic.

In the saddle directly below Greyrock is a junction where the Summit Trail meets the Meadow Trail coming in from the left. From here, it is 0.5 mile to the top of Greyrock Mountain. From this vantage point, it is hard to imagine a trail up the steep rock. Amazingly, the trail follows an intricate path along breaks and fractures on the southeast face of the mountain toward the summit.

The rounded domelike summit of Greyrock Mountain is formed by a process called *exfoliation,* in which giant slabs of *granite* have fallen off in huge sheets. When the granite first intruded the surrounding metamorphic rock, it was deeply buried under heavy layers of rock. As it later uplifted, its load lightened, causing the granite to crack, forming sheet joints along lines parallel to the outer surface of the mountain. As weathering and freeze-thaw action attacked the rocks, the outer rock layers were shed like layers of onion skin, creating this distinctly rounded landform called an exfoliation dome.

For the return hike, you can loop back along the Meadow Trail or retrace your steps along the Summit Trail for the shortest route back to the trailhead.

LAKE AGNES AND NOKHU CRAGS

Hike 2

FALLOUT OF A GRANITIC INTRUSION

A Tertiary granitic intrusion created the jagged Nokhu Crags by thrusting them aside. Both are dramatically juxtaposed today along the shore of Lake Agnes.

DISTANCE ■ 2.5 miles round trip (1.6 miles round trip to Lake Agnes)

ELEVATION ■ 10,320 to 10,720 feet

DIFFICULTY ■ Moderate

TOPOGRAPHIC MAPS ■ USGS Mount Richthofen; Trails Illustrated #200

GEOLOGIC MAP ■ 2

KEY REFERENCE ■ 2

PRECAUTIONS ■ Use caution when climbing around on the talus slopes along the lakeshore. Camping and fires around the lake are prohibited.

FOR INFORMATION ■ Colorado State Forest

About the Landscape: The jagged spires of the Nokhu Crags are pieces of an ancient sea floor that now stand 2,000 feet upright to reflect dramatically in Lake Agnes, located near Cameron Pass in the Never Summer Mountains. The Crags are formed from layers of 75 million-year-old Cretaceous Pierre Shale which were tilted vertically and metamorphosed by the hot magma of a granitic intrusion that surged up from below. Renewed uplift of the Front Range over the past 10 million years has shoved the *granitic pluton* and its Crags up through the surface to create a dramatic alpine setting.

Unlike other areas of the Front Range, which are cored by Precambrian *basement rocks* more than 1 billion years old, the Never Summer Mountains took shape from much younger granitic rocks that intruded the area "only" 28 million years ago. These granitic rocks are leftovers from *magma* chambers that once fueled a spate of volcanic eruptions. Although the volcanoes have long since eroded away, their granitic foundation and its accompanying Crags have climbed to alpine heights.

Trail Guide: To reach the Lake Agnes Trailhead, drive north from Fort Collins on US Highway 287 (which is also Colorado Highway 14 along this stretch) for 10.5 miles. Turn left and follow Colorado Highway 14 for 66 miles as it winds along the Cache La Poudre River and over Cameron Pass. About 3 miles after Cameron Pass, turn left at the sign for Lake Agnes and American Lakes (if you are coming from the west, this turn is about 7 miles east of the small town of Gould). After paying for a park pass at the State

Lake Agnes fills a cirque below the Nokhu Crags.

Forest entrance station, drive 2.3 miles over a steep gravel road to the trailhead.

Above the parking area, the jagged outline of the Nokhu Crags towers over the treeline, marking a tumultuous past of magmatic activity. Notice the light-colored granitic *dikes* that have intruded the darker Nokhu rocks in a crosscutting pattern on the hillside above the crags, hinting at the igneous interplay in the area.

From the trail register, the route immediately starts the 400-foot climb up to Lake Agnes. About 0.5 mile from the trailhead, a break in the trees provides a great view of the Nokhu Crags rising nearly 2,000 feet straight up. These rocks were once deposited as mud on an ancient sea floor that has since hardened into the Pierre Shale. *Shale* is typically a soft, easily eroded rock, but here, heat from the intruding magma has metamorphosed the shale to *hornfels,* making it hard and resistant to erosion. The greenish-yellow tint of the outcrops is not minerals in the rock but rather lichens coating the surface.

Lake Agnes comes into view about 0.8 mile from the trailhead. A scramble onto rock outcrops to the left gives you a clear view of the lake. Lake Agnes fills a *cirque* scoured by Pleistocene *Ice Age glaciers.* Towering above the lake to the south is the rounded granitic summit of Mount Richthofen.

A trail worn by fishermen follows the western shoreline of the lake. Notice that the dark, fine-grained rocks along the trail have weathered from the slopes above. This is hornfels, the once-soft and crumbly Pierre Shale now altered by the heat of the granitic intrusion.

After several hundred yards, it's necessary to climb a short distance up the slope to the right to avoid the low cliffs along the lake. The trail then continues along the shore. As you emerge beyond the trees, notice that all the rocks underfoot are now granitic. These rocks are mostly *granodiorite* with abundant dark *hornblende* crystals. You have crossed the boundary, or contact, between the metamorphosed Pierre Shale and the Mount Richthofen intrusion. Look to the opposite side of the lake (eastward) for a good view of this contact between the contrasting rock types. The *talus* slope turns from reddish on the left (well-baked hornfels) to gray on the right (Mount Richthofen Granodiorite). Follow the color change upward to see where the layered rocks that make up the Nokhu Crags end and the massive igneous intrusive rocks begin. Imagine a molten pluton deep within the earth boiling up through a hardened ancient sea floor, baking it and tilting it aside as it rose. Millions of years later, the pluton and its tilted fallout would rise above the surface to form the dramatic landscape before you.

The trail eventually peters out where the loose talus slopes meet the shoreline. After taking in the serene beauty of Lake Agnes and the spectacular geologic setting, retrace your steps back to the trailhead.

LITTLE YELLOWSTONE CANYON

Hike 3

HEADWATERS OF THE COLORADO RIVER

The origin of the mighty Colorado River is found through Rocky Mountain National Park's back door in volcanic Little Yellowstone Canyon.

DISTANCE ■ **5 miles round trip**

ELEVATION ■ **10,175 to 9,400 feet**

DIFFICULTY ■ **Moderate**

TOPOGRAPHIC MAPS ■ **USGS Fall River Pass; Trails Illustrated #200**

GEOLOGIC MAP ■ **1**

KEY REFERENCE ■ **2**

PRECAUTIONS ■ **The Little Yellowstone Canyon bottom can be reached only by scrambling upstream from where the trail meets the Colorado River. Be careful as rocks can be loose and slippery. Overnight camping at designated sites requires a backcountry permit.**

FOR INFORMATION ■ **Rocky Mountain National Park**

About the Landscape: Borne from the melting snowfields that flank the summits around La Poudre Pass, the mighty Colorado River begins as a mere trickle on its 1,400 mile journey from Rocky Mountain National Park to the Gulf of California. Here at its headwaters, the river gathers strength enough to shape a narrow canyon through colorful layers of volcanic ash and lava, products of the explosive volcanic activity in this region of the Front Range between 28 and 24 million years ago. This canyon, called Little Yellowstone, is named after similar volcanic formations in the Grand Canyon of the Yellowstone, in Wyoming's Yellowstone National Park.

Trail Guide: This hike enters Rocky Mountain National Park through the "back door" at the Never Summer Trailhead in Roosevelt National Forest. A longer alternative hike (about 10 miles round trip) starts at the Colorado River Trailhead along Trail Ridge Road within the park.

To reach the Never Summer Trailhead, drive north from Fort Collins on US Highway 287 (which is also Colorado Highway 14 along this stretch) for 10.5 miles. Turn left and follow Colorado Highway 14 for 61 miles as it

Eroded spires of volcanic tuff and breccia in Little Yellowstone Canyon

winds along the Cache La Poudre River to the Long Draw Road (Forest Road 156). Turn left and follow this well-maintained gravel road for 13.4 miles to where it ends at the trailhead.

The hike begins by following a maintenance road along the Grand Ditch. This hand-dug canal was constructed near the turn of the century to supply the blossoming cities along the Front Range with water diverted from the Colorado River drainage over to the east side of the Continental Divide. After several hundred yards, the route enters Rocky Mountain National Park, and just beyond, it passes a National Park Service patrol cabin at La Poudre Pass on the Continental Divide.

From the patrol cabin, continue along the ditch road. The outcrops along the road are shiny Precambrian *basement rocks* of *schist* and *gneiss*. The lighter colored veins that cut through these dark *metamorphic rocks* are composed of igneous *pegmatite* that contains large crystals of *quartz* and *feldspar*. You are looking at evidence of the multiple events that created Colorado's basement.

At the point where the road makes a big bend to the right, the snow-clad spine of the Never Summer Mountains comes into view on the western skyline. On the left (east) across the ditch, is the headwaters of the Colorado River. Here, the river is just a quiet stream flowing through a lush alpine meadow, belying the power it commands farther downstream where it carves the Grand Canyon and supplies much of the southwestern United States with water. This is the hike's best view of the Colorado River headwaters.

Around the bend, a change occurs in the rock outcrops along the ditch bank to the right. Gone are the metamorphic rocks of the Precambrian basement. The rocks are now reddish-brown *volcanic rocks*. Notice the angular rock fragments "floating" within a finer-grained material. This rock is a volcanic *breccia* forged as a mixture of ash and rock fragments that cascaded down a mountainside during the explosive volcanic eruptions that smothered this region about 28 to 24 million years ago.

About 1 mile from the patrol cabin, the ditch road meets the Little Yellowstone Trail (look for the sign). Follow this trail left down the forested hillside for about 1 mile, where it emerges along the rim of Little Yellowstone Canyon.

Although the canyon walls are too steep to see down to the river, the views of the layered volcanic rocks that the river has etched are spectacular. The light-colored layers upstream (to the left) appear to be slanted at nearly a 45-degree angle, probably tilted by faulting long after the volcanic activity ceased. The more colorful lavender layers downstream are soft ash layers that have eroded into loose slopes without any vegetation. The rocks underfoot along the rim are also hardened layers of volcanic ash. The ash both fell from the air and flowed down the mountains in hot, glowing clouds of ash and rock debris. This material cooled and solidified to form volcanic breccia and *tuff* (mostly ash).

The trail continues following the forested rim of the canyon and then winds down to meet the Colorado River about 3 miles from the trailhead. Along the way, it passes the junction and sign for the Stage Road Trail on the right, which climbs back up to meet the Grand Ditch road.

Athough there is no maintained trail upstream along the Colorado River through Little Yellowstone Canyon, adventurous hikers may want to scramble carefully upstream into the canyon for a river-level view of the volcanic layers and rock spires that the river has eroded. Be prepared to get your feet wet, as it is necessary to cross the river several times.

Return to the trailhead by the route you came, or perhaps make a detour by hiking up the Stage Road back to the Grand Ditch road and then back to the trailhead.

GLACIER GORGE

Hike 4

An Ice Age Quarry in Rocky Mountain National Park

Explore a glacially sculpted landscape on the hike to Mills Lake in Glacier Gorge.

DISTANCE ■ **5 miles round trip**

ELEVATION ■ **9,240 to 9,960 feet**

DIFFICULTY ■ **Moderate**

TOPOGRAPHIC MAPS ■ **USGS McHenrys Peak; Trails Illustrated #200**

GEOLOGIC MAP ■ **3**

KEY REFERENCE ■ **3**

PRECAUTIONS ■ **Please be careful when climbing along rock cliffs above the waterfalls near the trail.**

FOR INFORMATION ■ **Rocky Mountain National Park**

About the Landscape: Glacier Gorge is a classic *hanging valley* in the heart of Rocky Mountain National Park. Here, Colorado's *basement rocks* were quarried by ice as it pushed over the terrain again and again during the *Ice Age.* Everywhere there is evidence of the glaciers that engulfed the landscape, including Mills Lake, a shallow rock basin carved from basement rock by ice. Today, melting snow surges down Glacier Gorge in summer, cascading over Glacier Falls at the steep lip of the hanging valley.

Trail Guide: To reach the Glacier Gorge Trailhead, drive west 3.5 miles from downtown Estes Park on US Highway 36 to the Beaver Meadows Entrance Station. Turn left onto Bear Lake Road and drive 9.5 miles to the trailhead at Glacier Gorge Junction. During the summer months, the parking area is often filled by 8:00 A.M. A free shuttle bus from the entrance station will drop you near the trailhead if you do not arrive early.

The hike begins across the road from the parking area. The first 0.7 mile is a gentle climb to Alberta Falls amidst large boulders of *granite* scattered along the trail. Called glacial *erratics,* these boulders hitchhiked down the valley frozen in glacial ice and were then left stranded as the ice retreated.

Glacial erratic perched on the shoreline of Mills Lake

A close look at these rocks reveals elongate, pink *feldspar* crystals, a characteristic of the local Silver Plume Granite that intruded the area about 1.4 billion years ago. The rectangular feldspar crystals are oriented approximately parallel to one another, aligning in the direction of flow of the *magma* as it slowly cooled during the igneous intrusion. Alberta Falls cascades over outcrops of the Silver Plume Granite. Look along the outcrops above the falls for glacially polished surfaces and *striations,* lines scratched in the rock by stones frozen in the ice.

Above Alberta Falls, the trail switchbacks toward the base of the Glacier Knobs, glacially rounded outcrops of metamorphic basement rock. At the 1.4 mile point, the trail meets the East Longs Peak Trail on the left. Continue straight ahead among boulders of dark *schist* that become more common as the trail continues to climb. The Glacier Knobs, the high rounded outcrops ahead, are made of this schist. These *metamorphic rocks* are 1.7 billion years old and, along with the granite that intruded into the schist, form the uplifted basement core of the Front Range.

About 1.9 miles from the trailhead, the trail to Glacier Falls and Mills Lake splits off to the left from the trail that continues up Loch Valley to Sky Pond. After turning left at the junction, the trail immediately crosses a bridge over Icy Brook. It becomes more difficult to follow as it crosses outcrops of schist, but just keep heading uphill. Off to the left, you will hear Glacier Falls, where Glacier Creek cascades from Glacier Gorge, the hanging valley above. For a good view of the falls, hike a short distance left off the trail toward the thundering sound of water.

As the trail reaches the level of Glacier Gorge, follow the cairns (rock pile markers) to Mills Lake. About 100 yards before you reach the lake, look for an area of dark rock surrounded by schist. The dark rock is an *intrusive igneous rock* called diorite that appears to be floating in the schist. This is the remains of a once-continuous *dike* that was deformed during metamorphism 1.7 billion years ago.

Mills Lake itself lies in a shallow, glacially carved rock basin with numerous islands poking above the surface of the water. This lake is named after Enos Mills, a naturalist who explored, wrote about, and fostered the creation of Rocky Mountain National Park. Mills Lake is a pleasant place to lean against a glacial erratic boulder along the shoreline and ponder the *Ice Age* when ice completely filled Glacier Gorge and all the other major valleys in Rocky Mountain National Park. The alpine scenery of Colorado's Rockies is largely the work of these glaciers. Ice more than 1,000 feet thick etched the once-rounded summits into jagged peaks and scoured the stream-carved valleys into the broad U-shaped valleys of today.

Although Mills Lake is the turnaround point for this hike, and a great picnic spot, the trail continues along the east shoreline of Mills Lake to Jewel Lake, another small, shallow lake. Above Jewel Lake, the trail continues up Glacier Gorge for 2.2 miles to Black Lake, then ultimately climbs to Frozen Lake. However far you choose to explore, return to the trailhead by retracing your steps.

CHASM LAKE

GLACIAL REFLECTIONS

Chasm Lake lies in a cirque chiseled into the east face of Longs Peak in Rocky Mountain National Park.

DISTANCE ■ **8.4 miles round trip**

ELEVATION ■ **9,400 to 11,800 feet**

DIFFICULTY ■ **Strenuous**

TOPOGRAPHIC MAPS ■ **USGS Longs Peak; Trails Illustrated #200**

GEOLOGIC MAP ■ 3

KEY REFERENCE ■ 3

PRECAUTIONS ■ Be sure to get an early start to avoid being above treeline during afternoon thunderstorms. The last 0.25 mile to Chasm Lake climbs up bare rock ledges—please watch your step. Overnight camping with a Backcountry Permit is allowed in designated sites only.

FOR INFORMATION ■ Rocky Mountain National Park

About the Landscape: For ambitious hikers, the unforgettable trek to Chasm Lake to greet dawn's golden light begins at 4:00 A.M. Those willing to forego the sunrise will still be impressed by this *Ice Age* landscape.

Longs Peak is the most prominent landmark along the Front Range

Colorado's basement rocks exposed on the east face of Longs Peak

north of Denver. The familiar flat-topped peak is the highest summit in Rocky Mountain National Park, rising 14,255 feet above sea level. Chasm Lake lies in a glaciated *cirque* basin at the base of the peak's east face.

The flat-topped summit of Longs Peak probably hails from the *Rocky Mountain Surface,* a flattened landscape beveled along the Front Range during the long period of erosion that followed uplift during the Laramide Orogeny. Final uplift of the modern-day range during the past 10 million years activated rivers and streams that dissected the Front Range, isolating once-connected segments of the Rocky Mountain Surface, such as Longs Peak, in the process.

Trail Guide: To reach the Longs Peak Trailhead, drive south from Estes Park 9.7 miles on Colorado Highway 7. Turn right at the Park Service sign for Longs Peak and drive to the trailhead located near the Ranger Station at the end of the road. Be warned that during the summer months, the parking area at the Longs Peak Trailhead is often full by 4:00 A.M.! Most hikers, however, are bound for the summit, leaving Chasm Lake in quiet solitude at sunrise.

For the first several miles, the Longs Peak Trail winds uphill through the forested hillside of Pine Ridge. The *erratic* boulders along the trail were left behind by *glaciers* that conveyored them down from the flanks of Longs Peak during the Ice Ages.

After crossing the cascades of Alpine Brook, the trail continues to climb and emerges above treeline. The summit of Longs Peak is now in full view to the left of Mount Lady Washington directly ahead. From this point, the trail zigzags through an extensive boulder field along the flank of the Mills Moraine, named after Enos Mills, the founder of Rocky Mountain National Park. The Mills Moraine is a *lateral moraine* in which *basement rocks,* plucked from the surrounding peaks by glaciers, accumulated along the margins of the glacier to form the long, huge pile you are now navigating.

Boulders of banded *gneiss* and swirled *schist* become more abundant the higher you climb on the moraine. The dark, shiny layers within the schist are mostly *mica,* which alternates with light-colored layers of *quartz* and *feldspar.* Several different kinds of *granite* are scattered about, including gray, pink, and a coarse-grained variety with elongate crystals of feldspar. In certain boulders, these large feldspar crystals are aligned parallel to one another in the direction of the flow of magma that continued during cooling. This is a characteristic of the 1.4 billion-year-old Silver Plume Granite that makes up Longs Peak.

About 3.7 miles from the trailhead, the Longs Peak Trail reaches the junction with the Chasm Lake Trail in the saddle located along the crest of the Mills Moraine. Bear to the left and follow the Chasm Lake Trail as it traverses downhill along the north flank of a glaciated valley that cuts into the east slope of Longs Peak. In the U-shaped valley below, a series of glaciated basins, each bejeweled with its own lake, stair-steps up to the amphitheater below Longs Peaks where Chasm Lake is located (still hidden from view).

As the trail approaches the head of the valley, it climbs over the ledge at the top of Columbine Falls, then follows along a marshy flat to a Park Service patrol cabin. To reach Chasm Lake, scramble up the ledge behind the cabin following the rock cairns (rock piles). Once you are at the top of this last giant rock step, Chasm Lake comes into view.

Chasm Lake lies in a spectacular cirque basin chiseled into the base of Longs Peak's east face. The sheer east face, which rises more than 2,400 feet straight up, is the highest cliff in the Southern Rockies. It is a rock cathedral, excavated by Ice Age glaciers along vertical *fractures* in the granite. By filling the fractures with water and expanding them with ice, the glaciers wedged rocks from the cliff, continually enlarging the cirque and moving the steep headwall of the rock basin back into the mountain. The dirty-looking snowfield perched on the talus slope at the base of the cliff is the last vestige of the Mills Glacier, a probable remnant of the *Little Ice Age.*

As you begin to retrace your steps back to the trailhead, notice the boulders perched precariously on the rock ledges bordering Chasm Lake. These were left behind by the last glacier that filled the cirque. Look for polished surfaces and striations, evidence of the forceful scouring by rocks grinding beneath the moving ice.

ARAPAHO GLACIER

Hike 6

COLORADO'S LARGEST GLACIER

One of the southernmost glaciers in North America hangs on as a Little Ice Age remnant below the serrated Indian Peaks.

DISTANCE ■ **7 miles round trip**

ELEVATION ■ **10,120 to 12,700 feet**

DIFFICULTY ■ **Strenuous**

TOPOGRAPHIC MAPS ■ **USGS Monarch Lake and East Portal; Trails Illustrated #102**

GEOLOGIC MAP ■ **4**

KEY REFERENCE ■ **4**

PRECAUTIONS ■ **Due to the popularity of the Indian Peaks, a National Forest Service permit is required for backcountry camping between**

June 1 and September 15. The Arapaho Glacier is located in a watershed set aside for the City of Boulder and is off limits to hikers. Old mines are dangerous—please be careful.

FOR INFORMATION ■ Boulder Ranger District

About the Landscape: Outstanding alpine scenery and proximity to Denver and Boulder make the Indian Peaks one of the most popular destinations in all of Colorado. A series of *cirques* lines the eastern flank of the range, some of which harbor remnant glaciers from the Rockies' frozen past. This hike leads to a view of Arapaho Glacier, one of the southernmost glaciers in North America and the largest remaining glacier in Colorado.

Trail Guide: To reach the Fourth of July Trailhead, drive west from Boulder on Colorado Highway 19 to the town of Nederland. In Nederland, take Colorado Highway 72 and go 0.5 mile south to Boulder County Road 130 (sign for Eldora Ski Area). Turn right and drive on a rough dirt road for 7.9 miles along the north fork of Middle Boulder Creek to the trailhead.

The hike begins by following the Arapaho Pass Trail, a well-maintained route that climbs a gentle grade along the north side of Boulder Creek Valley.

Boulders of ancient *gneiss* and *schist* lie along the trail revealing that, along with the rest of the Front Range, the Indian Peaks are cored by a broad uplift of Precambrian *basement rock.* After several hundred yards, look for a giant boulder to the right of the trail. This rock is a banner example of the Boulder Creek Granodiorite, one of the oldest igneous intrusions in Colorado, dated at 1.7 billion years old. This rock is called *granodiorite* because it contains a higher percentage of dark minerals than *granite* and is intermediate between granite and diorite.

After 1 mile, the trail meets the junction with the Diamond Lake Trail. Keep to the right and continue traversing up the side of the valley. Look for a rock promontory to the left of the trail to gain a panoramic view. Do not be alarmed, but you are standing amidst a geologic zone of weakness, albeit an ancient one. The upper reaches of the Boulder Creek Valley trace the Arapaho Pass Fault. *Faults* create zones of weakness along which streams and glaciers can more easily penetrate the landscape.

Two miles from the trailhead, the Arapaho Pass Trail intersects the Arapaho Glacier Trail. Turn right on the Glacier Trail and look for the Fourth of July Mine near the trail junction. The collapsed mine entrance is located near the machinery rusting on the tailings pile. Between 1914 and 1937, more than 100 tons of reportedly gold and silver ore were removed from this mine shaft which extends 2,000 feet underground. Ore bodies and veins of precious minerals are often associated with fault zones, such

Arapaho Glacier is Colorado's largest.

as the Arapaho Pass Fault, where mineral-laden fluids can easily flow along the broken and fractured rock. The Indian Peaks are located at the eastern limit of the Colorado Mineral Belt, a northeast–southwest trend of fault zones where most of the state's productive mines are found.

From the mine, the Arapaho Glacier Trail climbs up the ridge to the northeast. At the first switchback, the boulders in an extensive boulder field to the left of the trail display a variety of metamorphic textures. A number of boulders contain garnet, a dark red mineral formed during intense metamorphism. Other boulders show stretched, folded, and contorted textures much like the swirled layers in a marble fudge cake. All these rocks are from the Precambrian metamorphic core of the Indian Peaks.

After many switchbacks and long traverses across the alpine tundra, the trail reaches the saddle east of South Arapaho Peak. In the cirque below the jagged summits and sheer faces of North and South Arapaho Peaks is the Arapaho Glacier. Snow and ice fill the cirque basin. The glacier itself appears "dirty" compared to the relatively fresh melting snow that partially obscures the old glacial ice. Near the front tip of the glacier, an aquamarine lake of silty glacial meltwater is bordered by an end moraine of rock debris that was transported by the retreating sheet of ice. The fracture near the top of the glacier, called a bergschrund, was formed as the ice cracked as it moved downslope. This is an indication that this is indeed a moving glacier, not just a permanent snowfield.

Although the Arapaho Glacier continues to form in the cirque and grind downhill, it's overall size is diminishing. It is probably a remnant of the *Little Ice Age,* a cold, wet period that began about 700 years ago. Modern-day glaciers in the Rockies are mere ice cubes compared to the mighty glaciers that carved the Indian Peaks during the last major advance of ice that ended about 15,000 years ago.

Although the Arapaho Glacier Trail continues to the east, this hike returns to the trailhead via the same route. As you hike back down, the spectacular alpine terrain of the Indian Peaks is ahead of you. Be sure to take time to enjoy the view.

CHICAGO LAKES

The Mount Evans Batholith

The Mount Evans Batholith is unveiled high in the Rockies where it has been sculpted by ice into sheer cliffs that tower over stair-stepped Chicago Lakes.

DISTANCE ■ **8 miles round trip**

ELEVATION ■ **10,650 to 11,760 feet**

DIFFICULTY ■ **Moderate**

TOPOGRAPHIC MAPS ■ **USGS Georgetown, Idaho Springs, and Mount Evans**

GEOLOGIC MAP ■ **5**

KEY REFERENCE ■ **5**

PRECAUTIONS ■ **The trail to the upper lake encounters some large boulders— watch your step.**

FOR INFORMATION ■ **Clear Creek Ranger District**

About the Landscape: The Chicago Lakes Trail leads to a glacial master-piece on Mount Evans' northeast side. Upper and Lower Chicago Lakes stair-step up to a *cirque* surrounded by towering cliffs.

Mount Evans (14,264 feet) dominates the central portion of the Front Range west of Denver. Best known for having the highest paved road in North America, the bulk of Mount Evans is composed of the Mount Evans *Batholith,* a major *granitic* intrusion into Colorado's Precambrian basement that uplifted along with the rest of the Front Range. Mount Evans was later carved by *Ice Age glaciers* into a rugged landscape of U-shaped valleys, sheer rock faces, and artistically sculpted cirques.

Trail Guide: To reach the Chicago Lakes Trailhead from Denver, drive west on Interstate 70 to Idaho Springs (Exit 240). Turn left, crossing over the Interstate, and follow the Mount Evans Highway (Colorado Highway 103) 13.4 miles to the Echo Lake Campground. Parking for the trailhead is located at the entrance to the campground. The trail starts across the road just below the entrance station for the Mount Evans Highway.

The trail begins by traversing a forested hillside and skirting the shore-line of Echo Lake. An abundance of huge, rounded boulders suggest this hillside is part of a glacial moraine, formed by the material transported and cast aside by glaciers carving the *granitic* slopes of Mount Evans.

The trail then follows down an even grade. About 0.5 mile from the trailhead, a continuous outcrop left of the trail provides a close-up view of the Mount Evans Batholith. This *batholith* emerged about 1.4 billion years ago when *magma* pushed up into surrounding *metamorphic rocks.* This igneous intrusion cooled slowly to form a variety of granitic rocks, most predominantly the rock type called *granodiorite* (a granitic rock darker than granite and intermediate between granite and diorite).

The arrangement of rock types in this outcrop appears very complex. Although medium to dark gray granodiorite makes up most of the forma-tion, the outcrop is also highly fractured and crosscut by intrusions of *quartz* and *pegmatite,* a granitelike rock with very large crystals. Several particularly thick (4 to 5 feet wide) pegmatite veins, containing prominent pink *feldspar* crystals, cross the trail.

The U-shaped Chicago Creek Valley comes into view as the trail steepens. After a series of switchbacks, the trail crosses a log bridge over Chicago Creek at about the 1-mile point. On the other side of the creek, the trail intersects a maintenance road that leads uphill to the Idaho Springs City Reservoir. The trail follows this road for about 1 mile, then enters the Mount Evans Wilderness at the trail register just past the two summer cabins beyond the reservoir.

From the wilderness boundary, the trail climbs through an old burn area

67

View looking down cascades to Lower Chicago Lake

for about the next 1.5 miles. Sheer rock cliffs come into view on the opposite side of the valley.

About 3.5 miles from the trailhead, Lower Chicago Lake comes into view. The downstream end of the lake is dammed by a glacial moraine that chokes the outlet stream with boulders. At the upper end of the lake, a spectacular waterfall spills from Upper Chicago Lake, cascading several hundred feet over a rock ledge that extends across the valley.

The trail continues around the north side of Lower Chicago Lake, keeping to the slope several hundred feet above the lake. About halfway around is a junction with a trail that leads down to the shoreline. To reach Upper

Chicago Lake, keep to the right. Several hundred yards beyond the junction, the trail encounters a field of huge boulders that have tumbled down from the cliff above. The trail crosses the lower end of this boulder field (not too difficult), then climbs steeply to the upper lake.

The setting for Upper Chicago Lake is a showcase for glacial artistry. The cirque where the lake is located forms a natural amphitheater with cliffs rising vertically nearly 2,000 feet. Permanent snowfields cling to fractures in the sheer rock faces. Along the rock bench that separates the upper and lower lakes, glacial *erratics* perch precariously on rounded outcrops worn smooth by moving ice. These boulders were left behind as the valley's last glacier melted. The rock types that make up these boulders are a mixture of the medium-gray granodiorite and the pink granite of the Mount Evans Batholith.

Before heading back to the trailhead, take time to explore the cascades spilling from the upper lake. The view down the notch of the Lower Chicago Lake is breathtaking—but watch your step! Looking beyond the lower lake toward the High Plains, you will see that the classic U-shape of the glacial valley befits a textbook.

Hike

8

ROCK CREEK TRAIL

SMOOTH GRANITIC SUMMITS

The rounded crest of the Platte River Mountains tells a tale of erosion and ice.

DISTANCE ■ **8 miles round trip**

ELEVATION ■ **9,720 to 11,500 feet**

DIFFICULTY ■ **Moderate**

TOPOGRAPHIC MAPS ■ **USGS Mount Logan and Observatory Peak; Trails Illustrated #105**

GEOLOGIC MAP ■ **5**

KEY REFERENCE ■ **None**

PRECAUTIONS ■ **During the summer, avoid being caught above treeline during afternoon thunderstorms.**

FOR INFORMATION ■ **South Park Ranger District**

About the Landscape: The Platte River Mountains have distinguished themselves by eroding into smooth, rounded surfaces rather than imitating their craggy neighbors throughout the rest of the Front Range. Like the other mountains, the little-known Platte River Mountains are part of an uplifted block of Precambrian *basement rock*. What makes them unique is the nature of their *granitic* erosion and their total immersion in ice during the *Ice Age*. Both actions contributed to their distinctly dome-shaped peaks.

Sweeping views of the Front Range and South Park can be enjoyed from a perch atop the rounded outcrops at the crest of the range. Although not far from Denver, this area receives little use compared to other Front Range destinations.

Trail Guide: To reach the Rock Creek Trailhead from the Denver area, drive 48 miles west from Evergreen on US Highway 285. About 2 miles after crossing Kenos Pass, turn left onto Lost Park Road (sign for National Forest access). Follow this graded road for 7.5 miles, then turn left onto Forest Road 133 (sign for Rock Creek and Ben Tyler Trail). Signs lead to the trailhead 2.1 miles from the turn. The last 0.25 mile can be muddy and rutted, so you may need to park before reaching the trailhead.

The trail starts out in the forest following a gentle grade up along Rock Creek. For about the first 0.25 mile, Rock Creek forms an impressive series of cascades as it tumbles over rounded Precambrian boulders. Along the trail, boulders of *granite* and *gneiss* form part of an old road leading to the ruins of a logging camp at about the 0.5-mile point. After 2 miles, the trail leaves the creek and climbs a steady grade up a forested ridge.

About 3 miles from the trailhead, the trail crosses several alpine meadows. Trees become sparse and South Park comes into view to the west. South Park is the fault-bounded valley that separates the Front Range from the Mosquito Range to the west.

As the trail emerges above treeline along the flank of a wind-swept ridge, look for the first accessible rock outcrops below the trail to the left. It's worthwhile taking a moment to investigate. This outcrop represents the margin of a 1.4 billion-year-old granite intrusion that pushed up through older 1.7 billion-year-old *metamorphic rocks*. An interesting mixture of metamorphic gneiss and *schist* is surrounded by intrusions of granite. The gneiss and schist are very twisted and contorted in places due to the intrusion. In other areas, the metamorphic rocks are completely absent and the outcrop is only granite. In several boulders, isolated pieces of the gneiss and schist appear to float in the granite. These are "undigested" pieces of rock, called zenoliths, that were cast into the igneous brew at some point during the intrusion but did not melt into magma.

Back on the trail, granite paves the way as you approach the saddle along the crest of the Platte River Mountains. The saddle is a very broad area of soggy tundra. For the best view of the surrounding countryside, scramble up to the top of the granite outcrops to the right of the trail where you will see a sweeping view of the Front Range.

Cascades over Precambrian basement along Rock Creek

Immediately to the northwest are the rounded summits of South Twin Cone (12,265 feet) and Mount Blaine (12,303 feet), two of the highest peaks in the Platte River Mountains. These domes have been rounded by a process called *exfoliation,* an erosion pattern common for granite intrusions. When *magma* intrudes and hardens into granite, the resulting *pluton* spends its initial existence buried under heavy layers of earth. If the pluton is uplifted to the surface, as has happened here in the Platte River Mountains, the pluton may crack as the pressure is relieved. In exfoliation, rock layers spall off in sheets along these cracks or sheet joints that develop parallel to the outer surface of the outcrop or mountaintop. When the Platte River Mountains uplifted through overlying layers, sheets of granite gradually peeled off like the layers of an onion, creating these distinctly rounded landforms.

Their roundedness was enhanced during the Pleistocene Ice Age when the Platte River Mountains were not carved by but rather engulfed in glacial ice. Instead of sculpting jagged summits, the ice completely covered and then ground down their already rounded summits into the smoothed landforms of today.

The hike back to the trailhead retraces the same route. In some places, it is possible to lose the trail going downhill through the trees, so keep a sharp lookout for the trailblazes on the trees.

Hike

9

THE CRAGS

PIKES PEAK'S SPINY WEST SIDE

An easy trail leads to an area of unusual granite formations on the west side of Pikes Peak.

DISTANCE ■ **4 miles round trip**

ELEVATION ■ **10,080 to 10,800 feet**

DIFFICULTY ■ **Easy**

TOPOGRAPHIC MAPS ■ **USGS Pikes Peak and Woodland Park; Trails Illustrated #137**

GEOLOGIC MAP ■ **6**

KEY REFERENCE ■ **6**

PRECAUTIONS ■ **Use extra care when scrambing among The Crags.**

FOR INFORMATION ■ **Pikes Peak Ranger District**

About the Landscape: Due in part to its colorful history and prominent stature, Pikes Peak is perhaps the most famous landmark in Colorado. Most visitors drive the Toll Road to the 14,110-foot summit. This hike explores a magical area of eroded rock formations on the back, or west, side of Pikes Peak, away from the crowds. Here the Pikes Peak *granite* has cracked and weathered into magnificent sculptures called The Crags.

Located along the southern Front Range near Colorado Springs, Pikes Peak is a huge uplifted block of Precambrian *granite.* This large mass of intrusive *igneous rock,* called the Pikes Peak Batholith, welled up as *magma* within the earth's crust about 1 billion years ago, making it some of the "youngest" Precambrian *basement rock* in Colorado. The Pikes Peak granite is generally pink in color, but it weathers to a distinctive red-orange soil that is visible along roadsides throughout the area.

Trail Guide: To reach the The Crags Trailhead, drive west 22 miles from Colorado Springs on US Highway 24 to the town of Divide. Turn left onto Colorado Highway 67 heading south toward Cripple Creek. After 4.8 miles, turn left again onto Forest Road 383 at the sign for The Crags Campground. Drive 3.4 miles to the campground. The trailhead is located at the upper end of the campground loop.

The trail begins by following a well-worn path along Fourmile Creek. Several hundred yards from the trailhead, large boulders that have tumbled off the slope on the left rest along the trail. Meet the Pikes Peak granite, a pinkish rock with interlocking crystals of *quartz* (gray to translucent) and *feldspar* (pink to buff). Dark, elongate crystals of biotite *mica* are also scattered throughout the rock. The 1 billion-year-old Pikes Peak granite is part of a large *batholith* exposed here at Pikes Peak and in the Rampart Range to the north.

The trail traverses several meadows and provides glimpses of towering granite outcrops that rise above the forest. After about a mile, the trail passes some granite formations on the left. Farther on, another granite tower meets the trail on the right. These formations have prominent horizontal *fractures* that segment the outcrops like huge disks stacked on top of one another. This arrangement seems precarious and certainly will topple over in time. As you will see when you reach The Crags, fractures in the Pikes Peak granite have influenced these unusual horizontal and vertical weathering patterns in the rock.

About 2 miles from the trailhead, the route climbs through a forested ravine until it reaches a rocky ledge with a view. On the right, the granite spires of The Crags climb up the flank of Pikes Peak toward the treeless skyline. From this viewpoint, the trail continues uphill to the left where it becomes indistinct as it winds through the trees. Simply continue climbing until you emerge on a rocky ridge. A wonderland of unique landforms is before you. These are "The Crags."

Eroded spire of Pikes Peak granite at The Crags

The unusual rock outcroppings of The Crags are caused by weathering in places where the granite is laced with countless *fractures*. These fractures, which are oriented both horizontally and vertically, are the result of a combination of events that have stressed the granite over its 1 billion-year-old life. The vertical fractures first formed during the continued flow of *magma* while the huge batholith cooled and were later augmented as the rock was shaken when Pikes Peak and the rest of the Front Range was uplifted during the *Laramide Orogeny*. The horizontal fractures were more likely caused by expansion of the granite as the weight and pressure of overlying rock were relieved by erosion during uplift.

Once a fracture is formed, water from rain and snowmelt seeps into it and, upon freezing, expands and wedges the rock apart. Over time, the rock breaks apart and disintegrates along zones that follow the fractures, creating a variety of interesting landforms. Weathering along vertical fractures creates steep landforms such as the spires and pinnacles before you.

After exploring the nooks and crannies along the ridge, you may choose to simply return by the route you came. If you are feeling adventurous, however, there is an alternate route that scrambles down the ridge to the west (toward the ravine between the spires) and makes a short loop back to the main trail along Fourmile Creek.

Hike 10

PETRIFIED FOREST TRAIL

FLORISSANT FOSSIL BEDS NATIONAL MONUMENT

Massive petrified tree stumps provide a snapshot of ancient life.

DISTANCE ■ 1-mile loop

ELEVATION ■ 8,320 to 8,360 feet

DIFFICULTY ■ Easy

TOPOGRAPHIC MAPS ■ USGS Lake George; Trails Illustrated #137

GEOLOGIC MAP ■ 7

KEY REFERENCE ■ 7

PRECAUTIONS ■ Please stay on the marked trails. Fossil collecting is strictly prohibited without a permit (issued only to approved research projects affiliated with a museum or university). Please do not remove any materials from the National Monument.

FOR INFORMATION ■ Florissant Fossil Beds National Monument

About the Landscape: About 35 million years ago, a lush, ancient forest was frozen in time as flows of ash and mud from a series of violent volcanic eruptions solidified it in place. Although the forest regenerated, it was buried twice more. Renewed uplift of today's Front Range and erosion of its overlying layers have brought the remnants of this forest to the surface in the mountains west of Pikes Peak. At the Florissant Fossil Beds, detailed impressions of thousands of plant and insect fossils and numerous petrified stumps of giant redwood trees paint a picture of this Colorado forest that once was.

A short loop hike along the Petrified Forest Trail leads past several impressive giant fossil redwood stumps and the light gray *shale* beds of the Florissant Formation which contain the fossil treasure trove. Although the trail does not wind through any active excavation sites, an amazing variety of specimens from the fossil beds is on display at the National Monument Visitor Center.

Trail Guide: To reach Florissant Fossil Beds National Monument, drive 35 miles west from Colorado Springs on US Highway 24 to the small town of Florissant. Turn left onto Teller County Road 1, drive 2 miles south, then turn right at the marked entrance road to the Visitor Center. Pick up a self-guided trail map then start on the Petrified Forest Trail behind the Visitor Center.

The first part of the trail is paved and leads to large petrified redwood stumps. First, on the right, is a petrified stump of an extinct redwood tree (*Sequoia affinis*) roughly 13 feet in diameter. Today, three species of trees related to these ancient redwoods still exist: the coastal redwood native to California's northern coast, the giant sequoia of the inland Sierra Nevada, and the dawn redwood of central China. The petrified stumps and needles fossilized here are almost identical to contemporary coastal redwoods.

This means that, 35 million years ago during the Oligocene, a warm and humid climate like that of modern coastal California prevailed in this part of Colorado. Giant redwood trees grew along meandering streams that flowed across the eroded terrain of the *Rocky Mountain Surface.*

In this particular part of Colorado, the reign of the redwoods was interrupted when violent volcanic eruptions from the now-extinct Mount Guffey in the Thirtynine Mile Volcanic Field (about 15 miles to the west) periodically smothered this landscape with mudflows. The stumps still stand where the mudflows caught them. The flows solidified into *tuff,* a

Giant petrified redwood stump at Florissant Fossil Beds

rock composed of mostly volcanic ash. Over time, percolating ground-water saturated the entombed bases of the once-towering redwoods with silica-rich solutions that petrified (or permineralized) the wood.

The tented enclosures on the left beyond the first fossil stump are protective cases for other stumps, including a "petrified trio" of stumps entwined together. Just beyond the enclosures the trail splits in two. Follow the Petrified Forest Trail to the right.

As you follow the trail, go back in time and imagine that, around you, the forest growth has regenerated since the earlier volcanic flows. Once again, streams wind through a lush forest. There are no ponderosa pines and aspens like today but rather giant redwood, beech, cottonwood, and hickory trees. Insects buzz through the dense canopy and butterflies flutter in sunlit openings.

This lush, ancient scenery is now compressed into the Florissant Formation beneath your feet. About 0.25 mile from the trailhead, a spur trail to the left leads to the most famous fossil site in the formation where, in just 5 days in 1871, fossil insect specialist Samuel Scudder collected more than 5,000 specimens from this ancient forest bed.

The layers of the Florissant Formation represent the mud, silt, and volcanic ash that washed into ancient Lake Florissant. The lake was created by mudflows, similar to the earlier flows that preserved the stumps, which blocked a stream drainage and created a natural dam. As water backed up behind the dam, thousands of insects, leaves, and seeds from the regenerated forest settled into the lakebed. The lakebed sediment compacted into shale, and the insect and plant remains transformed over time into carbon compression fossils; traces of life "frozen" in the rock.

Back on the main trail, about 50 yards past the junction to Scudder's pit, you arrive at the "Big Stump," one of the largest petrified stumps in the National Monument, with an incredible 38-foot circumference. This redwood stood nearly 250 feet tall and was 700 years old when it was buried!

Before you is the entire story of the Florissant Fossil Beds. Exposed at the base of the cut-bank surrounding the fossil stump is the gray ash layer, or tuff, that first smothered the redwood forest. Sitting on top of the tuff and forming the bench at the base of the slope are the light gray, fossiliferous lake shales of the Florissant Formation. The rounded outcrops above the shale layer are a volcanic *breccia* deposit from the later volcanic eruption that ultimately buried ancient Lake Florissant, protecting the lakebed from erosion and preserving its riches.

From the Big Stump, the trail turns east, winds around the tops of several unexcavated stumps, and circles back to the Visitor Center.

GREENHORN MOUNTAIN

VOLCANIC ROCKS PRESERVE THE ROCKY MOUNTAIN SURFACE

Greenhorn Mountain rose with the rest of the Rockies, but its flat surface was sealed by a resistant volcanic layer.

DISTANCE ■ **3 miles round trip**

ELEVATION ■ **11,440 to 12,220 feet**

DIFFICULTY ■ **Easy**

TOPOGRAPHIC MAPS ■ **USGS San Isabel and Badito Cone**

GEOLOGIC MAP ■ **8**

KEY REFERENCE ■ **8**

PRECAUTIONS ■ **There is no shelter from summer thunderstorms on Greenhorn Mountain's bare summit.**

FOR INFORMATION ■ **San Carlos Ranger District**

About the Landscape: Greenhorn Mountain stands tall as the southernmost erosional remnant of a volcanic surge that blanketed wide areas of the *Rocky Mountain Surface* in the southern Front Range beginning about 35 million years ago. Although the mountain kept up with the rest of the rising Rockies over the past 10 million years, its volcanic summit uniquely survived while most of the volcanic rocks in the region tumbled downstream. On Greenhorn Mountain, exposures of *rhyolite tuff* and *breccia* are protected under a resistant cap of *andesite lava.*

Greenhorn Mountain lies at the southern end of the Wet Mountains, the southernmost of the Precambrian-cored uplifts that define Colorado's Front Range. Although sometimes not considered part of the Front Range, the Wet Mountains share a common geologic history with their counterparts to the north and are thus included here.

Trail Guide: To reach the Greenhorn Mountain Trailhead from the west on US Highway 69, turn onto Gardner Road (Forest Road 634) 1.5 miles west of Gardner and drive to the intersection with Greenhorn Mountain Road (Forest Road 369). From the intersection, turn right and drive 15 miles to the trailhead at the end of the road. Coming from the east on US Highway 165, turn onto Forest Road 360 at the sign for Ophir Campground and drive to the intersection with Greenhorn Mountain Road (Forest Road 369). Turn left and drive to the trailhead.

The trailhead is located in an open meadow directly below Greenhorn Mountain. Boulders of *granite* and *gneiss* surround the parking lot. About 50 yards from the trailhead, these rocks appear in a rounded outcrop to

Rock field formed by freeze-thaw action on the North Peak of Greenhorn Mountain

the left of the trail. They are part of the 1.7 billion-year-old Precambrian basement that cores the Wet Mountains.

The Greenhorn Trail passes through a narrow stand of spruce trees before starting to climb along the base of Greenhorn Mountain. The rocks underfoot here are completely different from the basement rocks near the trailhead. Red and gray volcanic rocks line the trail. These are fragments of the rhyolite tuff and andesite lava that crown Greenhorn Mountain. Within them are clues that hint at extremely violent volcanic explosions.

An outcrop of gray andesite is exposed on the left just below the first switchback. Notice that the rock contains very few visible crystals. Because crystals form slowly, this is an indication that the lava spewed rapidly from the volcano and cooled very quickly.

At the second switchback, there is an assortment of angular red boulders to the left of the trail. This rock is a volcanic breccia which forged from a mixture of ash and rhyolite fragments ejected during an explosive eruption. The white material between the rock fragments is a network of tiny *calcite* crystals. The calcite crystallized from hot, mineral-laden water that percolated through the breccia, effectively cementing the rocks together and making the outcrop resistant to erosion.

The trail continues climbing and crosses a *talus* slope of andesite. An outcrop of this rock occurs to the right of the trail. This is the resistant caprock of Greenhorn Mountain. The unusually flat appearance of Greenhorn and of all the Wet Mountains was preserved by this caprock. When the *Rocky Mountain Surface* formed on the top of the eroded Laramide mountains, the volcanics spread across the flattened southern region, preserving its form. As the region rose again, most of the volcanic rocks that once blanketed much of the Wet Mountains eroded downstream, leaving Greenhorn's summit as the main reminder of this fiery episode.

About 2 miles from the trailhead, the trail reaches a grassy saddle between the limbs of the horseshoe-shaped North Peak of Greenhorn Mountain. In many areas along North Peak, fields of frost-heaved rocks make the going rough. These rocks were broken by the freeze–thaw action of ice. During the colder months and during the night, surface water that has seeped down along *fractures* in the rocks freezes. As the ice crystals grow and expand, they break the rocks apart along the fractures.

This freeze–thaw action, called frost wedging, pushes the rocks up and to the side, slowly working them into the prominent patterns before you. These rock fields are called *felsenmeers,* a German word meaning "sea of rocks." On the steeper slopes below you, these rock fields look like tongues of soil and rock as they move slowly downhill, a process called solifluction.

If thunderstorms are not threatening, take time to climb to one of the high points on North Peak. At the top, a sweeping view of the High Plains stretches out to the east as far as the eye can see. Below you are the tilted sedimentary layers that flank the Wet Mountains uplift. These are remnants of the layers that tilted up when the Wet Mountains first emerged during Laramide mountain building, 70 million years ago.

After taking in the view, return to the trailhead by retracing your steps back down the mountain.

Chapter 2
THE FLATIRONS

The red, angular *flatirons* of Colorado are remains of the Rocky Mountain "trap door," the rock layers that pushed up and tilted back when the Rockies first emerged during the *Laramide Orogeny*. The flatirons region, a narrow belt of upright sedimentary rocks that stretches along the Front Range between Fort Collins and Colorado Springs, also encompasses other trap door remnants, although these do not stand today as do the well-known flatirons.

The rocks that form the flatirons derive from several different geologic formations. After the *Ancestral Rocky Mountains* rose about 300 million years ago, a long period of erosion washed sand and gravel downstream, piling it into *alluvial fans* at the mouths of canyons. Along the ancestral Front Range Highland, which was located about where the Front Range is today, windswept dunes formed from the eroded sand. The riverborne alluvial fans became the present-day Fountain Formation, and the wind-blown dunes became the Lyons Formation.

After the Ancestral Rockies eroded, laying down this rock pile, subsequent layers of sediment accumulated. Morrison Formation mud from

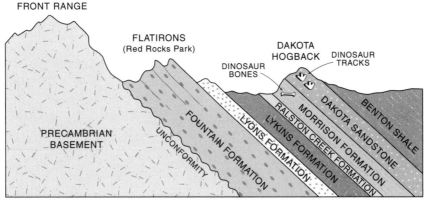

Cross-section showing inclined sedimentary layers along the flatirons at Dinosaur Ridge

dinosaur-ridden swamps and the Dakota sandstone, a marine sediment from the Cretaceous Seaway, buried the Ancestral Rockies core and the layers at its flanks.

As the Laramide Orogeny pushed Precambrian cores upward about 70 million years ago, the Fountain Formation, the Lyons Formation, and the other overlying sedimentary layers may have originally arched over the emerging mountains. Eventually these sedimentary rocks eroded downslope, leaving resistant flatirons and *hogbacks* of the Fountain Formation, Lyons Formation, and sandstones of the Dakota Group intact along the eastern flank of the mountains.

The terms flatiron and hogback are often used interchangeably. As used here, hogbacks are ridges of resistant, steeply inclined sedimentary layers such as the familiar "Dakota hogback." Flatirons, in contrast, are more triangular-shaped landforms formed by erosion of hogbacks, such as the flatirons of the red Fountain Formation exposed at Roxborough State Park. Both of these features are loosely termed "The Flatirons" when referring to their regional occurrence along the east flank of the Front Range.

As the Laramide mountains crumbled, their cores and the adjacent flatirons became buried in debris. Further layers of sediment accumulated on top of them in subsequent eras. Finally, in the uplift that brought the Rockies to their present heights during the past 10 million years, the remains of their original trap door, the resistant flatirons and hogbacks, emerged above the rubble.

EROSION OF THE ANCESTRAL ROCKIES

All of the rocks that the *Ancestral Rocky Mountains* carried upward 300 million years ago, including their basement core and thick layers of marine *sedimentary rocks,* eventually crumbled into a mixture of *sandstone* and *conglomerate.* These *sediments* hardened into a coarse formation that can still be found in several places within Colorado today.

These sedimentary rocks are exposed in four major areas. East of the Ancestral Rockies, countless streams flooded across a wide, sloping apron of sediment, called an *alluvial fan.* This fan-shaped debris pile hardened into rock now called the Fountain Formation which today forms the colorful *flatirons* that extend from Boulder to Colorado Springs. Between the two Ancestral Rockies ranges, sediments washed downslope, lining the *Central Colorado Trough* and hardening into today's Maroon Formation to the north and the Sangre

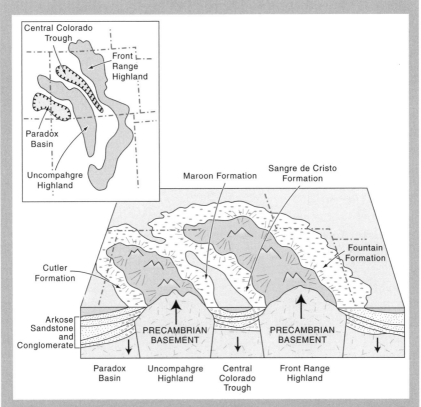

Erosion of the Ancestral Rocky Mountains

de Cristo Formation to the south. Farthest west, sediment washed down the Ancestral Rockies' western slope to fill the Paradox Basin, becoming today's Cutler Formation of the Colorado Plateau.

The rocks that compose these formations are very coarse grained, containing large chunks of *quartz* and *granite* that have not worn down. In addition, a significant amount of *feldspar* is found among the larger grains. Unlike quartz, which is very resistant to weathering and makes up the bulk of most sandstones, feldspar is much less resistant and disintegrates fairly rapidly into clay. A sandstone containing an abundance of feldspar is called an *arkose sandstone.* The presence of arkose sandstone and large conglomeratic particles in Ancestral Rockies *strata* indicate that the particles have not abraded during lengthy times in transport. The distinctly coarse sediments reveal their origins on mountainous heights that were once very nearby.

DINOSAUR RIDGE

Hike 12

THE "DINOSAUR FREEWAY"

A short roadside trail crosses a Dakota hogback where dinosaur tracks and bones are preserved in the rocks.

DISTANCE ■ 2 miles round trip

ELEVATION ■ 5,972 to 6,200 feet

DIFFICULTY ■ Easy

TOPOGRAPHIC MAP ■ USGS Morrison

GEOLOGIC MAP ■ 9

KEY REFERENCE ■ 9

PRECAUTIONS ■ Please be alert for traffic along the road. State law forbids collecting rocks or fossils anywhere on Dinosaur Ridge.

FOR INFORMATION ■ Dinosaur Ridge Visitors Center

About the Landscape: Dinosaur Ridge is one of the world's most famous dinosaur fossil localities. Here, only a stone's throw from downtown Denver, is an easy walk through time that leads past dinosaur tracks, bones, *ripplemarks,* and other traces of Colorado's vanished life and ancient environments.

Dinosaur Ridge is formed from easily eroded Jurassic *sandstone* and *mudstone* layers that are protected by a resistant ridge, or *hogback,* of Dakota sandstone. On the west side of the Dakota hogback, dinosaur bones were unearthed in the 150 million-year-old Morrison Formation of Jurassic age. In addition, dinosaur tracks have also been uncovered on the east side of the ridge in sandstones of the Dakota Group. Since the track-bearing layers in the Dakota can be traced from Colorado southward into New Mexico, the Dakota Group has been dubbed the "dinosaur freeway."

Trail Guide: To reach Dinosaur Ridge, drive west from Denver on Interstate 70 to exit 259 (Morrison). From the offramp, turn left (south) and drive 1.4 miles on Colorado Highway 26 and 93 (also called the Alameda Parkway) to a junction where Colorado Highway 26 turns east (straight ahead leads to the town of Morrison). Bear left at the junction and follow Colorado Highway 26 up the backside of Dinosaur Ridge. Near the top of the ridge, the road makes a hairpin turn and heads downhill to the Visitors Center and parking area on the left, about 1.5 miles past the junction.

From the parking area, dinosaur "footprints" painted on the pavement lead you to the start of the trail which follows along a road. As the trail heads up the ridge along the roadside, seventeen interpretive signs point

Dinosaur tracks in Dakota Group sandstone, Dinosaur Ridge

out key geologic features that tell the story of the ancient landscape where the dinosaurs lived.

The first part of the trail travels through gray rocks of the 100 million-year-old Benton Shale. Going back in time, you are walking here on the bottom of the *Cretaceous Seaway* in water hundreds of feet deep. In shallow water up toward shore, silt and sand are settling to one day become the sandstones of the Dakota Group.

As the road starts its gentle climb up the ridge, sloping layers of sandstone in the Dakota Group form the steep hillside of the hogback. The water around you in that ancient seaway is getting shallower here along the swampy coastline. Ripplemarks form as waves and currents shift the sands carried to the shoreline by rivers. Logs and branches from the swampy shoreline fall into the sand to leave permanent imprints. Plants from the lush forests in nearby areas along the coast will one day become coal deposits.

About halfway up the hogback, there is a large interpretive display at the dinosaur trackway site. Imagine, as you stand along the shoreline of the Cretaceous Seaway, herds of dinosaurs trampling the sand as they walk by, leaving behind impressions of their feet. Gentle waves wash mud over the tracks, preserving the traces of their passing beneath a thin, dark layer that will become shale. In all, ten different layers along Dinosaur Ridge contain tracks from seventy-eight animals that once used this "dinosaur freeway."

As the road approaches the crest of the ridge, it passes through the shallow coastal beach, swamp, and lagoon environments where ripples in the sand have been preserved and burrowing invertebrates have become trace fossils.

At the crest, the road turns sharply to the right at a hairpin turn and then heads downhill, crossing the boundary, or contact, between the Cretaceous rocks of the Dakota Group and the older Jurassic layers of the Morrison Formation. You are now walking along a river system that is 150 million years old. Sediment laid down in these rivers has become the red, purple, and gray-green mudstone layers and interbedded sandstones of the Morrison Formation. The contact between this and the Dakota is an *unconformity,* a gap in the sedimentary record that in this case spans more than 25 million years. Somehow you have managed to pass over 25 million years of rivers that ran right by here.

About halfway down the hill, distorted layers at the base of a sandstone ledge mark the passing of a large dinosaur. It is likely that the huge, plant-eating sauropod dinosaur called brontosaurus made these "dinosaur bulges" as it walked heavy-footed right by here, probably using its long neck to graze high in the trees in the woodland along the river.

The last stop on our walk back in time across Dinosaur Ridge is along an ancient river channel that has become a famous dinosaur bone quarry. The first dinosaur bones ever collected from the Morrison Formation were found near here in 1877. As you imagine walking along this ancient river, notice that bones are washing downstream. Once they are buried in sediment, they will slowly become fossilized as they absorb the silica-rich water.

When you complete the walk through time, simply retrace your steps back across Dinosaur Ridge to your vehicle parked in the present day at the Visitors Center.

FOUNTAIN VALLEY

Rocky Mountain Trap Door Shards

A gentle hike near Denver takes you among spectacular sandstone formations that were tilted skyward during the rise of the Rocky Mountains.

DISTANCE ■ 2.25-mile loop
ELEVATION ■ 6,200 to 6,000 feet
DIFFICULTY ■ Easy
TOPOGRAPHIC MAP ■ USGS Kassler
GEOLOGIC MAP ■ 10
KEY REFERENCE ■ 10
PRECAUTIONS ■ Although trails are clear and wide, watch for poison ivy.
FOR INFORMATION ■ Roxborough State Park

About the Landscape: Fountain Valley in Roxborough State Park is a geologic standout near Denver's back door. Here, the colorful *sedimentary rocks* of the Fountain Formation are standing on end in spectacular fashion along the front of the Rocky Mountains. Rising from lush oak woodlands, these *flatiron* sculptures record the tale of both the *Ancestral Rocky Mountains,* uplifted 300 million years ago, and the 70 million-year-old *Laramide Orogeny,* precursor to the present-day Rocky Mountains.

Also exposed within the park are resistant ridges of the Permian Lyons Formation and *hogbacks* of Cretaceous Dakota sandstones which stand above the landscape in much the same way as the Fountain Formation. Roxborough State Park was the first park in Colorado's state park system to be designated both a Colorado Natural Area and a National Natural Landmark.

Trail Guide: To reach the Fountain Valley Trailhead from Denver, drive south on US Highway 85 to Titan Road, 4 miles past Colorado Highway 470. Turn right and go west for 2.7 miles until you reach Roxborough Park Road on the left. Turn left and drive south for 4.7 miles on this gravel road. Turn left at the Roxborough Fire Station and enter the park (just before the intersection with North Rampart Range Road). Coming from the south on Interstate 25, take Exit 183 (Sedalia/Littleton) and drive north on US Highway 85 about 14 miles to Titan Road and continue as described above.

In the park, the gravel road turns to pavement after about 1.3 miles. The road parallels a hogback of Dakota sandstone off to the west, then crosses the Dakota hogback 1.6 miles from the park entrance. After only

Tilted sedimentary layers of the Fountain Formation have eroded into colorful flatirons in Roxborough State Park.

another 0.5 mile, enter the parking area for the first great view of the red rock flatirons of the Fountain Formation.

Take a moment to look at the outcrop of red rock at the north end of the parking area. The coarse-grained nature of this *sandstone* is typical of the rocks of the Fountain Formation. Look closely to identify both quartz (glassy) and *feldspar* (light gray) particles within the rock. Due to the abundance of feldspar, this rock is called an *arkose sandstone*. Also, note the fist-sized quartz cobble emerging from the rock face. This large quartz fragment washed down from the eroding Ancestral Rockies with the rest of these sediments that make up the Fountain Formation.

After a stop at the Visitor Center, follow the wide gravel trail north for about 100 yards to the Fountain Valley Overlook. Turn left up the short spur trail for a panoramic view of the overall landscape. To the north, the colorful flatirons of the Fountain Formation trail toward the Denver suburbs. Looking south, notice the steep incline, or dip (about 60 degrees), of the rock formations. Imagine these tilted layers extending up over the Front Range hills to the west. As the ancient Laramide mountains uplifted from below, pushing a rigid block of *basement rocks* upward, the overlying sedimentary layers tilted and warped up over them. Since that time, erosion has removed the overlying layers of rock, leaving behind these tilted sandstone flatirons (looking like a half-opened trap door) along the flank of the mountains.

Back on the main trail, after a short distance is an intersection where the trail loops back on itself. Go left (or clockwise) where the trail winds among the rock pinnacles. The walk through the valley here is extremely scenic. Off to the right, fins of sandstone rise above the oak trees. Farther along, a ridge of sandstone forms a wall to the right of the trail. This is the Lyons Formation, a layer of wind-blown dunes deposited on top of the Fountain Formation which also pushed open with the Rocky Mountain "trap door." The trail eventually crosses to the other side of this ridge at the historic homestead of Persse Place.

Heading back to the south, the trail climbs a slight grade with a Dakota hogback off to the left (east). The Dakota formed from sand deposited along a coastal beach area as the *Cretaceous Seaway* flooded Colorado about 100 million years ago. This layer tilted upward with the Fountain and Lyons Formations as the Rockies emerged and has since eroded down to this resistant hogback.

Near the top of the rise, take the turnoff for the Lyons Overlook on the right. This short side trail provides the best view in the park and should not be missed. An observation platform offers a commanding view of the Fountain Formation red rock flatirons set against the rising foothills of the Front Range. As you approach the viewpoint, notice the patterned surfaces of the Lyons sandstone on the lefthand side of the trail. These are *cross-beds* marking the advancing crests of wind-blown sand dunes along the flank of the Front Range highland of the Ancestral Rockies about 250 million years ago.

The trail continues downhill from the Lyons Overlook and joins the trail that returns back to the Visitor Center. You have now come full circle.

GARDEN OF THE GODS

PIKES PEAK TRAP DOOR

Hike 14

Fins of sandstone, bent skyward by the emerging Rockies, scenically frame Pikes Peak.

DISTANCE ■ **0.5-mile loop**
ELEVATION ■ **6,400 to 6,450 feet**
DIFFICULTY ■ **Easy**
TOPOGRAPHIC MAP ■ **USGS Cascade**
GEOLOGIC MAP ■ **11**

KEY REFERENCE ■ 11

PRECAUTIONS ■ To limit erosion in this high-use area, please remain on the paved trails at all times.

FOR INFORMATION ■ Garden of the Gods Visitor Center

About the Landscape: The Garden of the Gods is one of the all-time classic geologic views and one of the most photographed spots in Colorado. Here, the rounded summit of Pikes Peak is framed by the trap door fins of Fountain and Lyons Formation sandstones that were pushed up and open as the Rockies uplifted.

The Fountain Formation was formed by *Ancestral Rockies* sediment that eroded down the mountains and formed a *sandstone* skirt along their base. Winds later laid down the Lyons sandstone by whipping across the high plains and piling sand in dunes on top of the Fountain Formation. The massive fins of rock that remain standing above the surrounding landscape were the best cemented (or "glued" together) portions of these sedimentary rock layers.

These layers were tilted back as the Rocky Mountains pushed upward during the *Laramide Orogeny* about 70 million years ago. At first, the layers bent gently as the mountains pushed upward. But the overlying rocks eventually gave way and broke along a zone called the Rampart Range Fault. Less resistant parts of the sandstone beds eroded away, leaving the striking flatiron and fin formations that we see standing on end today.

Trail Guide: To reach the Central Garden Trail for this short hike, follow Garden of the Gods Road west for 2.4 miles from Interstate 25 (exit 146) in Colorado Springs. Where Garden of the Gods Road turns south and becomes 30th Street, continue south for 1.5 miles and turn right onto Gateway Road at the entrance to the park. Ahead, Pikes Peak is framed between two towering fins of the Lyons Formation called the Gateway Rocks. Follow the signs to the main parking area at the north end of Juniper Way Loop road.

Before starting down the trail, take time to walk up the Juniper Way Loop road for a look at the Rampart Range Fault where the sedimentary "trap door" broke apart as the Rockies rose. Be sure to walk on the right side of the road in the pedestrian/bike lane. About 50 yards above the parking area, the *fault* is in view at the north end of North Gateway Rock. Look near the base of the towering outcrop where Fountain Formation boulders on the west (right) side of the fault are bent up against the massive vertical wall of the Lyons Formation. The line where these broken

▶ *Spectacular fin of sandstone in the Lyons Formation along the Rampart Range Fault*

rock layers meet is the fault surface. This is a *reverse fault* where the Lyons sandstone thrust up and over the Fountain Formation.

Back at the parking area, start the hike by following the paved Central Garden Trail south between North Gateway Rock on the right and a ridge of white rock on the left. Both these vertical rocks are sandstones of the Lyons Formation. The oxidation state of minute iron-bearing minerals within the rock determine its color. When iron oxidizes it "rusts," staining the rock red. This happened to the Lyons sandstone long ago in the desert environment where the *sediment* was first buried. At some point, long after the rocks were dyed red and buried, the chemistry of the water seeping through the rock layers changed and some of the sandstone layers were bleached white.

After about 0.10 mile, the trail forks. Stay to the right and walk through the gap between the Gateway Rocks. Then bear left toward the rock spire in the middle called Sentinel Rock. This rock is a vertical portrait of a place where the wind-blown Lyons sands and the stream-deposited Fountain sediments long ago met and interfingered. On the south face of this spire is a layer of *conglomerate.* A close look reveals pebbles of quartz and feldspar characteristic of the Fountain Formation bound into the fine-grained sandstone from the Lyons' wind-blown dunes. These pebbles were deposited within a river channel that flowed between sand dunes. On the west side of the spire look for *ripplemarks* at eye level. They are traces of the stream currents that flowed here about 250 million years ago.

Continuing south, take the right fork at the next junction and follow a short loop trail around a number of thin fins of red sandstone. Look for *cross-beds* in these towering sandstone outcrops that mark the shifting crests of ancient wind-blown dunes. Bear left at several trail junctions to stay on the loop that leads back to Sentinel Rock. After passing back through the gap between the Gateway Rocks, bear left to return to the trailhead.

Chapter 3
THE PARK AND GORE RANGES

The Park and Gore Ranges are a long strand of epic mountains that mark the western edge of Colorado's Rockies, trending south from Wyoming's Sierra Madre into the center of the state. Like the other ranges from the *Laramide Orogeny,* the Park and Gore are mega-uplifts of Precambrian *basement rock.* These mountains are bounded on each side by a system of north–south trending *faults* and are separated from the Front Range by the basins of North Park and Middle Park where upward movement did not keep pace with the emerging mountains.

Around the Park and Gore Ranges, many of the faults that define the intricacies of their form have long histories. Only the most recent faulting episodes have defined the character of the landscape that we see today.

The steep western edge of the Gore Range is bounded by a major break in Colorado's rocks called the Gore Fault. This particular fault activated during the Precambrian and many subsequent times throughout Colorado's geologic history. It reactivated 300 million years ago during the Pennsylvanian and defined the western boundary of the Front Range highland of the *Ancestral Rockies,* a major mountain range that stretched eastward to near where the Front Range rises today.

Debris flowed both east and west off this highland, filling basins, such as the *Central Colorado Trough,* with *sediment.* The red sedimentary rocks exposed on the west side of the present-day Gore Range, called the Minturn Formation, are the same age as the red rocks of the Fountain Formation exposed in the *flatirons* along the Front Range.

Today, the Gore Fault connects with the Mosquito Fault to the south along the west side of the Mosquito Range. To the north, the Gore Fault connects with the faults that bound the west side of the Park Range. These are Laramide faults that activated 70 million years ago to bring the modern ranges upward for the first time. Then, between 33 and 12 million years ago, great volumes of volcanic ash and debris exploded from these faults across much of the Park Range in repeated episodes of volcanism that spewed material from both east and west. The Rabbit Ears Range that connects the Park Range to the Front Range and divides North and Middle Parks was a major volcanic field during this time.

These faults also bordered the renewed uplift that has occurred over the past 10 million years, when the ranges surged up to their now-familiar heights. In the Park Range, more than 150 hot springs, including Steamboat Springs, simmer at the surface of this fault system, enabling the earth's deep pressure cooker to let off some steam.

Much later, *Ice Age glaciers* made their advance across the highest peaks of the Park and Gore Ranges. Fashioning jagged peaks, U-shaped valleys and serrated edges, they carved drama into the monumental summits.

FEATURES OF IGNEOUS INTRUSIONS

Deep within the earth, molten rock or *magma*, which is relatively buoyant, rises through denser surrounding rock. It pushes its way through cracks and *fractures*, sometimes emerging above ground. When it does, the spectacular results are volcanoes and lava flows. But when magma is trapped underground, forming a *pluton*, it cools slowly and is "frozen" within the crust, hidden from view. Over time, uplift and erosion may expose the "plumbing system" of these igneous intrusions.

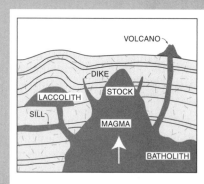
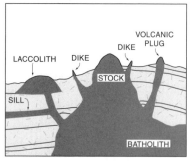

A. Before erosion   B. After erosion

Features of plutons are described on the basis of their size or shape. A *batholith* is the largest type of igneous intrusion. The Pikes Peak batholith is the best example of this in Colorado. A *stock* is a smaller pluton, generally covering less than 60 square miles. The Spanish Peaks are classic textbook examples of stocks. Both stocks and batholiths have no particular shape. They represent reservoirs of molten rock that pooled at depth within the earth.

Dikes and *sills* are features of igneous intrusions that have particular shapes. A dike forms where magma has forced its way into fractures that cut vertically through layers of surrounding rock. After the surrounding rock erodes, dikes may jut out as steeply inclined walls of rock. They are dramatically exposed around the base of the Spanish Peaks. In contrast, a sill forms where magma has squeezed between horizontal layers of rock. Sills form tabular sheets of rock that create plateaus or mesas when exposed by erosion. A *laccolith* is a thicker variation of a sill in which magma squeezes between sedimentary layers and domes the overlying layers. Ute Mountain, in the extreme southwestern corner of Colorado, is a classic example of a laccolith.

Magma rising up through a vertical tube or conduit that feeds a volcano at the surface may leave behind a volcanic neck or plug. This feature is the "throat" of an ancient volcano, bared by erosion. Hahns Peak is a good example of a volcanic plug.

Hike 15

HAHNS PEAK

Eroded Core of a Tertiary Volcano

This short hike culminates atop the core of a "recent" volcano.

DISTANCE ■ 3 miles round trip

ELEVATION ■ 9,369 to 10,839 feet

DIFFICULTY ■ Moderate

TOPOGRAPHIC MAP ■ USGS Hahns Peak

GEOLOGIC MAP ■ 12

KEY REFERENCE ■ 12

PRECAUTIONS ■ The last section of the trail is steep and traverses over loose rocks—watch every step. Parts of the area are private property—please keep to the old roads and trail. The peak is a dangerous place to be during a lightning storm.

FOR INFORMATION ■ Hahns Peak Ranger District

About the Landscape: The bald, rocky summit of Hahns Peak to the north of Steamboat Springs is visible from miles away. Although the conical profile of the mountain looks like a volcano, its shape is the result of erosion of the volcanic neck or plug rather than being shaped by volcanic eruptions that constructed a cone at the surface. A trail and network of mining roads leads to an old fire lookout on the summit for a commanding view of the Park Range and northern Colorado.

Hahns Peak is the easternmost of a group of eroded volcanic mountains that once existed west of the Park Range. These peaks, which include the Elkhead Mountains, were the conduits for volcanic eruptions that pierced the earth's surface between 12 and 10 million years ago. At the time when these Tertiary volcanoes were active, northern Colorado was covered with a blanket of *sedimentary rocks.* The volcanic eruptions buried the *sediments* beneath a pile of volcanic ash, *lava,* and *breccia.*

With renewed uplift of Colorado over the past 10 million years, these volcanic rocks and the sedimentary layers below them were largely removed by erosion. The resistant cores of the once-buried volcanic centers now rise above the surrounding landscape.

Trail Guide: To reach the Hahns Peak Trailhead, drive 29 miles north from Steamboat Springs on the Elk River Road (Routt County Road 129) to the

Approaching the summit of Hahns Peak

The first snow on Maroon Bells is reflected in Maroon Lake, White River National Forest.

Columbine Falls cascade down Longs Peak below Chasm Lake, Rocky Mountain National Park

The Front Range's Nokhu Crags rise above Lake Agnes, Colorado State Forest

▶ *Conglomerate above Willow Lake, Sangre de Cristo Range, Rio Grande National Forest*

An imminent storm causes eerie lighting on volcanic tuff, Wheeler Geologic Area, La Garita Wilderness, Rio Grande National Forest

Tilted red rocks (flatirons) in Fountain Valley, Roxborough State Park

Moss campion, a tundra wildflower, adorns this granitic rock, Indian Peaks Wilderness, Roosevelt National Forest

▶ *Dawn light glows at Horseshoe Cirque, Mosquito Range, Pike National Forest.*

White Canyon carved in the Chalk Cliffs at Mount Princeton, San Isabel National Forest

A mountain of shifting sand against the foot of the Sangre de Cristo Range, Great Sand Dunes National Monument

Sunrise silhouettes Rabbit Ears Peak, Routt National Forest.

Columbine General Store. Turn right onto Forest Road 490 and follow this dirt road staying left at the first fork. Stay left again at the second fork. Although the road continues up the side of the mountain, the trailhead is marked by signs at the edge of a meadow. Be aware that there is private property behind a locked gate nearby.

The hike begins by following the road. Stay right at the fork only a short distance from the parking area. The road immediately starts to climb steeply through the forested hillside. At first, most of the rocks along the road are light to medium gray volcanic *rhyolite.* However as you continue, sedimentary rocks become increasingly common. The most obvious is a pebble *conglomerate.* These rocks are part of the Dakota *sandstone* formed by 100 million-year-old sediments from the inland *Cretaceous Seaway* that once covered most of Colorado. These easily eroded rocks have endured the *Laramide Orogeny,* the explosive emergence of Hahns Peak, and the renewed uplift of the mountains, making them an unusual sight at high altitude.

About 0.5 mile from the trailhead, the Hahns Peak Trail leaves the road and starts up the slope to the right (look for the Forest Service trail sign). The trail winds upward among chunks of Dakota sandstone and conglomerate. As the trail leaves the forest and climbs through open meadows, the sedimentary rocks give way to light-colored rhyolite. This is the *igneous rock* that makes up the core of Hahns Peak.

After about 0.75 mile from the old road below, the trail meets a miner's cabin at the T junction with another old road. Turn left and follow this road as it climbs to the saddle on the north side of the mountain.

For the final 0.25 mile of the hike, the trail climbs up loose rocks to the summit. Step by step, you become very familiar with the rock that forms the core of Hahns Peak. Most of the rock is tan to gray rhyolite with abundant white *feldspar* crystals. Many of the feldspar crystals have weathered out, leaving behind small holes or pits throughout the rock. Much of the rock has iron stains along fractures. This is the result of alteration of the rock by hot gases and liquids during, or after, the eruptions.

At the summit, you are standing at a point once deep within a volcano through which ash and lava once rocketed across the landscape. To the west are the eroded roots of the Elkhead Mountains which were active about the same time as Hahns Peak. To the east are the glaciated peaks of the Park Range.

If clouds are building, do not linger too long on the summit to avoid the real danger of lightning. Use caution climbing back down the mountain, as footing is often unstable.

FISH CREEK CANYON

A GLACIATED HANGING VALLEY

Scenic waterfalls and contorted basement rock are on view along this popular trail above Steamboat Springs.

DISTANCE ■ **4 miles round trip**

ELEVATION ■ **7,480 to 8,800 feet**

DIFFICULTY ■ **Moderate**

TOPOGRAPHIC MAPS ■ **USGS Steamboat Springs; Trails Illustrated #118**

GEOLOGIC MAP ■ **13**

KEY REFERENCE ■ **None**

PRECAUTIONS ■ **Use caution climbing over rocks and ledges near the waterfalls. This is a very popular trail; avoid weekends if possible.**

FOR INFORMATION ■ **Hahns Peak Ranger District**

About the Landscape: The popular Fish Creek Canyon Trail leads to a spectacular glaciated hanging valley in the southern portion of the Park Range above Steamboat Springs. The trail through Fish Creek Canyon climbs above Fish Creek Falls to reach an upper falls that spills from a higher *hanging valley.* Exposed along the trail are Precambrian *basement rocks,* swirled and contorted by metamorphic events that occurred 1.7 billion years ago. Uplifted many times and now bared by erosion, these rocks were polished and striated by the *Ice Age glaciers* that carved the canyon.

Trail Guide: To reach the Fish Creek Canyon Trailhead from downtown Steamboat Springs, turn east onto 3rd Street, then make an immediate right after the Post Office onto Fish Creek Road. Drive 3 miles uphill through a residential area to the Fish Creek Falls parking area.

The hike begins by following a well-constructed trail downhill for about 100 yards to a bridge at the base of Fish Creek Falls. The outcrops along the first part of the trail are Precambrian *metamorphic rocks* that are part of the uplifted core of the Park Range. A number of different rock types are present, including *schist, gneiss,* and a dark-colored metamorphic rock called amphibolite. Cross-cutting veins of *quartz* and *feldspar* add to the complex patterns, hinting at the basement rock's tumultuous past.

At the bridge across Fish Creek is a great view of Fish Creek Falls. A variety of metamorphic basement rocks in the cascades below the falls are worn smooth by the water. The number of people on the trail dramatically decreases once you get beyond the falls.

From the falls, the trail climbs up a forested hillside into the hanging valley of Fish Creek Canyon, scoured by Ice Age glaciers and left "hanging"

The upper falls in Fish Creek Canyon

above the more deeply carved Yampa River Valley. *Erratics* of all sizes are scattered along the trail and among the trees. These boulders were transported and left behind by the glaciers that carved the canyon. As the trail emerges from the trees, polished outcrops appear on the right. The horizontal scratches on the rock surface, called *striations,* were formed by rocks embedded in glacial ice and carried with it. The weight and pressure of the thick ice sheet that once flowed over the place where you stand were great enough to carve grooves in the outcrop as the captured rocks were ground against it.

About 1 mile from the trailhead, the trail crosses Fish Creek to the north side of the canyon. The trail begins to climb more steeply and reaches a section blasted into a sheer rock face. Light-colored *pegmatite* veins cross the trail. One of the veins is about 5 feet thick, with very large quartz and feldspar crystals, revealing these to be igneous intrusions that cooled slowly enough to form large crystals.

The trail continues over solid bedrock and soon reaches an area where there are more striations left behind in the rock by moving glaciers. The outcrops along the trail and extending up the hillside appear streamlined, with grooves worn by the glaciers all across their surfaces. The rocks themselves are highly contorted gneiss and schist. In places, there appear to be intrusions of *granitic* rocks and light-colored veins of quartz and feldspar.

On the opposite side of the canyon are huge, angular blocks of basement rock that form a boulder field of *talus* above the creek. These rocks do not have the rounded shapes that usually result from transport by glaciers; instead, these were dislodged from the cliffs above by frost action. Water from rain and snowmelt seeps into fractures in the rock, expands as it freezes, and wedges the rock apart. Eventually the force of gravity brings the rock mass crashing down the canyon wall. There are more boulders on the north-facing wall where the process is more active; this is because the north side remains in shadow and is colder than the rest of the canyon during most of the year.

As the trail tops the crest of the next ridge, another waterfall comes into view. This is the upper falls of Fish Creek Canyon. This cascade spills from a side canyon, an even higher hanging valley above the canyon we have traversed. A short spur trail leads down to the creek for a good view of the falls as they spill over what was once the junction between two glaciers.

Although the main trail continues beyond the upper falls for another 3 miles up to Long Lake and eventually the Continental Divide, the upper falls is the turnaround point for this hike. Simply return to the trailhead by the route you came.

Hike 17 — RABBIT EARS PEAK

ERODED FLOWS OF VOLCANIC ROCK

This easy hike leads up to the unusual volcanic Rabbit Ears for an exploration of their origins.

DISTANCE ■ **5 miles round trip**

ELEVATION ■ **9,600 to 10,650 feet**

DIFFICULTY ■ **Easy**

TOPOGRAPHIC MAP ■ **USGS Rabbit Ears Peak**

GEOLOGIC MAP ■ **14**

KEY REFERENCE ■ **13**

PRECAUTIONS ■ **Use caution climbing around the base of the peak. When coming back down, watch out for volcanic pebbles that act like ball bearings beneath your feet.**

FOR INFORMATION ■ **Hahns Peak Ranger District**

About the Landscape: Standing erect at the crest of the Park Range, the twin volcanic outcrops on Rabbit Ears Peak are a prominent landmark at Rabbit Ears Pass between Steamboat Springs and Kremmling. A gentle hike traversing hills and meadows climaxes at the two towers of volcanic rock where a close look reveals that they are not the neck of a volcano as they are often assumed to be. They are actually layers of extruded *volcanic rock* that cooled at the surface rather than intrusive rocks that solidified deep within the neck of a volcano.

The volcanic material that makes up the "Rabbit Ears" was extruded from the Rabbit Ears Range to the east. These volcanic mountains mark the roots of ancient volcanoes that spewed ash and lava across north-central Colorado between 33 and 23 million years ago. Over time, the explosive flows of ash and *lava* buried areas of Precambrian *basement rock* at the crest of the Park Range. Erosion has now shaped these volcanic layers into the unique Rabbit Ears of today.

Trail Guide: This popular hike to Rabbit Ears Peak follows a jeep trail still in use. (Note: a vehicle with high clearance is required.) To reach the Rabbit Ears Trail, drive 19 miles southeast from Steamboat Springs on US Highway 40 to Rabbit Ears Pass. Turn left (north) at the sign for Dumont Lake Campground and follow Forest Road 315 (part of old US Highway 40) for 1.5 miles to a historic marker. Turn left onto Forest Road 311 and drive 0.25 mile to the junction with Forest Road 291, turn right and park.

This hike follows the jeep trail (Forest Road 291) all the way to the base of Rabbit Ears Peak. Boulder-strewn sections of the road will make you glad you are not driving. The road winds through open meadows and stands of spruce where wildflowers are plentiful during summer. The best panoramic views of the Rabbit Ears are from the meadows about 1 mile from the trailhead.

About 2 miles from the trailhead, the road climbs steeply and ends abruptly near the base of the Rabbit Ears. With care, scramble up to a higher ledge along the outcrop. From there, follow the well-worn path a short distance to the saddle between the towers of volcanic rock.

Layer of volcanic ash exposed at the Rabbit Ears

The Rabbit Ears provide several good clues that they are made up of *extrusive igneous rock* that cooled at the earth's surface rather than intrusive rock that cooled deep within the neck of a volcano. Although the outcrop seems chaotic at first glance, stand back where you can see a crude horizontal layering to the rocks. The outcrop appears to be constructed from several layers stacked one atop the other. In particular, there is a light gray ash layer that extends laterally along part of the cliff face. Such an arrangement could not have formed within a volcanic pipe, where material would be moving vertically toward a vent at the surface. Rather, this layer formed from ash spread out across the landscape during repeated eruptions of an explosive volcano.

The lower part of the peak is composed of dark *basalt* lava. Tiny holes in the rock called *vesicles* were formed from gas trapped within molten rock. Some of the vesicles appear elongated, having stretched as the lava moved while cooling. The lack of any visible crystals in the rock suggests it cooled rapidly at the earth's surface, rather than cooling slowly underground.

On top of the basalt lava is a wild and chaotic outcrop of broken volcanic rocks called *breccia.* Dark boulders of basalt appear to be "floating" in a jumble of smaller rocks and pebbles. Many of the smaller rocks are red rocks filled with vesicles. This rock is called scoria and forms from highly gaseous basalt lava with a frothy consistency. The great mix of rock types in the breccia suggests that they joined in an external volcanic flow of glowing ash and rock debris, not from the interior of a volcano.

In the upper part of the outcrop, there are white crystals that seem to bind the rocks together. Look closely at some of the fallen boulders along the base of the cliff. The white material is *calcite* that was crystallized from hot gases or fluids moving through the rock after the eruption. The calcite has effectively "cemented" the rocks together, making the outcrop very resistant to weathering. This calcite cement may be one reason why the Rabbit Ears have withstood the forces of erosion through time.

Use extreme caution when climbing down from the outcrop, and then retrace your path back to the trailhead.

BOOTH FALLS

Cascades along the Gore Fault

View upturned sedimentary layers along the Gore Fault and Booth Falls, a cascade over Precambrian igneous rocks.

DISTANCE ■ **4 miles round trip**

ELEVATION ■ **8,400 to 9,800 feet**

DIFFICULTY ■ **Easy**

TOPOGRAPHIC MAPS ■ **USGS Vail East; Trails Illustrated #108**

GEOLOGIC MAP ■ **15**

KEY REFERENCE ■ **14**

PRECAUTIONS ■ **Use caution exploring rocky ledges around Booth Falls. This is a very popular trail and should be avoided on weekends. Please park only in the designated parking area, not in front of the private residences nearby.**

FOR INFORMATION ■ **Holy Cross Ranger District**

About the Landscape: A hike up Booth Creek to picturesque Booth Falls in the southern Gore Range provides easy access to a view of colorful *sedimentary rocks* juxtaposed against uplifted *basement rock* along the Gore Fault.

The Gore Fault once formed the western boundary of the Front Range highland in the *Ancestral Rocky Mountains*. Sediments stripped off the crest of the Ancestral Rockies were deposited in the adjoining basin to the west, called the *Central Colorado Trough*. These sediments became the colorful sedimentary layers of the Minturn Formation (Pennsylvanian) and Maroon Formation (Permian). Reactivation of the Gore Fault during the *Laramide*

Orogeny pushed Precambrian basement rocks up against these sedimentary layers, bending them upward in the process.

Trail Guide: To reach the Booth Creek Trailhead from Vail, drive 4.5 miles east from Vail Village (Interstate 70, Exit 176) along Frontage Road to Booth Falls Road. Turn left and drive through the residential area to the parking area at the end of the road. Coming from Denver, take Interstate 70 to Exit 180 and drive 0.8 mile west along the Frontage Road and turn right onto Booth Falls Road. Turn right and drive to the parking area at the end of the road.

The trail begins by climbing a moderate grade through an aspen grove. The large *limestone* boulder just beyond the trail register is from the Minturn Formation. A close look at the rock reveals abundant fossil fragments, including *brachiopods,* stems of *crinoids*, and even a few solitary corals. These organisms lived in a warm, shallow sea that filled the Central Colorado Trough between the uplifted ranges of the Ancestral Rockies during the Pennsylvanian about 300 million years ago.

About 0.25 mile from the trailhead, the trail crosses outcrops of limestone arranged like stepping stones along the path. The fluting in the surface is the result of weathering. Over time, rainwater has slowly dissolved the limestone, creating the gutterlike appearance.

The trail enters a meadow at about 0.5 mile from the trailhead where sedimentary layers of the Minturn Formation come into view high on the west side of the canyon. These rock layers consist of an interbedded sequence of red *sandstone* and maroon *conglomerate* eroded from the Front Range highland of the Ancestral Rocky Mountains. Sandwiched in between these layers are beds of gray limestone that formed when the Central Colorado Trough was periodically flooded by seawater.

The Gore Fault comes into full view 1.5 miles from the trailhead. At this point, the trail crosses a broad meadow. Across the creek on the opposite (west) side of the canyon, the once horizontal layers of the Minturn Formation are bent sharply upward. To the right (north) of these upturned layers on the other side of the fault lie the jagged rocks of the Precambrian basement. The Gore Fault runs along this abrupt change in the rocks in a steep ravine covered by *talus* and vegetation. During the Laramide Orogeny, which began roughly 70 million years ago, Precambrian basement rocks pushed up against the Pennsylvanian sedimentary layers of the Minturn Formation. In the process, the Minturn layers were upturned to their nearly vertical positions along the *fault.*

At the far end of the meadow, the trail climbs a series of switchbacks to an overlook of Booth Falls. As the trail climbs, it crosses the Gore Fault on the east side of the canyon. Keep a close eye out for the change from sedimentary rocks along the trail (the last of which is maroon conglomerate) to Precambrian *granitic* rocks. At this point, you are standing on the ancient Gore Fault. Once across the fault, Precambrian boulders of *granite, granodiorite,* and *gneiss* form the steep, rocky slopes above the trail.

At about 2 miles from the trailhead, the trail reaches a rock outcrop with a view of Booth Falls. Here, Booth Creek cascades more than 50 feet over a resistant ledge of Precambrian rock into the canyon below. Booth Falls probably first formed along the fault zone of the Gore Fault, where Booth Creek flowed over resistant Precambrian rocks on the upthrown side of the fault while eroding away the softer Minturn sedimentary layers on the downthrown side of the fault. Over time, the falls have carved headward into the Precambrian rocks, slowly cutting back away from the fault to where they fall today.

Booth Falls is a convenient turnaround point for this hike. The trail, however, continues climbing up through the Precambrian rocks to Booth Lake, another 3 miles beyond the falls. To return, retrace your steps back to the trailhead.

The Gore Fault is well exposed on this hillside above Booth Creek, where tilted sedimentary layers on the left end abruptly against Precambrian basement rocks on the right.

Chapter 4
THE SAWATCH AND MOSQUITO RANGES

Like two out-stretched arms, the Sawatch and Mosquito Ranges border either side of central Colorado's Arkansas Valley. These once-connected limbs of a great *Laramide Orogeny* highland, called the Sawatch uplift, became separated as the *Rio Grande Rift* forced the landscape apart.

The lofty summits of the Sawatch Range, Colorado's tallest mountains, stand along the west side of the Arkansas Valley. Fifteen "fourteeners" mark the crest of the range, including Mount Elbert (14,433 feet), the highest peak

Old miner's shack in the Mosquito Range

in all the Rockies. To the east, the Mosquito Range parallels the Sawatch Range and separates the Arkansas Valley from South Park, the valley on its east side.

As distinct as these mountains seem today, the Sawatch and Mosquito Ranges rose together as a single, broad mountain uplift during the Laramide Orogeny. This second largest of the Laramide uplifts after the Front Range was cored by Precambrian *basement rocks* that pushed up from below, buckling overlying sedimentary layers into a broad *anticline* that encompassed both ranges.

This once-great mountain range has since split apart by the faulting that formed the Arkansas Valley. This faulting began about 30 to 26 million years ago along the northern end of a network of interconnected valleys called the Rio Grande Rift. Ultimately, the Arkansas Valley down-dropped and separated the two great ranges.

Along with the rest of Colorado, the Sawatch and Mosquito Ranges have been elevated to their present heights over the past 10 million years. Erosion has exposed rugged basement rocks along their crests, and *Ice Age glaciers* have etched their summits into the craggy silhouettes we see today.

THE COLORADO MINERAL BELT

Colorado's Rocky Mountains are rich with minerals. Since the time gold was first discovered in 1858, more than $5.5 billion worth of gold, silver, lead, zinc, copper, and molybdenum have been extracted. Nearly all of the economically important mineral deposits are located within a narrow belt that cuts diagonally across Colorado's Rockies, from the San Juan Mountains near Durango, to the Front Range north of Boulder. This trend is called the *Colorado Mineral Belt*.

The groundwork for mineralization was laid during the Precambrian when mountain building caused major fault systems to develop. These zones of northeast–southwest trending *faults, fractures,* and shear zones, called the Colorado Lineament, became "scars" in the *basement rock* that influenced the orientation of later events. The Colorado Mineral Belt follows the southern margin of this ancient fault system.

During the *Laramide Orogeny,* between about 70 and 45 million years ago, masses of molten magma and hot mineral-rich fluids began to rise through these ancient faults and fractures, creating a string of Laramide-age intrusions that cut diagonally across the mountain uplifts.

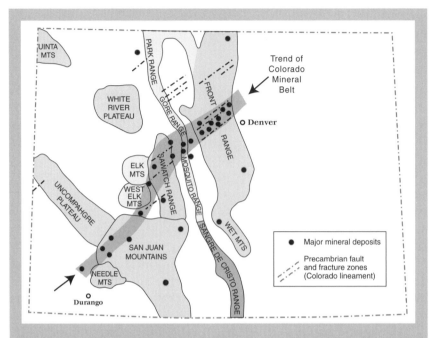

Trend of
Colorado
Mineral
Belt

○ Denver

● Major mineral deposits

Precambrian fault
and fracture zones
(Colorado lineament)

As *magma* cools at depth, a hot "broth" or hydrothermal solution enriched with dissolved minerals separates from the *pluton*. Within the cooling magma, atoms of metals such as gold do not fit into growing crystals of *feldspar* and other minerals, so they eventually become concentrated in the remaining water-rich magma. These fluids may mix with groundwater that seeps downward from the surface through fractures in the rock and circulates around the magma. Where the water is hottest, more minerals are dissolved. Eventually, these fluids may move into the surrounding rock and create concentrated ore deposits, as has happened all along Colorado's Mineral Belt.

MOUNT ELBERT

THE TOP OF COLORADO

Hike to the summit of Mount Elbert, Colorado's highest peak.

DISTANCE ■ **8 miles round trip**
ELEVATION ■ **10,080 to 14,433 feet**
DIFFICULTY ■ **Strenuous**

TOPOGRAPHIC MAPS ■ USGS Mount Elbert and Mount Massive; Trails Illustrated #127

GEOLOGIC MAP ■ 16

KEY REFERENCE ■ None

PRECAUTIONS ■ This trail is very steep and requires hiking several hours above treeline. Be sure to get an early start to avoid being caught by afternoon thunderstorms.

FOR INFORMATION ■ Leadville Ranger District

About the Landscape: Mount Elbert is the pinnacle of the Rocky Mountains. It is a steep, tough hike to the *basement rocks* at the "top of Colorado," but on a clear day, the view from this summit is grand enough to make you forget your aching feet. At 14,433 feet above sea level, it is Colorado's highest peak and the second highest peak in the lower forty-eight states after California's Mount Whitney (14,494 feet). Surrounded by close contenders, Mount Elbert is the highest of fifteen mountains that rise over 14,000 feet in the Sawatch Range.

Trail Guide: The Mount Elbert Trail follows the northern route to the summit from the Elbert Creek drainage. Two other routes from the south begin near Twin Lakes.

To reach the Mount Elbert Trailhead, drive 4 miles west from Leadville on US Highway 24. Turn right onto Lake County Road 300, then drive 0.8 mile and turn left at the sign for Halfmoon Campground. Drive 1.3 miles to the next intersection (Forest Service sign indicates the Halfmoon Drainage). Turn right and follow this bumpy gravel road (which becomes Forest Road 110) for 5.9 miles to the trailhead located on the left past the Elbert Creek Campground.

This hike starts out by following a section of the Colorado Trail. The trail climbs immediately up a steep *lateral moraine* that bounds the south flank of Halfmoon Creek drainage. Rounded boulders of Precambrian basement *igneous* and *metamorphic rocks* were left behind here by a glacier that once flowed through this drainage. All of the mighty peaks of the Sawatch Range were once laden with glacial ice. Their craggy summits and moraine-edged slopes are classic examples of the work of glaciers.

About 1 mile from the trailhead, the Mount Elbert Trail splits off to the right. The Mount Elbert Trail climbs up a forested slope, emerging above treeline after about 1 mile from the intersection. Here, the steep, rocky east flank of Mount Elbert comes into view. Sorry, but the rounded peak on the skyline is only a false summit.

For about the next 1 mile, the trail continues its steep climb up a series of long switchbacks to the top of a ridge. Here, a *cirque* carved into Mount

Exclamation at Mount Elbert's summit—Colorado's highest point and the tallest peak in the Rockies

Elbert's east face comes into view. Note the small tarn (glacial lake) in the cirque basin. Back toward the east, there is also a great view of the Arkansas Valley, the northern limit of the *Rio Grande Rift*. Notice the mounds and ridges of lateral and *end moraines* left behind by *Ice Age glaciers* on the valley floor. Turquoise Lake to the north and Twin Lakes to the south are located in basins created by *end moraines*. Man-made dams have enhanced these natural basins to form the lakes.

The trail continues along the ridge, weaving through outcrops of Precambrian basement rock. This 1.7 billion-year-old metamorphic rock is banded with *gneiss* and *schist* and crosscut in places by intrusions of light-colored crystalline *pegmatite*. Look at the complex pattern on the head-wall of the cirque on the left to see these textures in large scale. This confusion of rocks tells the story of the geologic chaos that reigned as Colorado first began to take shape during the Precambrian. Imagine the powerful forces of uplift that brought these basement rocks up to this great height.

The last 1 mile to Mount Elbert's summit is very strenuous. After reaching the false summit, the trail leads toward another steep outcrop that appears to be the summit, but upon reaching its crest, the true summit comes into view a short distance beyond. A brass benchmark marks the highest point.

From here, the view is breathtaking. To the north, Mount Massive, only 12 feet lower than Elbert, dominates the skyline. Westward, jagged mountains extend as far as the eye can see. With perfect weather conditions, it is possible to pick out Maroon Bells and Snowmass Mountain near Aspen. Extending southward is the line of majestic fourteeners in the central Sawatch Range. To the east, the Mosquito Range, the opposite limb of the once-great Sawatch uplift, forms the skyline above Leadville.

After taking in the view from the top, use extreme caution negotiating the steep trail back down the mountain to the trailhead.

Hike 20

ASPEN GROTTOS

An Ice Age Cavern

Explore a slot canyon carved in solid granite.

DISTANCE ■ **0.5 mile round trip**

ELEVATION ■ **9,500 to 9,540 feet**

DIFFICULTY ■ **Easy**

TOPOGRAPHIC MAPS ■ **USGS New York Peak; Trails Illustrated #127**

GEOLOGIC MAP ■ **16**

KEY REFERENCE ■ **15**

PRECAUTIONS ■ **Use extreme caution when scrambling around on the rocks entering the Grottos.**

FOR INFORMATION ■ **Aspen Ranger District**

About the Landscape: The Aspen Grottos (also called the Ice Caves) is an easily accessible underground cavern along the Roaring Fork River near Aspen. Unlike most caverns, which are created where limestone is dissolved by water, the Grottos are carved in solid Precambrian *granitic* rock (1.4 billion-year-old quartz monzonite).

The Grottos formed when the Roaring Fork River was swollen with meltwater from receding *Ice Age glaciers* about 15,000 years ago. The meltwater coursed over the granitic bedrock carrying rocks and other debris that sculpted the cavern's walls through abrasive action. Today, the river has abandoned the channel through the Grottos, leaving behind a slot canyon with windows open to the sky.

Trail Guide: To reach the Grottos Trailhead, drive 8.5 miles east from Aspen on Colorado Highway 82. Continue 0.9 mile past Weller Campground to an unmarked road on the right. Turn here and drive a short distance to the parking area and trailhead.

The short trail to the Grottos starts out by crossing a bridge over the Roaring Fork River and following a portion of the Old Stage Road. There

Window to the sky, Aspen Grottos

are two bridges at the edge of the parking lot. Take the bridge on the right to cross the river.

About 50 yards past the bridge is a broad outcrop of Precambrian granitic rock to the left of the trail. A number of boulders perch on top of the bedrock. These large, round *granitic* boulders, called glacial *erratics,* were transported down the valley by a glacier and left behind when the ice melted.

Just past the erratic boulders is a small sign for the "Ice Caves" that points left. Turn off the Old Stage Road and follow the most well-worn trail through the trees. Stay to the left where the trail forks. As you pass another large erratic boulder on the left you are nearing the Grottos. The trail veers right and ends at an area of glacially scoured granitic bedrock. Continue up the smooth rock surface until you see an opening in the rock. This is the entrance to the Grottos. Scramble carefully down through the opening to the cave floor.

Once you are inside the Grottos, notice the smooth, fluted walls of the cave. These formations were sculpted by *sediment* and rock debris carried along by flowing water that followed *fractures* in the bedrock, gradually scouring out and enlarging the cavern where you are standing today.

The windows open to the sky are forming as huge blocks of rock fall from the roof. These rocks are strewn at your feet. Seasonal water seeps into the overhead fractures and expands as it freezes, wedging the rock apart until it crashes down under the influence of gravity. Ice that collects inside the Grotto during the winter may remain frozen for much of the year, thus giving it the name "Ice Caves."

Today, the Roaring Fork River flows a short distance to the north of the Grottos. Once you return to the parking area, walk across the other bridge (to the left) and continue about 30 yards to a picturesque waterfall. Here the river is carving and fluting the granitic bedrock much like it did when the Grottos were formed thousands of years ago.

Hike 21

HORSESHOE CIRQUE

SEDIMENTARY LAYERS LINE AN ALPINE CIRQUE

Hike below tilted sedimentary layers that form a picturesque cirque in the Mosquito Range.

DISTANCE ■ **2 miles round trip**
ELEVATION ■ **12,271 to 12,320 feet**
DIFFICULTY ■ **Easy**

TOPOGRAPHIC MAPS ■ USGS Mount Sherman; Trails Illustrated #110

GEOLOGIC MAP ■ 16

KEY REFERENCE ■ 16

PRECAUTIONS ■ The access road for this hike crosses old mining claims on private land. Please respect all signs and hike only around Horseshoe Cirque, which is located on National Forest land. Old mines are dangerous—please do not enter open tunnels.

FOR INFORMATION ■ South Park Ranger District

About the Landscape: Horseshoe Cirque is a striking landform in central Colorado's Mosquito Range. Tilted *sedimentary rocks* once deposited on ancient sea floors have been sculpted by *Ice Age glaciers* into imposing horseshoe-shaped cliffs along the east flank of Horseshoe Mountain. These layers of marine deposits form the walls of Horseshoe Cirque above Leavick Tarn, the larger of two shallow glacial lakes.

It is unusual to find sedimentary rocks exposed in Colorado's high country. As these one-time sea-floor materials uplifted to crown the mountains of the Mosquito Range, most of the *sediments* were stripped off by erosion. The beds exposed at Horseshoe Cirque are remnants of the layers that were pushed up during the huge Laramide Sawatch uplift that once extended from the Mosquito Range on the east to the Sawatch Range on the west.

Trail Guide: To reach the start of this hike, drive 1.5 miles south of Fairplay on Colorado Highway 9 and turn right on Park County Road 18 (at the sign for National Forest access). Follow this maintained gravel road along Fourmile Creek 11.2 miles to an unmarked road on the left that crosses a culvert over the creek. Turn left and follow this old mining road 1.6 miles uphill to where it reaches an abandoned mine tunnel on a sharp switchback. Park on the level area in front of the mine tunnel.

Start by walking toward the Horseshoe cliffs along the north side of the lake visible from the parking area. Although this hike does not follow an established trail, the terrain is easy to negotiate.

Boulders of *limestone* are scattered on the hillside above the shoreline of the lake. These gray and tan rocks are mostly from the Mississippian Leadville Limestone, which was deposited on a 350 million-year-old sea floor and which now forms the upper part of the cliffs and hillsides of Horseshoe Cirque. These relatively soft sedimentary layers have managed to hang on through earthquakes, uplifts, glaciers, and millions of years of rain, sleet, and snow.

An interesting feature in some of the gray limestone boulders is the presence of round, dark spots smaller than a dime. These are called oncolites. They represent small accumulations of algae that formed in warm, shallow water and were rolled back and forth by currents to become shaped like balls. Oncolites are common in lower Paleozoic rocks that were deposited in the seas that covered much of Colorado during this time.

The Leadville Limestone is the host rock for many of the large ore bodies in central Colorado, including the Leadville Mining District, from which more than $0.5 billion worth of silver, lead, zinc, gold, and copper have been mined in the Arkansas Valley on the west side of the Mosquito Range.

At the far end of the first lake, a stream drains from the higher lake called Leavick Tarn. A tarn is a lake that fills a glacially formed rock basin or *cirque.* Follow the stream to the Leavick Tarn and around its shoreline to an outcrop of pink granite on the far side of the lake. These granite rocks are part of the 1.7 billion-year-old Precambrian basement that uplifted to form the Mosquito Range.

After crossing a soggy meadow, look for an outcrop of white *quartzite* along the shore of Leavick Tarn. The "quartzite" in this outcrop is actually a hard *sandstone* cemented together by *quartz,* not the *metamorphic rock* quartzite, which is fused together by heat and pressure. This quartzite layer is also visible just above the Precambrian basement *granite* on Horseshoe Cliffs. This is the Cambrian age Sawatch Quartzite, the oldest Paleozoic rock formation in central Colorado. Here, along the base of the Horseshoe Cliffs, these 500 million-year-old Paleozoic rocks are found directly on top of the granite basement; this *unconformity* represents a gap in time of more than 1 billion years.

Imagine that you have suddenly arrived at the beach. You stand on a shoreline of soft, sugary sand that borders hills of ancient basement rock that will one day be covered by the Cambrian sea as it advances from the west.

Coming back to the present, climb to the top of the low hills east of

Oncolites in limestone at Horseshoe Cirque

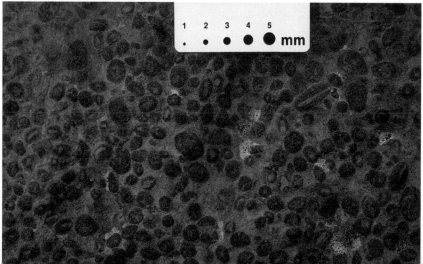

Sedimentary rocks still cap the Mosquito Range at Horseshoe Cirque.

Leavick Tarn for a great view of the Horseshoe Cirque and surrounding landscape. These hills are composed of limestone and were scoured by advancing glaciers many times during the Pleistocene Ice Age. Large *erratic* boulders of pink granite left behind by the ice sheets are perched on top of the limestone outcrops.

From this point, the hike back to the parking area is a simple matter of crossing the outlet stream spilling from the lower lake and climbing a short distance back to your vehicle.

Chapter 5
THE RIO GRANDE RIFT

Beginning 30 to 26 million years ago during the Oligocene, Colorado began to pull apart as though the Rocky Mountains were caught in a tug-of-war between the High Plains and the Colorado Plateau. As the mountains pulled slowly apart, the landscape between them stretched and thinned, creating a network of deep, down-faulted valleys called the *Rio Grande Rift*. The Rift divides the crest of Colorado's Rocky Mountains from the upper Arkansas Valley near Leadville, and continues south through the San Luis Valley and into New Mexico along the Rio Grande.

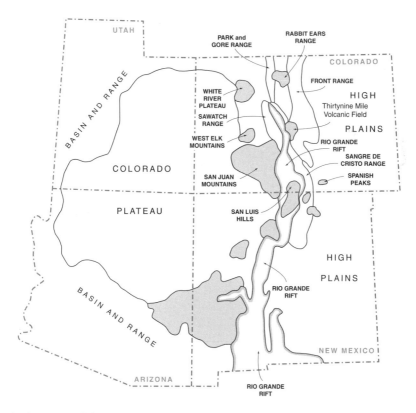

The location of the Rio Grande Rift

This tectonic *rifting* most likely originated from friction as a piece of the Pacific Plate (called the Farallon Plate) *subducted*, or descended, beneath North America. This caused huge reverberations inland and initiated the zone of spreading along the rift where the land was stretched and thinned as *magma* began to well up from below. As the magma pushed higher, the tremendous heat from the molten rock caused swelling and expansion at the surface, further stretching the landscape. Geologists still debate whether stretching along the rift began because of upwelling from below, or if upwelling from below began because the land was stretching.

As the Colorado Plateau and the High Plains moved away from each other, the eroded stubble of the Laramide uplifts stretched apart. To accommodate this motion, the Colorado Plateau slowly rotated a few degrees in a clockwise direction, reactivating old *faults* and tearing a gash in the remains of the Southern Rocky Mountains. During this movement, which intensified about 10 million years ago and continues today, the land adjusted to the tension in the rocks. Some mountain-size blocks subsided, forming down-dropped *grabens* such as the Arkansas and San Luis Valleys. Others tilted and uplifted, creating steep *fault-block* mountains, or horsts, such as the Sawatch and Sangre de Cristo Ranges.

Coincident with this action, a phase of volcanic activity spread across much of Colorado as magma pushed to the surface through the faults and

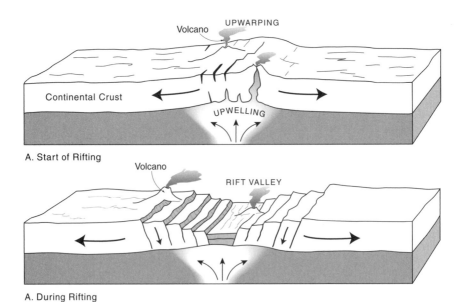

A. Start of Rifting

A. During Rifting

Development of a rift valley

fractures in the rocks. Although all of the volcanic activity of this period was not directly related to the Rio Grande Rift, the Rift was a major fault zone that was and still is affected by the volcanics. Even today, hot springs bubble to the surface from faults along the margins of the Rift, in such places as Princeton Hot Springs in the Arkansas Valley.

The Rio Grande is a relative latecomer to the Rift. Only within the last 5 million years, after renewed uplift of the Southern Rockies to their present heights, did rivers flow off the mountains and down the rift to become the Rio Grande.

CHALK CLIFFS

Hike 22

WHITE CLIFFS FLAG A GEOTHERMAL AREA

Explore the brilliant white Chalk Cliffs of the Mount Princeton Hot Springs area.

DISTANCE ■ **3 miles round trip**

ELEVATION ■ **8,400 to 8,800 feet**

DIFFICULTY ■ **Easy**

TOPOGRAPHIC MAPS ■ **USGS Mount Antero; Trails Illustrated #130**

GEOLOGIC MAP ■ **17**

KEY REFERENCE ■ **17**

PRECAUTIONS ■ **Use caution when exploring side canyons. Beware of flash floods and rockfalls. Please respect private property and give a wide berth to horses on trail rides from the lodges nearby.**

FOR INFORMATION ■ **Salida Ranger District**

About the Landscape: This easy exploration along the base of the brilliant white 1,600-foot-high Chalk Cliffs that flank Mount Princeton (14,197 feet) is best concluded with a soak at the nearby Mount Princeton Hot Springs Resort. It is no coincidence that these stunning white cliffs rise in the same place that hot springs percolate to the surface. It is the hot groundwater here at the western margin of the Rio Grande Rift that caused these massive granite cliffs to become whitewashed.

Between 30 and 26 million years ago, as the *Rio Grande Rift* zone began to stretch apart, the earth's crust thinned, allowing *magma* to well up close to the surface along the western margin of the rift. Groundwater flowed around this magma, heating up to become geothermal. The hot groundwater was full of dissolved minerals, and as the water circulated around the *granitic batholith,* these white hydrothermal minerals, called zeolites, filled the *fractures* in the rock. The hot springs at the surface today indicate that zeolites may still be forming deep below.

During the faulting and uplift along the western margin of the Rio Grande Rift over the past 10 million years, the once deeply buried granitic rocks with zeolite-filled fractures were carried upward as Mount Princeton rose. The southern flank of the mountain weathered to reveal the white cliffs.

The Chalk Cliffs are not made of the "chalk" used on blackboards nor are they made of the rock geologists call chalk, which is a fine-grained *limestone* made famous by England's White Cliffs of Dover. Rather, these Chalk Cliffs are the originally gray granitic batholith turned white by the zeolites that weather out of exposed fractures in the rocks.

Trail Guide: To reach the Chalk Cliffs trailhead, drive 8 miles south from Buena Vista on US Highway 24 to the turnoff for the Mount Princeton Hot Springs. Drive 7.2 miles on County Road 162 to the trailhead located on the right. A Forest Service information kiosk marks the trailhead.

From the parking area, a segment of the Colorado Trail winds east along the Chalk Cliffs. It follows a gentle, tree-covered slope formed by granitic boulders and other rock debris that has washed off the cliffs. Note the unusual white powdery soil underfoot.

The grayish granitic rocks along the trail are from the 36 million-year-old Mount Princeton batholith. The specific rock type is quartz monzonite, a type of granite best identified by microscope. It contains less than 10 percent *quartz* and roughly equal amounts of two different *feldspar* minerals (orthoclase and plagioclase). A close look at the rock reveals that the light-colored feldspar crystals are peppered with dark flakes of *mica* and *hornblende.*

At about the 0.5-mile point, keep left at the junction and continue hiking along the cliffs. Note that the prominent rock face ahead is highly fractured, displaying a maze of white veins. These are zeolite-filled fractures.

After about 1 mile from the trailhead is another junction. The Colorado Trail continues straight ahead, paralleling the base of the cliffs eastward. Take the left fork, turning north toward the prominent canyon that breaches the Chalk Cliffs.

The trail leads upslope, becoming confused in several places as branches split off. Simply continue toward the mouth of the canyon. After about 0.25 mile from the junction, the trail meets the bright white cliffs adjacent to the canyon's entrance. From this point, find your way along a trail that leads down into a wash and follow the wash to explore up the canyon. This wash and the canyon it flows through have been carved by flash floods. Be sure not to investigate further if the weather looks threatening.

The Chalk Cliffs

A short way up the wash is a prominently veined section of cliff on the left. This is a good outcrop for investigating the powdery, white zeolite minerals that fill the fractures in the granitic rock. Rub your hand along the veins and look at the powder on your hand. These are zeolites, the minerals precipitated from hot groundwater that percolated along fractures in this granite. This powder now coats the cliffs around you and forms the white soil along the trail. When the wind blows, the powder billows into white clouds.

The wash continues up for about another 0.25 mile where it finally ends against the cliffs. Return to the mouth of the canyon by following the wash back downhill. As an alternative to returning directly back to the parking area, look for side trails leading to the right along the base of the cliffs as you climb out of the wash and exit the canyon. These side trails lead to a number of interesting nooks and crannies along the cliffs. Ultimately, these trails merge with the Colorado Trail and lead back to the parking area.

GREAT SAND DUNES NATIONAL MONUMENT

Hike 23

GIANT WIND-BLOWN DUNES

Climb barefoot up the tallest sand dunes in North America to observe modern geologic processes in action.

DISTANCE ■ As far as you want to go!

ELEVATION ■ 8,050 to 8,700 feet

DIFFICULTY ■ Easy to moderate

TOPOGRAPHIC MAP ■ USGS Zapata Ranch

GEOLOGIC MAP ■ 18

KEY REFERENCE ■ 18

PRECAUTIONS ■ Be sure to stay oriented in the dunes so as not to lose your way. Avoid dunes during thunderstorms. In summer, the surface sand on the dunes gets very hot and can burn your feet.

FOR INFORMATION ■ Great Sand Dunes National Monument

About the Landscape: The Great Sand Dunes are alive. They are a place where *sediment,* namely sand, is actively being deposited. On windy days, *ripplemarks* and *cross-beds* form before your eyes.

For thousands of years, wind has swept eroded grains of Colorado's Rockies into North America's tallest dunes. The foot of the Sangre de Cristo Range in the San Luis Valley serves as the dust pan that collects this nearly 10-mile-wide mountain of sand.

Trail Guide: To reach Great Sand Dunes National Monument, drive 14.5 miles east from Alamosa on US Highway 160. At the junction with Colorado Highway 150, turn left (north) and drive 19.3 miles to the park entrance. This hike starts at the Dunes parking area, a left turn 0.4 mile north of the Visitor Center.

Kick off your shoes and follow the established paths from the parking area to Medano Creek. In front of you is the great mountain of sand, but you must first cross the creek to get to the dunes. As you cross, contemplate the importance of this watery boundary that plays a major role in keeping the dunes in place. Upstream, the creek captures sand blowing off the dunes, preventing the dunes from crossing the riverbed. The creek curves around the dunes, transporting the sand downstream where prevailing winds from the southwest blow the sand upwind to the northeast— and back onto the dunes.

Once across Medano Creek, traverse the broad sandflat that borders the dunes. Fist-sized cobbles of *gneiss* and *granite* poke above the sand. These Precambrian rock fragments were eroded from the Sangre de Cristos and deposited across this flat during floods. The black sand grains are magnetite, a mineral worn from the *igneous* and *metamorphic basement rocks.*

The first dunes you come to are low, relatively flat dunes that are easy to walk across. As the dunes steepen, the going is easier along their crests

Climbing the Great Sand Dunes

where the undulations are fairly gentle. Only about 30 percent of the sand now beneath your feet is from the Sangre de Cristos. Most of the grains are tiny fragments of *volcanic rock* such as ash and lava that came from the San Juan Mountains across the valley.

If you could have stood in this place about 15,000 years ago, the Rio Grande would have flowed directly toward you from the San Juan Mountains and turned abruptly south near this point. At that time, the river was swollen with meltwater and debris from the disappearing glaciers at the end of the last *Ice Age.* Gradually, the Rio Grande has moved southwestward away from this ancient sharp bend, creating the gently curved channel of today. Its old channels dried into oxbow lakes and mounds of loose sand and silt. Since the prevailing winds here travel to the northeast across the San Luis Valley directly toward the notch in the skyline above the dunes, the old Rio Grande riverbed sands were picked up and swept by wind toward the mountains where eddies and turbulence caused the wind to drop its load.

Today, the wind continues to rework this great sand pile, mounding it higher and higher and causing the dunes to migrate across one another. Periodic storms from the northeast work against this standard pattern and blow the sand in the opposite direction. These reversing winds pile the sand even higher and help to keep the dunes from marching up the mountains.

As you walk, you may notice that the sand beneath the surface is wet. Like a big sponge, the Great Sand Dunes soak up the meager rainfall and groundwater pooled below the surface of San Luis Valley. This water wicks up through the sand pile and helps to stabilize the dunes. In places where the wind has swept the dry surface sand away, the moist layer below reveals rows of lines that parallel the dune crests. These lines trace cross-beds created by the crests of the dunes that constantly migrate as advancing sands blow forward to form new crests.

If the wind picks up, sheets of sand may roar against your legs and ankles. The complex wind patterns swirling off the crests of the dunes form ripples at your feet. Slowly, the dunes transform, and the record of their movement is preserved in buried patterns.

Over the crest of the next dune, or perhaps after reaching the highest dune 750 feet above the valley floor, simply reverse your direction and head down the dunes to the parking area. Retracing your steps, however, may be difficult. The footsteps you left behind may have vanished by the time you return, the slate wiped clean by recent movements of the sand.

Chapter 6
THE SANGRE DE CRISTO RANGE

The Sangre de Cristo Range attained its statuesque skyline by emerging as an "island" while the floor sank around it. This makes the Sangre de Cristos a *fault-block* mountain range that towers above the valleys that flank it.

The Sangre de Cristos began in Pennsylvanian and Permian time as layers of *sedimentary rocks* that filled the *Central Colorado Trough* when the *Ancestral Rocky Mountains* eroded. During the *Laramide Orogeny,* this sedimentary rubble pile, now a *conglomerate* called the Sangre de Cristo Formation, was jostled as *basement rock* rose from below in a huge *anticline* that encompassed today's range and the San Luis Valley. Along the eastern edge of this uplift, the upward movement was hindered by the Wet Mountains. As the uplift pushed against them, a series of *thrust faults* developed that pushed the basement rock up and over the younger sedimentary conglomerate. At least eight thrust faults stacked up tilted slabs of rocklike shingles to form the Sangre de Cristo Range, and since then, some of the rocks have eroded away. Today, red conglomerates of the Sangre de Cristo Formation are found on the highest peaks in the range squeezed between thrust faults within the Precambrian basement.

The dramatically steep incline of today's Sangre de Cristo Range began to develop as the *Rio Grande Rift* shook up the region's *faults* between 30 and 26 million years ago and was accentuated as this movement intensified about 10 million years ago. During this shake-up, the San Luis Valley down-dropped along normal faults, including the Sangre de Cristo Fault, a major fault that borders the steep western face of the Sangre de Cristos. To the east, the Wet Mountain Valley also down-dropped along a major fault, but to a far lesser degree. At the same time, the Sangre de Cristo mountain block uplifted and tilted. The result was a mountain range bordered on the east and west by down-dropped valleys.

Ice then swept down the flanks of the Sangre de Cristos during the *Ice Age,* completing the skyline with jagged peaks and U-shaped valleys. Alhough this glacial carving makes them resemble other Laramide ranges to the north, they are unlike the mountains in Colorado's Rockies, which are basement-cored anticlinal uplifts. The Sangre de Cristos stand tall as a fault-block mountain range.

WILLOW LAKE

Hike 24

GLACIATED CRESTONE CONGLOMERATE

At scenic Willow Lake, a waterfall cascades over a cliff of Crestone Conglomerate.

DISTANCE ■ **10 miles round trip**
ELEVATION ■ **8,800 to 11,720 feet**
DIFFICULTY ■ **Strenuous**
TOPOGRAPHIC MAPS ■ **USGS Crestone and Crestone Peak**
GEOLOGIC MAP ■ **19**
KEY REFERENCE ■ **19**
PRECAUTIONS ■ **Be prepared for the nearly 3,000-foot elevation gain on this hike. Avoid getting caught above treeline during summer thunderstorms. Camping is prohibited within 300 yards of Willow Lake.**
FOR INFORMATION ■ **Saguache Ranger District**

About the Landscape: The imposing Sangre de Cristo Range is dissected by a series of glaciated valleys that harbor pristine alpine lakes in their upper reaches. One of the most scenic is Willow Lake, a glacier-gouged, bare-rock basin with a spectacular waterfall spilling over a cliff at its upper end.

The hike to Willow Lake traverses a steep glaciated valley past numerous waterfalls. It also crosses the Crestone Thrust Fault where, during the formation of the Sangre de Cristos, Precambrian *basement rock* pushed up and over the younger Crestone Conglomerate, the 6,000-foot-thick upper member of the Sangre de Cristo Formation.

Trail Guide: To reach the South Crestone Trailhead, turn onto the T-Road at the sign for Crestone, south of Moffat on Colorado Highway 17. Drive 12.8 miles to Crestone and turn right at the stop sign onto Galena Road (a Forest Service sign here says Willow Creek Trail 2 miles). Follow this gravel road (which becomes Forest Road 949), bearing right at the fork, to the trailhead at the end of the road.

Follow the trail to Willow Lake which splits from the South Crestone Trail about 50 yards from the trailhead and immediately crosses Crestone Creek. Bear left at the next fork and head uphill through the meadow to where the trail register is located.

For about the next 1.5 miles, the trail switchbacks up a forested ridge that separates Crestone Creek from the Willow Creek drainage to the south. The colorful *conglomerate* boulders that make up this ridge are part of the glacial *end moraine* deposited by the glaciers that carved Willow Creek Valley.

As you climb the switchbacks to the top of the ridge, notice the steep, jagged outcrops on the north wall of Crestone Creek Valley. These rocks are Precambrian basement rocks, part of the elevated basement that shaped the western edge of the Sangre de Cristo Range.

From the top of the ridge, the trail descends a moderate grade, then contours along the north side of Willow Creek Valley. Although not

The 300 million-year-old Crestone Conglomerate, Willow Lake Trail

visible, the trail crosses the Crestone Thrust Fault somewhere along this section. You are walking along the place where, 70 million years ago, basement rock rumbled up through flat layers of Crestone Conglomerate and bent them back to form the Sangre de Cristo Range.

A short distance after passing a spur trail to the right, you meet the first outcrop of sedimentary Crestone Conglomerate on the east side of the fault. Here, colorful mixtures of red to maroon *sandstone* and conglomerate are exposed to the left of the trail. Rounded pebbles of white *quartz* appear to be floating in the sandy *sediment*. A close look reveals pebbles and angular grains of *feldspar,* making this outcrop a conglomeratic *arkose sandstone.* These coarse sediments were eroded about 300 million years ago from the southern part of the Uncompahgre Highland (called the San Luis Highland), part of the western segment of the *Ancestral Rocky Mountains.*

As the trail begins to switchback up the north wall of the valley, it reaches the boundary of the Sangre de Cristo Wilderness (note the sign) about 2 miles from the trailhead. At about the 3-mile point, the trail is blasted into a sheer rock face where it (treacherously!) crosses a cascading stream. Ahead is the waterfall that cascades from the hanging valley above.

Next, the trail meets Willow Creek and crosses to its south side. It switchbacks steeply from the creek for about the next 0.5 mile to the top of the rock ledge. As you reach the top, the trail levels out, although it is still another 1.5 miles to the lake.

Follow the trail through the forest and then scramble up some rock outcrops to lake level. The view of Willow Lake is breathtaking. A substantial waterfall spills over a steep cliff at the upper end of the lake. Where you stand, glaciers once flowed as rivers of ice, carving this staircase of valleys. The lake itself is set in a huge bowl gouged by the glaciers from solid rock. *Striations* in the conglomerate outcrops along the lakeshore were scratched by rocks trapped within the moving ice. The steep cliff at the far end of the lake formed as the glaciers plucked huge fractured blocks of rock from the rock wall.

If time and energy permit, it's worthwhile to work your way carefully around the north side of the lake to the top of the cliff. From this vantage point, there is a great view looking west across Willow Lake into the San Luis Valley and across the *Rio Grande Rift* to the San Juan Mountains on the far skyline.

Although this is the turnaround point for this hike, the trail continues for over another mile to an upper lake at the extreme end of Willow Creek Valley.

LILY LAKE

GLACIATED BASEMENT ROCKS

Hike past cascading rivers and waterfalls to picturesque Lily Lake.

DISTANCE: **8 miles round trip**
ELEVATION: **9,840 to 12,350 feet**
DIFFICULTY ■ **Strenuous**
TOPOGRAPHIC MAPS ■ **USGS Blanca Peak and Mosca Pass**
GEOLOGIC MAP ■ **20**
KEY REFERENCE ■ **19**
PRECAUTIONS ■ **Beware of summer thunderstorms. Be sure to get an early start or make the hike an overnight backpack trip.**
FOR INFORMATION ■ **San Carlos Ranger District**

About the Landscape: The trail to Lily Lake follows the upper Huerfano River through a classic U-shaped glaciated valley to its headwaters in the melting snowfields below the north face of Blanca Peak. *Ice Age glaciers* carved the basement core of the mountains into a rugged landscape of jagged peaks and sheer rock cliffs. Lily Lake itself is located in a *cirque,* an almost circular rock basin carved into the *basement rock.* A climb past cascading streams and waterfalls to Lily Lake leads to dramatic views of jagged peaks and the twisted Precambrian basement rocks of the Sangre de Cristo Range.

Trail Guide: To reach the Lily Lake Trailhead, drive west 1 mile on Colorado Highway 69 from the small town of Gardner to Huerfano County Road 550. Turn left and drive west on this paved road (which turns into gravel) and follow the signs for the Lily Lake Trailhead. The road deteriorates as it approaches the trailhead, but is generally passable with a high-clearance two-wheel drive vehicle. If it gets too rocky, park at the State Wildlife Area and walk the final 6 miles to the trailhead.

In the canyon below the trailhead, the Huerfano River cuts a gorge through a pile of sand, gravel, and boulders that blocks the valley. This material is part of an *end moraine* dumped here by a glacier that sculpted the valley during the Ice Age.

The Lily Lake Trail begins by following an old mining road across the forested hills of the end moraine. As it comes down the slope of the moraine, the trail crosses the first of several lush meadows and narrow side streams. After about 0.5 mile, the cascades of the Huerfano River are close by on the left. The trail diverts from the river where a sign for Lily Lake points to the right. After crossing a forested ridge, the trail suddenly becomes indistinct where it skirts the next boggy meadow. Several Forest Service signs (with arrows) point the way to where the trail begins to angle up side slopes on the west side of the meadow.

For the next 2 miles, the trail follows a consistent grade upward along the west side of the valley. Glimpses of Blanca Peak (14,345 feet) come into view, providing a sneak preview of what lies ahead. Along this stretch, you encounter the first outcrops of basement rock. *Dikes* and veins of dark *igneous rock* (called amphibolite) occur within lighter colored exposures of *granite* and *gneiss.* These basement rocks are part of Colorado's 1.7 billion-year-old Precambrian basement which was metamorphosed and deformed many times to create these complex and contorted patterns. You will have numerous opportunities to study these ancient rocks up close as the trail gets steeper and you pause to catch your breath.

About 3 miles from the trailhead, the trail reaches a forested bench where it passes several deteriorating miners' cabins. Several historic digging sites dot the area around Lily Lake. Part of the land surrounding Blanca Peak was excluded from the Sangre de Cristo Wilderness because of existing prospects for gold, silver, and tungsten.

The Huerfano River flows through a gorgeous glaciated valley below Blanca Peak.

From the forested bench, the trail climbs steeply for about the next mile through an alpine meadow above treeline. The trail crosses and follows along several spectacular cascades and waterfalls spilling down from Lily Lake. As the trail starts to switchback across a rocky outcrop above the meadow, look at the boulder field to the right. This is a small *rock glacier,* a mixture of rock and ice that is creeping downhill. Note how the boulders have plowed the soil in front of them as they push downslope.

As the trail crests the next rise, Lily Lake comes into view. Lily Lake fills a circular basin called a cirque, the place where snow and ice accumulated to feed the Ice Age glaciers that carved the Huerfano Valley. You are looking at the place where those powerful rivers of ice were born. Imagine 1,000 feet of ice over your head, slowly beginning a descent across what were once rather rounded basement rock uplifts.

Take time to explore the rocky hills across the outlet stream to the left (south). Look beneath your feet as you walk to find places where the rocks were scratched and polished by boulders trapped within the moving ice. These grooves in the rocks are called *striations,* and their alignment indicates the direction of the ice flow.

From this vantage point above Lily Lake, there are sweeping views of Mount Lindsey (14,042 feet) to the east and the sheer north face of Blanca Peak towering above you to the south. These mountains are "uprooted" basement rocks of Colorado, pushed skyward during Laramide mountain building 70 million years ago.

After enjoying the alpine scenery that surrounds Lily Lake, return to the trailhead by the route you came.

Chapter 7
THE WHITE RIVER PLATEAU

The White River Plateau is a sort of tectonic afterthought. Although it is a bona fide Laramide uplift, it arched upward less than 50 million years ago, millions of years after all the other Rocky Mountains lurched skyward. It is a broad, flat-topped dome of high forested plateaus north of Glenwood Springs and the Colorado River.

Prior to its Laramide uplift, the White River Plateau was a relatively stable landscape. It was not involved in the uplift of the *Ancestral Rocky Mountains,* but was rather located in the basin between the ancient uplifts called the *Central Colorado Trough.* As mountains were uplifting and eroding nearby, the layers of Paleozoic marine *sedimentary rocks* in the White River region remained intact. For this reason, the White River Plateau preserves the best record of Paleozoic rocks in Colorado, a sequence nearly 8,000 feet thick. On top of the Paleozoic layers, more than 7,000 feet of Mesozoic desert, river, and marine *sediments* accumulated, resulting in a stack of sedimentary rocks nearly 15,000 feet thick!

This region is best known for the Flat Tops, where thick accumulations of Tertiary *lava* flows cap the northeastern part of the plateau. This created a landscape of flat-topped mountains and high plateaus that were later bejeweled with countless alpine lakes by *Ice Age glaciers.*

Following the Laramide uplift of the plateau, three periods of volcanic eruptions extruded lava flows between about 24 and 8 million years ago. Unlike the explosive eruptions in the Rockies, which collapsed into huge *calderas* and spread blankets of ash and volcanic debris, the volcanic activity in the Flat Tops region was dominated by repeated eruptions that flooded lava across the landscape like rivers, forming lakes of molten *magma.* This activity built a layered stack of *basalt* as thick as 1,500 feet. These *volcanic rocks* are resistant to erosion, protecting softer underlying sedimentary layers from disappearing and thus preserving the plateau landscape.

DEVILS CAUSEWAY

BRIDGE OF BASALT

A narrow arête formed of basalt connects vast alpine plateaus.

DISTANCE ■ 10-mile loop

ELEVATION ■ 10,280 to 11,800 feet

DIFFICULTY ■ Strenuous

TOPOGRAPHIC MAPS ■ USGS Devils Causeway, Orno Creek, and Trappers Lake; Trails Illustrated #122

GEOLOGIC MAP ■ 13

KEY REFERENCE ■ 20

PRECAUTIONS ■ Use extra care crossing the Devils Causeway and exploring along the cliff tops. Get an early start to avoid getting caught on top during afternoon thunderstorms.

FOR INFORMATION ■ Yampa Ranger District

About the Landscape: The Devils Causeway is a narrow bridge of *basalt* that connects two broad alpine plateaus. Like a setting out of an adventure movie, the crossing will test your confidence afoot. But alas, it is not necessary to make the crossing to enjoy the spectacular scenery of the Flat Tops.

The narrow bridge of basalt at the Devils Causeway was formed by *Ice Age glaciers* that carved the Flat Tops during the Pleistocene. The glaciers that filled the valleys on opposite sides of the Causeway etched away at the headwalls of the *cirques* along their upper reaches until only a narrow ridge, called an arête, remained.

Trail Guide: To reach the Stillwater Reservoir Trailhead, drive 17.3 miles west from Yampa on County Road 7 (Forest Road 900). The trailhead and parking area are located at the end of the road.

The trail starts out above the north shore of Stillwater Reservoir, which dams the upper reaches of the Bear River. Flat Top Mountain, the highest point in the Flat Tops (12,493 feet), rises above the lake to the east. The layered rocks that make up its cliffs were formed by repeated eruptions of *basalt lava.* The steplike cliffs result from slight differences in each lava flow's resistance to erosion.

While following above the lakeshore, look for an outcrop of basalt to the right of the trail. The rock is medium to dark gray with small holes, or *vesicles,* formed by gas bubbles trapped in the *magma* during cooling. This rock is called vesicular basalt. Some of the holes are filled with white *quartz* crystals. Some of the crystal-lined vesicles still have space left in the center for crystals to grow. These are called geodes.

Near the west end of the reservoir, about 0.5 mile from the trailhead, the trail forks where the trail register is located. This hike will make a loop, ascending by the East Fork Trail to the right, and returning via the Bear River Trail to the left.

Just after you turn right at the junction, the trail enters the Flat Tops Wilderness. This part of the trail traverses a hilly terrain of boulders and sediment left behind by the glaciers that widened and deepened Bear River Valley during the Ice Age. A number of small lakes fill depressions once occupied by blocks of melting glacial ice. These are called kettle lakes.

After you pass Little Causeway Lake, an example of a kettle lake, the trail starts to climb more steeply, affording great views of the giant cliff-lined amphitheater at the head of Bear Valley. A series of long switchbacks ends in a saddle above treeline about 2 miles from the trailhead. Here is the first expansive view of the rolling alpine tundra plain that caps the Flat Tops. Turn off the East Fork Trail at this point, which continues straight ahead, and climb the steep, rocky trail to the left.

Once you reach the top, the challenge of the Devils Causeway is before you. The Devils Causeway was formed by erosion at the head of Bear River Valley to the south and east and along the Williams Fork drainage to the north and west. During the Ice Age, glacial ice capped the high plateaus of the Flat Tops and spilled down into the surrounding valleys. These rivers of ice widened and deepened the valleys and, in the process, steepened the basalt cliffs by plucking rocks from their faces. Over time, the upper reaches of these valleys, called cirques, drew closer and closer, until only this narrow ridge or arête separated the two.

As you ponder the meaning of life and the risks of crossing the Devils Causeway, take in the dizzying views of the basalt cliffs that form the sweeping escarpments at the edge of the Flat Tops. Below the cliffs to the right are *rock glaciers,* lobe-shaped mounds of ice-cored rock that move slowly downslope.

The Devils Causeway is not as narrow as it appears, but it commands all your attention as you cross. Take your time, watch every step, and don't look down! If you have more sense than the rest, simply return to the trailhead the way you came.

But if you do cross, once you are on the other side, the trail crosses a vast expanse of tundra where it meets the Chinese Wall Trail coming in from the north (right). Great views of the Chinese Wall are seen from the trail looking west into the White River drainage. You may wish to deviate

The Devils Causeway is a narrow expanse of basalt that connects alpine plateaus called the Flat Tops.

to the north to gain a better view of this long, towering cliff of layered basalt.

To return to the trailhead, continue straight ahead instead, following the well-worn tracks to the junction with the Stillwater and Bear River Trails about 3 miles from the Devils Causeway. At the trail junction, turn left and follow the Bear River Trail back down to the junction with the East Fork Trail and then back to the trailhead.

Hike **27**

HANGING LAKE

A TRAVERTINE OASIS

Waterfalls spill over travertine into Hanging Lake, perched on ledges of Cambrian Sawatch Quartzite above Glenwood Canyon.

DISTANCE ■ **2.5 miles round trip**

ELEVATION ■ **6,100 to 7,190 feet**

DIFFICULTY ■ **Short but strenuous**

TOPOGRAPHIC MAPS ■ **USGS Shoshone; Trails Illustrated #123**

GEOLOGIC MAP ■ **16**

KEY REFERENCE ■ **None**

PRECAUTIONS ■ Easy access makes this a very popular trail—avoid weekends if possible. To keep the lake pristine, please remain on the boardwalk. Swimming is prohibited. Use caution when negotiating the steep sections of the trail.

FOR INFORMATION ■ Eagle Ranger District

About the Landscape: The hike up the steep trail to Hanging Lake is a climb out of Colorado's "basement" to emerge along the sandy shores of the ancient Cambrian sea that flooded western Colorado more than 500 million years ago. The Colorado River slices the southern end of the White River uplift, exposing an *unconformity* between Colorado's Precambrian *basement rocks* and the overlying Paleozoic sedimentary layers. Hanging Lake is perched high above, where flowing water over the eons has built a natural travertine dam, forming a surprising oasis that dangles on the walls of Glenwood Canyon.

Trail Guide: To reach the Hanging Lake Trailhead, drive 9 miles east from Glenwood Springs on Interstate 70 to the Hanging Lake exit rest area. If you are westbound, take the Grizzly Creek exit and double back to the Hanging Lake rest area. Park at the rest area and follow the bike trail upstream along the Colorado River for about 0.25 mile to the trailhead where Dead Horse Creek flows from a narrow side canyon on the left (north).

The hike up the canyon starts out by climbing steeply over a rocky trail through boulders that have tumbled off the cliffs above. The boulders are a mixture of dark *schist* and pink *pegmatite basement rocks* and blocks of the mostly gray Sawatch Quartzite. The term quartzite is used here to refer to hard *sandstone* cemented together by *quartz,* not the *metamorphic rock* quartzite in which sand grains are fused together by heat and pressure.

After passing the Deadhorse Trail, which splits off to the right at about the 0.25-mile point, the Hanging Lake Trail approaches the boundary between the basement rocks and the overlying sedimentary layers of the Sawatch Quartzite. The contact between these two contrasting rock types of widely different ages is an unconformity, a gap in Colorado's rock record that spans more than 1 billion years. During this vast amount of time, Colorado's ancient landscape was flattened by erosion to its Precambrian core, then bathed by the shallow Cambrian sea that deposited the Sawatch Quartzite.

About 0.5 mile from the trailhead, a prominent ledge of basement rock with pegmatite veins streaking through it (to the left of the trail) lies just below the level of the unconformity. Above here, the trail switches back and then climbs along a *talus* slope of boulders that are all Sawatch Quartzite. At this point, you have climbed out of Colorado's basement. Your feet

are now being washed by waves lapping along a sandy shoreline that existed during the Cambrian over 500 million years ago. Take a close look at these rocks to see the sugary texture of this quartz sandstone. From here on up, the walls of the canyon are a thick sequence of these sandstone layers stacked one on top of another.

The trail continues to climb steeply, crossing back and forth over Dead Horse Creek on a number of foot bridges. At about the 1-mile point, you will see a log shelter to the left of the trail with an outcrop of Sawatch Quartzite just behind it. At about eye level, there are faint *cross-beds* of thin, slanting lines formed by currents transporting sand along the former coastline.

Just past the shelter, a waterfall cascades down through the forested canyon wall to the creek on the right. This water is spilling from Hanging Lake above (not yet in view). Something curious happens beyond this point—the creek bed in the upper reaches of the canyon is bone dry! All of the water in Dead Horse Creek comes down the east fork, presumably from a spring above Hanging Lake. The west fork, where the bridge is located, flows only after heavy rains or in the spring when the snow is melting.

The last part of the trail to the lake is very steep and has a metal hand railing for safety. At the top, the trail becomes a boardwalk that skirts the lower shoreline of Hanging Lake. At the far end of the lake, Bridal Veil Falls spreads across the upper ledge and plunges into the lake. Below the boardwalk to the right, a lower waterfall cascades through the forest to the creek bed below.

The water spilling over the rock ledges where Hanging Lake is located has built up deposits of travertine, a limestone-like rock that forms from dissolved minerals that crystallize into a primarily *calcite* coating on rock surfaces. As the water has splashed over the ledges of Sawatch Quartzite, layer after layer of the travertine has accumulated, and in the process, a natural dam has been built that forms the lake. A short side trail leads to Sprouting Rock above the upper falls, where Dead Horse Creek has scoured through layers of travertine.

Hanging Lake is a pleasant oasis to just "hang out" before retracing your steps back to the trailhead.

◀ *Waterfall at Hanging Lake—an oasis above Glenwood Canyon*

Chapter 8

THE ELK MOUNTAINS

The Elk Mountains are the *Ancestral Rocky Mountains* reincarnated. The Precambrian *basement rock* and overlying *sedimentary rocks* that composed the Ancestral Rockies are now transformed into the famously scenic red and maroon layers of the distinctive Elk Mountains, which form the western border of Colorado's Rockies.

As the Ancestral Rockies crumbled in erosion during Pennsylvanian and Permian time, much of their *sediment* washed into the *Central Colorado Trough,* a *graben* that formed where a section of basement rock dropped down between the two rising mountain blocks of the Ancestral Rockies. The graben truly became a graveyard, an ancient stack of sedimentary rocks representing the once-great mountain range. This expansive pile of *shale, sandstone,* and *conglomerate* is known today as the Maroon Formation which is more than 10,000 feet thick near Aspen. The red color of the Maroon Formation is from a rustlike stain that coated the grains of sediment as they were buried more than 250 million years ago.

Today's Elk Mountains rose initially during the *Laramide Orogeny,* about 70 million years ago. Unlike the other Laramide mountains, they were not cored by basement rock that pushed up from below. Rather, the rock layers of the Central Colorado Trough were warped into a giant upward fold, or *anticline,* as the Sawatch Range uplifted to the east. As the Sawatch pushed higher, the Elk Mountain anticline was also carried higher. As uplift continued, the huge stack of sedimentary layers detached from the west flank of the Sawatch Range and slid downslope as a huge gravity slide. This action, which took place along a zone of weakness called the Elk Mountain Thrust Fault, moved a section of rock 4 miles thick and 30 miles across! This event took place in a geologic instant—perhaps less than 1 million years.

Following a long period of erosion that flattened the Laramide landscape, *magma* welled up during a major igneous event about 34 million years ago. During this period, volcanic fireworks began in the West Elk and San Juan Mountains. To their north, in the Elk Mountain area, the magma probably never reached the surface. Instead, as the magma pushed upward, it oozed along the Elk Mountain thrust fault and pooled to form two large

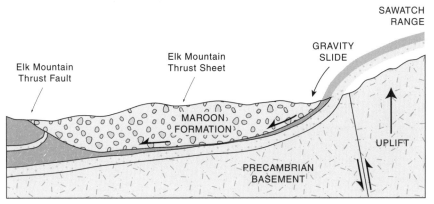

Generalized cross-section showing the Elk Mountain gravity slide about 70 million years ago

blisters that became the White Rock and Snowmass *plutons.* As these two massive igneous bodies intruded into the Maroon Formation, they pushed up the overlying sedimentary layers, creating a new mountain range from the old, ancestral rocks—the Elk Mountains.

When the magma cooled, it became *granodiorite,* a light-colored *granitic* rock. The Elk Mountains are riddled with many smaller intrusions of granodiorite that formed at about this same time. One of the most obvious features of this intrusive event is the "baked zones" where hot magma altered the Maroon Formation sedimentary rocks. The searing heat from the intruding magma cooked the adjacent sedimentary rocks, dramatically changing their color and appearance. The once red and maroon rocks were altered, or metamorphosed, into gray-green rock called *hornfels.* The igneous granodiorite intrusions and the greenish baked zones around them are visible on many of today's mountainsides. Boulders of granodiorite and hornfels are also found with sedimentary debris along many of the trails in the Elk Mountains.

The final chapter in the development of the Elk Mountain landscape took place during the past 10 million years as regional uplift brought the Elk Mountains (along with the rest of the Rockies) to their present elevations. As a result of this uplift, intense erosion and downcutting by streams dissected the area into a network of mountains and deep valleys. Finishing touches were applied by *Ice Age glaciers* that sculpted the valleys into their classic U-shapes and etched the shapes of the Elk Mountains' characteristic peaks.

MAROON BELLS

COLORADO'S MOST PHOTOGRAPHED PEAKS

Explore the Maroon Bells, picturesque peaks carved from the Maroon Formation sedimentary layers that once lined the Central Colorado Trough.

DISTANCE ■ **3.5 miles round trip**

ELEVATION ■ **9,560 to 10,120 feet**

DIFFICULTY ■ **Moderate**

TOPOGRAPHIC MAPS ■ **USGS Maroon Bells; Trails Illustrated #128**

GEOLOGIC MAP ■ **21**

KEY REFERENCE ■ **21**

PRECAUTIONS ■ **During summer months, get an early start to avoid afternoon thunderstorms. Expect crowds on weekends.**

FOR INFORMATION ■ **Aspen Ranger District**

About the Landscape: The twin peaks of the Maroon Bells are the most photogenic mountains in Colorado. Towering in the Elk Mountains near Aspen, the Maroon Bells are shaped from a deep pile of red and purple *sedimentary rock* layers, called the Maroon Formation, that accumulated in the *Central Colorado Trough* about 250 million years ago as the *Ancestral Rocky Mountains* eroded. They contrast markedly with other mountains in the Rockies because they are layered, maroon in color, and have bell-like shapes.

Famous photographs of the Maroon Bells have been taken from Maroon Lake. This hike follows along Maroon Lake to a second lake above it, called Crater Lake, which offers another opportunity to photograph the mountain reflections.

Trail Guide: To reach the Maroon Lake Trailhead, drive 0.5 mile west from Aspen on Colorado Highway 82 to the Maroon Creek Road (Forest Road 125). Turn left (south) and drive 5 miles to the Forest Service entrance station, then continue another 4.5 miles to the trailhead at the upper parking area. During the summer months, the road to Maroon Bells is closed to private vehicles between 8:30 A.M. and 5:00 P.M. Day hikers must take a bus from the Ruby Park Bus Station in downtown Aspen. Backpackers may enter at any time and can park in the overnight parking lot.

From the parking area, the trail follows the shoreline of Maroon Lake, the most famous spot for photographing the Maroon Bells. The layered twin peaks command the skyline to the west and are reflected perfectly in the lake when the water is still. From this view, the southernmost peak

Time for reflection, Maroon Lake

(on the left) is Maroon Peak (14,156 feet) and the peak to its right is North Maroon Peak (14,014 feet). Since their final uplift during the past 10 million years, wind, water, and ice have etched these peaks into their characteristic shapes.

Note the classic U-shape of the glaciated valley above Maroon Lake. Maroon Lake itself, however, was not hollowed by glaciers like so many other alpine lakes in the Rocky Mountains. Instead, the lake was formed by landslide debris that tumbled down from the bare rock slopes on the north side of the valley, damming Maroon Creek. Look at the slopes that rise steeply on the right. Several scarred areas reveal where landslides have broken loose in the past.

Follow the shoreline trail to the far end of Maroon Lake. Here, the trail crosses two bridges over Maroon Creek and then meets the Maroon Bells–Snowmass Trail. Keep left and continue following the Scenic Trail (marked on the sign) as it climbs a series of switchbacks across a *talus* slope.

This is a good place to look at the maroon-colored rocks up close. These boulders are of the red and purple *sandstones* and *conglomerates* of the Maroon Formation. Some gray *granitic* boulders are mixed in with the maroon sedimentary rocks. These granitic rocks are formed from the *magma* that once intruded along *faults* and *fractures* within the Maroon Formation, carrying the sedimentary pile upward on its shoulders to form the Elk Mountains.

At about the 1-mile point, the trail reaches a triple junction. Both the Scenic Trail (to the left) and the Maroon Bells–Snowmass Trail (to the right) lead back to Maroon Lake. To continue toward Crater Lake, follow the Maroon Bells–Snowmass Trail straight ahead.

For about the next 0.5 mile, the trail winds among large boulders that choke the valley above Maroon Lake. These boulders are also from landslides that tumbled down from the steep slopes to the north. Note that some boulders of the normally red and purple Maroon Formation appear

Large crystals of feldspar in the granitic rock that intruded the Maroon Formation

gray-green. This color transformation was created by heat from the intruding granitic *plutons* that altered the sedimentary rocks into this gray-green *metamorphic rock* called *hornfels;* note, however, that the heat did not change the rock enough to destroy its original texture.

As Crater Lake comes into view, the trail heads downslope from the boulder field. A short spur trail to the left leads to the shoreline of the lake and connects with the West Maroon Creek Trail. If you want to make the extra effort, the Maroon Bells–Snowmass Trail continues to the right, climbing steeply to the northwest up Minnehaha Gulch nearly 3 miles to Buckskin Pass. (This additional hike is strenuous, but the view of Snowmass Peak makes it worth the effort.)

Like Maroon Lake, Crater Lake was formed by landslides and rockfalls that dammed Maroon Creek. The trail winds through jagged, angular boulders distinctly different from those of glacial moraines which become rounded from abrasion during glacial transport.

After reflecting on the Maroon Bells from Crater Lake, return to the parking area by the same route or, more directly, back along the Maroon Bells–Snowmass Trail.

CATHEDRAL LAKE

TOWERS OF BAKED ANCESTRAL ROCKIES
SEDIMENTARY ROCKS

Maroon Formation sedimentary layers, baked hard by igneous intrusions, form picturesque Cathedral Peak.

DISTANCE ■ 6.4 miles round trip

ELEVATION ■ 9,880 to 11,866 feet

DIFFICULTY ■ Strenuous

TOPOGRAPHIC MAPS ■ USGS Hayden Peak; Trails Illustrated #131

GEOLOGIC MAP ■ 22

KEY REFERENCE ■ 21

PRECAUTIONS ■ During summer months, get an early start to avoid afternoon thunderstorms. This is a very popular trail, so plan for a weekday hike if possible.

FOR INFORMATION ■ Aspen Ranger District

About the Landscape: Although not as famous as the nearby Maroon Bells and much more difficult to reach, the jagged spires of Cathedral Peak are hidden jewels within the Elk Range. Reached by a safe but steep trail,

Cathedral Lake lies in a picturesque *cirque* below the layered towers of this mountain.

As with other summits in the area, Cathedral Peak formed when the sedimentary layers of the Maroon Formation were pushed upward from below, about 34 million years ago, by a huge *pluton* of *granodiorite*. Instead of rising to the surface, the *magma* spread out in thick, irregular layers that cooled slowly underground. The heat from the igneous intrusion baked the surrounding rocks, transforming the softer red and maroon sedimentary layers into hard, green-gray metamorphic rocks called *hornfels*.

Today, erosion has uncovered the "plumbing system" of these intrusions in the Elk Mountains. An almost circular ring of granodiorite surrounds Cathedral Peak and nearby Castle Peak, presumably underlying the mountains where it invaded along the Elk Mountain Thrust Fault.

Trail Guide: To reach the Cathedral Lake Trailhead, drive 0.5 mile west from Aspen on Colorado Highway 82 to the Maroon Creek Road traffic light (Forest Road 125). Turn left and then make an immediate left again onto the Castle Creek Road (Forest Road 102). Drive 12.3 miles south and turn right onto a gravel road (sign for trailhead). Drive 0.6 mile to the trailhead at the end of the road.

The trail starts out by climbing a moderate grade through an Aspen forest along a hillside formed by a glacial moraine. This unsorted pile of gravel and boulders was dumped here by the *glaciers* that scoured the Pine Creek drainage where Cathedral Lake is located. As the trail rounds the south side of the moraine, enjoy the great view of Castle Creek Valley below. A mere 20,000 years ago, a thick tongue of glacial ice reached all the way downstream to where Aspen sits today.

About 0.5 mile from the trailhead, Pine Creek cascades on the left as the trail crosses the boundary into the Maroon Bells–Snowmass Wilderness. Pine Creek tumbles over resistant ledges of granodiorite. This light to medium gray *intrusive igneous rock* cut into the sedimentary layers that make up the Elk Mountains. A close look at the rock reveals a fine-grained mosaic of *quartz* and *feldspar*, peppered with flakes of *mica* and needles of *hornblende*.

From here, the trail begins to climb more steeply as it parallels Pine Creek on the left. The trail makes its first switchback about 1 mile from the trailhead. A short distance ahead, Pine Creek forms an impressive waterfall left of the trail.

As the trail reaches the top of the switchbacks at about the 2.25-mile point, the rocks along the trail change. Gray-green rocks are now mixed in with the lighter gray *granodiorite*. You are at the margin where molten magma intruded into the Maroon Formation. The darker rocks here are baked sedimentary layers that have been altered to the *metamorphic rock* called *hornfels.* This change can also be recognized in the ridge to the north. The hornfels can be distinguished by its noticeable layering, because it was originally *sedimentary rock,* compared to the more jagged, irregular nature of the granodiorite.

For about the next 0.5 mile, the trail levels out where it crosses a series of expansive boulder fields stretching down from the cliffs to the right (north). Included now within the mix of rock types are red and maroon *sandstone, siltstone,* and smaller amounts of *conglomerate.* These sedimentary rocks are from the Maroon Formation which caps the ridge to the north. These rock layers were not metamorphosed to hornfels by the intrusion of granodiorite, probably because they were farther away from the heat.

After climbing a series of very steep switchbacks with outcrops of layered hornfels to the right of the trail, the trail reaches a fork just before the 3-mile point. A sign points right to Electric Pass and left to Cathedral Lake. From here it is less than 0.5 mile to the lake over the hummocky terrain of a *cirque* basin.

As the trail crests the last rise, Cathedral Lake comes into view. To the north, the towering spires of Cathedral Peak form a spectacular backdrop. Notice that Cathedral Peak and all the cliffs rising above the lake are composed of gray-green hornfels. Although broken by minor faults and fractures, the sedimentary layering in the cliffs is still very apparent. In places, the Maroon Formation retains its red color. Scan along the ridge that rims the cirque to the south and see if you can pick out the more irregular areas that mark probable intrusions of granodiorite.

After taking in the landscape, carefully retrace your steps back to the trailhead.

The well-worn trail to Cathedral Lake

Chapter 9
THE SAN JUAN MOUNTAINS

The tranquil alpine landscape of the San Juan Mountains belies their fiery past. About 35 million years ago, a rising *batholith* started the ignition in a series of volcanic events that would make Colorado's other mountain-building uplifts look sedate by comparison. The shaking and quaking that accompanied so many uplifts of *basement rock* were replaced here by rocketing explosions that flung magmatic material skyward, ultimately blanketing large parts of Colorado with red-hot embers. The San Juan Mountain volcanic field ultimately became the longest lived of these events.

For 14 million years during the Oligocene, layers of *lava, tuff,* and volcanic *breccia* almost completely smothered a broad *Laramide Orogeny* uplift called the San Juan Dome. Like other Laramide uplifts, by about 35 million years ago, erosion had beveled the San Juan Dome into a rolling upland called the *Rocky Mountain Surface.* The Oligocene fireworks buried this surface in the San Juans except for two hills of basement rock that later became the Needles and Grenadier Ranges.

In the San Juans, the style of volcanic activity occurred in three different phases that each lasted about 5 million years. The first volcanic phase, from 35 to 30 million years ago, was a series of classic explosions from tall, steep-sided volcanoes, called *composite volcanoes,* that looked and acted much like a large cluster of Mount St. Helens type mountains all breathing fire at once. Ash and lava flows of mostly *rhyolite* and *andesite* coalesced into a broad volcanic plateau that includes today's West Elk Mountains.

Beginning about 30 million years ago, the volcanic style changed to *pyroclastic,* in which explosive ash flow eruptions ejected great volumes of ash and rock. These eruptions were so sudden and powerful that the volcanoes collapsed under their own explosive thunder, forming huge depressions called *calderas.* In all, more than fifteen calderas formed in the San Juans, and their catastrophic eruptions smothered the landscape with red-hot ash flows. Unlike Oregon's Crater Lake, perhaps the world's most perfect caldera, the San Juan calderas did not form huge, easily recognizable bowls. Their forms are masked by faulting, later volcanic flows, and the collapse of new calderas within older ones.

Following the eruption, collapse, and burial of the calderas, hot mineralized

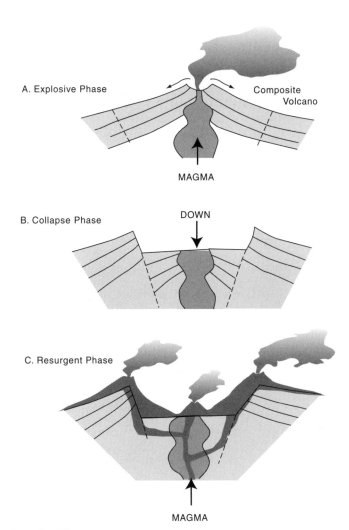

A. Explosive Phase

Composite
Volcano

MAGMA

B. Collapse Phase

DOWN

C. Resurgent Phase

MAGMA

Formation of calderas

fluid percolated along the *faults* ringing the calderas. This *hydrothermal* activity left behind a wealth of ore minerals in the highly fractured rocks of the San Juans.

The third and final stage of volcanic activity, from 26 to 22 million years ago, was a more sporadic episode in which increasing amounts of dark, fluid *basalt* lava oozed from the earth without tremendous fanfare. The basalt flows, which may have risen along deep faults flanking the emerging *Rio Grande Rift,* covered the San Juans and spilled into the adjacent San Luis Valley.

Before the San Juan volcanoes finally went to sleep about 22 million years ago, a last gasp of explosive activity formed the Lake City Caldera and ashflows. This completed the high volcanic plateau that became the San Juan Mountains.

As the San Juan region slowly rose with the rest of Colorado during the last pulse of uplift over the past 10 million years, the landscape was ravaged by torrential streams that widened their courses and deepened their canyons, carving the plateau into a mountainous landscape. Meanwhile, faulting and volcanic activity continued next door along the Rio Grande Rift, which nibbled at the eastern edge of the San Juans.

These mountains of fire were ultimately chilled in the *Ice Age* freezer that worked its magic on their peaks during the past 1.8 million years, carving mountaintops and valleys into the dramatic shapes of today's San Juan Mountains.

COLORADO'S VOLCANIC PAST

Colorado's most explosive fireworks began in middle Tertiary time about 35 million years ago, when boiling *magma* worked its way upward along cracks and fissures through Colorado's basement and

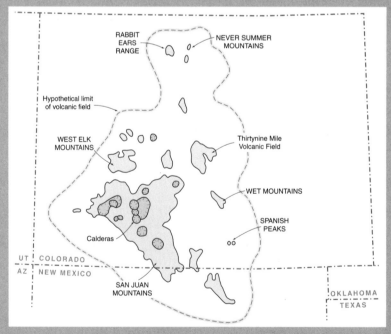

Extent of Colorado's mid-Tertiary age volcanic and intrusive rocks

overlying layers. This magma may have originated in the intense friction between grinding tectonic *plates* deep underground, the same action that pushed great blocks of *basement rock* skyward during the *Laramide Orogeny*. During this fiery phase, which lasted more than 15 million years, a chain of volcanoes stretched nearly all the way across Colorado, from the Never Summer Mountains and Rabbit Ears Range in the north, to the West Elk and San Juan Mountains in the south. Although many other eruptions and *lava* flows have occurred in Colorado's past, none matched the intensity of the middle Tertiary explosions. This activity spewed tremendous volumes of ash and volcanic debris that became the widespread layers of *tuff* and volcanic *breccia* we see today.

Outcrop of West Elk Breccia—a product of explosive volcanic eruptions

WEST ELK MOUNTAINS

Hike 30

CASTLES OF BRECCIA

Hike below towering cliffs of West Elk Breccia to Storm Pass for a view of The Castles, one of Colorado's most unique rock formations.

DISTANCE ■ 16 miles round trip

ELEVATION ■ 9,000 to 12,450 feet

DIFFICULTY ■ Strenuous

TOPOGRAPHIC MAPS ■ USGS West Elk Peak and Squirrel Peak; Trails Illustrated #134

GEOLOGIC MAP ■ 17

KEY REFERENCE ■ 22

PRECAUTIONS ■ Please respect the private property near the trailhead. Erosion of the West Elk Breccia results in loose footing along many parts of the trail. There is no shelter from lightning storms on Storm Pass. Please use existing campsites and camp away from the trail if possible.

FOR INFORMATION ■ Gunnison Ranger District

About the Landscape: The West Elk Mountains are the eroded remnants of an ancient volcanic field northwest of Gunnison. They are carved from a chaotic pile of volcanic rock called the West Elk Breccia, which consists mostly of angular volcanic fragments embedded in volcanic ash. Erosion has sculpted the West Elk Breccia into towering cliffs and ridges adorned with rock fins and pinnacles. The most unique of these rock formations, called The Castles, is a series of artistically sculpted spires that can be seen from Storm Pass, the destination for this hike.

The hike to Storm Pass traverses the length of Mill Creek. Although the route is strenuous in places, it can be completed as a long day hike. However, the hike makes for a perfect overnight backpack trip since several good campsites are located about 6.5 miles from the trailhead (1.5 miles below Storm Pass).

Trail Guide: To reach the Mill Creek Trailhead, drive north from Gunnison 2.8 miles on Colorado Highway 135 to Gunnison County Road 730. Turn left and follow this paved road 9.3 miles to the sign for Mill Creek. Turn left again onto Gunnison County Road 727 and follow this gravel road 3.5 miles to the trailhead at the end of the road.

The trail starts out following an old road along the south side of Mill Creek Valley. The road is cut into a moraine of cobbles and boulders left behind by the glaciers that carved the valley during the Pleistocene.

Scenic view of The Castles from Storm Pass

Several large boulders of volcanic *breccia* have rolled onto the trail, offering a glimpse of the West Elk Breccia that makes up the walls of the valley. The breccia is composed of dark, angular boulders of *andesite,* a gray, fine-grained *volcanic rock,* set in a cementlike matrix of volcanic ash. These rocks were forged in Oligocene time, between about 34 and 29 million years ago, during the first phase of San Juan volcanics when volcanoes emerged in explosive eruptions that spread huge volumes of ash and rock debris.

At about the 1.5-mile point, the route crosses Mill Creek. As the trail enters the meadow that leads down to the creek, the spectacular cliffs of West Elk Breccia are in full view, towering nearly 2,000 feet above both sides of the valley floor. After crossing the creek to the north side of the valley, the trail enters the West Elk Wilderness and follows a moderate grade through stands of aspen and spruce for about the next 2 miles.

About 3.5 miles from the trailhead, the trail passes through a gate and immediately climbs a steep switchback up a ledge of breccia. From the top of the ledge is a great view of the cliffs behind you. They are formed of chaotic masses of volcanic breccia, and angular volcanic boulders of all sizes protrude from their sheer rock faces. Towering pillars, spires, and fins rise from the clifftops. You can see where erosion along vertical *fractures* slicing through the cliffs has influenced the formation of these craggy outcrops. When water seeps into such fractures, it expands as it freezes, eventually wedging the rock apart and creating sculptures such as those before you.

For the next 3 miles, the trail traverses a mostly forested slope above Mill Creek. About 6.5 miles from the trailhead, the trail reaches the last stand of trees before beginning the steeper climb into Mill Basin below Storm Pass. This is the best area for camping below the pass. A spur trail off to the left leads to pleasant campsites. If you reach a steep switchback just past a waterfall on the right, you have passed the best camp areas.

Beyond the campsites, the trail climbs steeply, emerging above treeline where rock cairns (rock piles) mark the route. It is easy to miss the junction for Storm Pass. The cairn that marks this route is visible only if you are looking over your right shoulder because the trail to Storm Pass switches back to the right of the main trail. If you reach the stream-crossing in Mill Basin, the trail to Storm Pass is about 50 feet behind you on the right. The route is easy to see once you've missed it!

From the junction, the trail to Storm Pass is well marked and follows a series of long switchbacks to the pass. At Storm Pass, the spectacular rock formation called The Castles comes into full view. Although erosion has successfully attacked the rocks on all sides of its defining vertical fractures, the resistant Castles still stand like a fortress against the persistent forces of wind, water, and ice.

After taking in the majestic beauty of the craggy peak, return to the trailhead by the route you came.

CONTINENTAL DIVIDE

Hike 31

MEETING OF THE HEADWATERS AND THE GRENADIER RANGE

Hike a section of the Continental Divide Trail that brings you eye level with the remote Grenadier Range.

DISTANCE ■ **8 miles round trip**

ELEVATION ■ **10,760 to 12,700 feet**

DIFFICULTY ■ **Strenuous**

TOPOGRAPHIC MAPS ■ **USGS Howardsville and Storm King Peak; Trails Illustrated #140**

GEOLOGIC MAPS ■ **23, 26**

KEY REFERENCE ■ **23**

PRECAUTIONS ■ **Most of this hike is well above treeline. Be sure to get an early start to avoid afternoon thunderstorms.**

FOR INFORMATION ■ **Columbine Ranger District**

About the Landscape: This hike explores a segment of the Continental Divide Trail in the Weminuche Wilderness. Here the headwaters of the Rio Grande flowing eastward meet the headwaters of the westward-flowing waters that eventually find their way to the Colorado River. The trail provides a sweeping view of the jagged Grenadier Range, an island of *basement rock* jutting up amidst the San Juan volcanic mountains. This range is part of the huge San Juan Dome of Precambrian basement rock that uplifted during the *Laramide Orogeny,* 70 million years ago. Here, a localized uplift of *quartzite* basement rock, called the Grenadier Fault Block, arose between steep *faults* in the basement. Although volcanic flows later lapped at its feet, the *fault-block* remained intact during the San Juan explosive era to become a magnificent range of glacially carved metamorphic basement rock.

Trail Guide: To reach the Continental Divide Trailhead, drive 4.1 miles northeast from Silverton on Colorado Highway 110 (Alpine Loop Scenic Byway) to Howardsville. At the sign for Stony Pass, turn right onto Forest Road 589, a well-maintained gravel road. About 0.1 mile from the turn, stay right at the junction with Forest Road 4A. After another 1.6 miles, go right again where Stony Pass Road turns to the left. The maintained road ends near an old mine site where huge tailings piles line the banks of Cunningham Creek. If you do not have four-wheel drive, park at the end of the road to the left of the tailings pile and start your hike by climbing the trail to the right of the waterfall (add 1 mile to the round trip distance).

For those with four-wheel drive, follow the road that branches off to the right for 0.8 mile. It crosses the creek near the tailings pile and climbs a rough, rocky road to a hanging valley above the waterfall. After 0.8 mile, turn left down a narrow road that leads past a small tailings pile on the right and back across Cunningham Creek. The trailhead is located to the left just over the creek.

The Continental Divide Trail climbs up the east side of the valley above the trailhead. At first, the rocks are dominated by red-brown and purple *tuffs* and *breccias* from the first San Juan volcanic sequence that blanketed

Looking toward the rugged skyline of the Grenadier Range from the Continental Divide Trail

southwestern Colorado between 35 and 30 million years ago. *Metamorphic rock* fragments of *gneiss* and *schist* are also found along the trail. These rocks are weathering from exposures of 1.7 billion-year-old Precambrian basement.

After about 0.25 mile from the trailhead, the rocks change abruptly as the trail winds over an outcrop of gray *limestone.* Look closely for fossil fragments, mostly disk-shaped segments from the stems of *crinoids* that once lived on the ocean floor. These rocks are part of the 350 million-year-old Mississippian Leadville Limestone formed from an ancient shallow seaway that once covered this region. Much later, these sedimentary layers were dropped down between faults in the Precambrian basement and protected from erosion by the basement rock. Most of the mine workings across the valley are concentrated within this localized limestone layer because when *magma* and its hot, mineral-rich groundwater comes into contact with limestone, these minerals are readily precipitated.

The trail continues climbing, passing a junction at the 0.5-mile point. Follow the trail straight ahead, climbing through purple and blue volcanic tuffs and breccias.

After crossing a grassy meadow below rounded hills of *volcanic rocks,* the trail reaches a saddle where it meets the Continental Divide Trail, about 2 miles above the trailhead. You are now standing atop the Continental Divide. From this point, water draining to the east feeds the headwaters of the Rio Grande on its way to the Gulf of Mexico. Water flowing to the west eventually reaches the Animas River, which connects with the San Juan River on its way to the Colorado River and ultimately the Gulf of California.

From the saddle, follow the trail as it climbs a ridge to the south. Here there is a major change in rock type from the younger volcanic rocks you have been walking through. The rocky outcrops along the trail are now Precambrian basement rocks, mostly banded gneiss and schist crosscut by numerous veins of *quartz.* You are standing at the limit of a volcanic flow where molten debris flowed up against basement rock during the San Juan's first spate of volcanic eruptions 35 to 30 million years ago.

About .75 mile from the saddle, the trail reaches a junction. Continue straight ahead where the trail traverses a broad alpine meadow.

About 1 mile past this junction, the trail crests a gentle rise where you will see a large cairn (rock pile) on the right. Here, the jagged, glacially carved Grenadier Range dominates the view to the south. Together with the Needles, it is one of only two mountain ranges cored with basement rock to withstand the San Juan volcanic period. The Grenadier Range is too rugged and inaccessible for trails to penetrate, so this magnificent view of the craggy uplift will have to serve as the pinnacle for this hike.

The Continental Divide Trail continues across this vast, gentle alpine plateau and then begins to traverse more rugged terrain. To return to the trailhead after enjoying the view, simply retrace your steps.

BLUE LAKES PASS

The Mount Sneffels Intrusion

Hike to Blue Lakes Pass for an outstanding view of the Mount Sneffels intrusion and surrounding volcanics.

DISTANCE ■ 3.5 miles round trip (about 6 miles round trip without four-wheel drive)

ELEVATION ■ 12,200 to 13,000 feet

DIFFICULTY ■ Moderate

TOPOGRAPHIC MAPS ■ USGS Mount Sneffels; Trails Illustrated #141

GEOLOGIC MAP ■ 24

KEY REFERENCE ■ 24

PRECAUTIONS ■ Beware of the numerous old mine shafts in the area. Please respect the private land over which many of the old roads travel. Avoid the pass and surrounding summits during afternoon thunderstorms.

FOR INFORMATION ■ Ouray Ranger District

About the Landscape: The jagged spires of the Sneffels Range dominate the skyline in the western San Juan Mountains between Telluride and Ouray. Mount Sneffels stands out not only for its commanding presence as a "fourteener" but also because it has a different geologic make-up than the mountains that surround it. Mount Sneffels is part of an igneous intrusion that pushed upward through the layered volcanic rocks that form the bulk of the San Juan Mountains.

The rich mining history connected with this intrusion has left its mark with a network of old roads that lead to Yankee Boy Basin, a glacial *cirque* carved between Mount Sneffels (14,150 feet) and Gilpin Peak (13,694). The hike to Blue Lakes Pass winds through Yankee Boy Basin to the saddle between these two peaks for a commanding view across the serrated ridges and jagged peaks of the Sneffels Range.

Trail Guide: To reach the Blue Lakes Pass Trailhead from Ouray, drive 0.25 mile south on US Highway 550 to the turnoff for Box Canyon Falls. Turn right and follow Ouray County Road 361 for 12.4 miles to the information sign for Yankee Boy Basin. If you do not have a four-wheel drive

On the trail in the Sneffels Range below Blue Lakes Pass

vehicle, consider parking here and walking 2.4 miles to the trailhead (it's well worth the effort!). If you have four-wheel drive, follow the steep, narrow, and rocky road to its end at the trailhead in Yankee Boy Basin.

The trail starts out by crossing the lower reaches of a *talus* slope along the southeastern arm of Mount Sneffels. The rocks along the trail are mostly medium gray *granodiorite* that intruded as molten *magma* into the layered *volcanic rocks* now exposed in the surrounding mountains. After about 0.75 mile, the trail to the summit of Mount Sneffels splits off to the right. Continue straight ahead to the next junction with the trail to Wright Lake. Keep right and continue up the switchbacks to Blue Lakes Pass.

As the trail climbs to the pass, you can enjoy great views of Mount Sneffels rising to the north and Gilpin Peak across the valley to the south. Note the difference in the rocks that make up these two picturesque mountains. Mount Sneffels is composed of *intrusive igneous rock* that pushed up into the older volcanic layers about 32 million years ago. The mountain, which lacks any hint of horizontal layering, is laced with numerous *dikes* and vertical *fractures* that weather into countless needles and pinnacles along its flanks.

In contrast, Gilpin Peak is composed of mostly light-colored volcanic rocks arranged in horizontal layers. These layers are part of the thick sequence of ash and volcanic rock debris spewed in the repeated explosive eruptions that formed the San Juan Mountains between about 35 and 26 million years ago. These layers of *pyroclastic* rocks, mostly volcanic *tuff* and *breccia,* were derived from the Silverton and Lake City *Calderas* to the east.

Note the dikes of dark *igneous rock* that cut vertically through the horizontal volcanic layers that compose Gilpin Peak. These dikes were formed during the Mount Sneffels intrusive event. Much of the mining activity in the area exploited the minerals that precipitated along dikes similar to these. The red and yellow alterations in the rocks are caused by oxidation of iron-bearing minerals in the veins.

Blue Lakes Pass is located along a sawtooth ridge, which is actually an arm of the Mount Sneffels intrusion that reaches across to contact the layered volcanic rocks of Gilpin Peak. This narrow divide separates two glacial cirques—Yankee Boy Basin to the east and Blue Lakes Basin to the west.

The upper Blue Lakes are visible in the *hanging valley* directly below the pass. If the light is right, the lakes emit a deep, aquamarine color imparted by glacial rock dust, or "flour," in the water. A spectacular *rock glacier* meets the shoreline of the highest lake.

From the pass, hike back down to the first trail junction and bear right toward Wright Lake. After crossing a stretch of meadow and several switchbacks, the trail looks down on a rock glacier that flows from the flank of Gilpin Peak into Wright Lake. As this mass of rock and ice moves slowly downslope, the center moves faster than the margins, forming curved rock piles at the surface.

Follow the trail down to the shoreline of Wright Lake. If you parked at the upper trailhead, follow the jeep road to the left from the lake back to the parking area. If you parked down below, a trail from the south side of the lake contours above Sneffels Creek and meets the main four-wheel drive road about 0.5 mile down the valley.

BOX CANYON FALLS

THE OURAY FAULT AND AN ANGULAR UNCONFORMITY

Hike a short trail to Box Canyon Falls where Canyon Creek has carved a slot canyon into Precambrian quartzite.

DISTANCE ■ 1 mile round trip

ELEVATION ■ 7,900 to 8,000 feet

DIFFICULTY ■ Easy

TOPOGRAPHIC MAPS ■ USGS Ouray; Trails Illustrated #141

GEOLOGIC MAP ■ 25

KEY REFERENCE ■ 25

PRECAUTIONS ■ Part of this trail follows a boardwalk along a sheer cliff—watch your step!

FOR INFORMATION ■ Box Canyon City Park

About the Landscape: Box Canyon Falls cascades through a slot canyon carved by Canyon Creek into Precambrian *quartzite* uplifted along the Ouray Fault. The Ouray Fault is a major break in the rock layers along the north side of the Sneffels Range, where the Precambrian quartzite of the Uncompahgre Formation is pushed up against Paleozoic *sedimentary rocks.* Along the short trail to the falls, the view of the *fault* is dramatic and offers an opportunity to put your hand right on the surface of the fault itself. Another short trail to an upper viewpoint provides a classic view of an angular *unconformity,* where nearly flat-lying sedimentary layers of the Devonian Elbert Formation sit on top of vertical beds of Precambrian quartzite.

Trail Guide: Box Canyon Falls is reached by driving 0.25 mile north of Ouray on US Highway 550. Turn right at the sign for Box Canyon Falls, then bear right immediately and follow the gravel road to the City Park entrance and parking area. The trail begins at the fee station and follows a well-worn path past the junction with the Upper Canyon Trail (described below) to a boardwalk clinging to the canyon wall.

The thunderous roar of the falls increases dramatically as the trail approaches the canyon entrance. At the point where the boardwalk turns left into the canyon, look across at the opposite wall. A thin sliver of red rock, part of the Pennsylvanian Molas Formation, is smeared against gray Precambrian rocks along the Ouray Fault. These same red rocks are in the creek bottom farther to the right. You would have to climb high above the canyon to find the red rocks on the left side of the fault because the Precambrian rocks were pushed up along that side. This movement occurred during the

Angular unconformity above Box Canyon Falls

rise of the *Ancestral Rocky Mountains,* about 300 million years ago, when a huge *fault-block* of Precambrian basement was uplifted.

Take several more steps along the left of the boardwalk to where the red rocks of the Molas Formation meet dark Precambrian rocks across a *fracture* that extends into the canyon wall. This fracture represents the actual surface plane of the fault. On the left, the red sedimentary rocks are about 300 million years old. On the right, the rocks are at least 1.5 billion years old. This is a rare opportunity to put your hand right on a fault!

The boardwalk trail continues a short distance into the canyon to a viewpoint of the falls and an iron staircase that leads down to the creek bottom. Canyon Creek has carved a narrow slot canyon into the ancient Precambrian rock. The canyon has been fluted by the flowing water over vast stretches of time. This is certainly not a place to be in a flash flood!

The Upper Canyon Trail switchbacks up the hillside for less than 0.5 mile to a bridge across Canyon Creek above the falls, where the depth and narrowness of the canyon are quite impressive. The rock layer that the bridge spans is a thick bed of Precambrian quartzite in the Uncompahgre Formation. This rock was originally deposited as a *sandstone* at least 1.5 billion years ago, then the sand grains became fused together by heat and pressure (metamorphosed) into quartzite. Across the canyon upstream from the bridge, the quartzite layers stand almost vertically. The nearly horizontal layers on top are sedimentary layers of the Devonian Elbert Formation. The quartzite layers were tilted during Precambrian time, then eroded into a flat surface before the Devonian *sediments* were deposited in a shallow sea nearly 400 million years ago. This arrangement of rock layers is called an angular unconformity.

Before heading back down the trail, look down the canyon a short distance to where the white quartzite ends and very dark green rock begins. This dark layer is an igneous *dike* of basaltlike rock that intruded into the quartzite layers during the Precambrian. The movement along the Ouray Fault took place near this igneous dike. As the igneous material formed the dike, it followed along the same zone of weakness that later became the Ouray Fault.

After pondering the complex geology of this place, retrace your steps back down the trail to the path that leads back to the parking area.

WHEELER GEOLOGIC AREA

MOONSCAPE OF VOLCANIC TUFF

Hike in the central San Juan Mountains to Wheeler Geologic Area, once designated a National Monument.

DISTANCE ■ **14 miles round trip**

ELEVATION ■ **10,760 to 12,700 feet**

DIFFICULTY ■ **Moderate**

TOPOGRAPHIC MAPS ■ **USGS Pool Table Mountain, Half Moon Pass, and Wagon Wheel Gap; Trails Illustrated #139**

GEOLOGIC MAP ■ **26**

KEY REFERENCE ■ **26**

PRECAUTIONS ■ **To help protect this fragile area, please remain on the trails and do not climb on the rock pinnacles and steep slopes. This is a long hike; be sure to be adequately prepared.**

FOR INFORMATION ■ **Ouray Ranger District**

About the Landscape: The Wheeler Geologic Area is a unique landscape hidden in the central San Juan Mountains. Here, layers of volcanic ash were shaped by erosion into a compact landscape of pinnacles, spires, and narrow canyons. Located along the southern slope of the La Garita Mountains, the rocks of the Wheeler Geologic Area are soft, white layers of volcanic ash called the Rat Creek Tuff. The Rat Creek Tuff formed about 26 million years ago when an explosive eruption from the San Luis caldera spewed out a great volume of ash and rock debris.

The unique geologic landforms of the Wheeler Geologic Area are confined to a small area that was designated as a National Monument in 1908 by Theodore Roosevelt. Due to its remote location and difficult access, this status was withdrawn in 1950. In 1969, the U.S. Forest Service designated the 1-square-mile tract surrounding the rock formations as a "Geologic Area." Today, the Wheeler Geologic Area stands within the La Garita Wilderness.

Trail Guide: Although it is possible to drive the 14-mile four-wheel drive road from the Hanson's Mill Trailhead to within 0.5 mile of the rock formations, the road is reportedly "rough, rutted, and rocky" and recommended for high-clearance vehicles only. Hiking the 7-mile Wheeler Trail from the Hanson's Mill Trailhead may actually be faster than driving and makes for a pleasant overnight backpack trip.

To reach the Hanson's Mill Trailhead, drive 7.3 miles southeast from Creede, or 14.7 miles northwest from South Fork, on Colorado Highway 149 to Pool Table Road (Forest Road 600). Drive about 9.5 miles northeast over this maintained gravel road to the trailhead at Hanson's Mill (today just a pile of sawdust). From Hanson's Mill, Forest Road 600 becomes a four-wheel drive only route to the Wheeler Geologic Area.

The Wheeler Trail departs from the Hanson's Mill Trailhead and immediately deviates from the four-wheel drive road. About 1 mile from the trailhead, the trail enters the first of several meadows where it passes through boulder fields. To the west, cliffs of *volcanic rock* come into view in the canyons along East Bellows Creek.

The boulder fields and cliffs are made of a volcanic rock called welded *rhyolite tuff.* These rocks are red-brown to gray sprinkled through with rectangular, light gray crystals of *feldspar* and coppery flakes of *mica.* Welded tuff is created when volcanic ash (along with mineral crystals and rock fragments) is ejected during an explosive volcanic eruption. If the ash is hot enough at the time it is deposited, the particles fuse or "weld" together into solid rock during cooling.

At about the 2-mile point, the trail switchbacks down to meet East Bellows Creek. Crossing the creek in early summer may require getting your feet wet. Once across the creek, the trail follows along a *talus* slope below cliffs of welded tuff in Canyon Nieve. About 0.5 mile from the crossing, the trail heads up a side drainage. For about the next 3 miles, the trail climbs gentle grades through mostly open meadows, eventually leveling out as it crosses an expansive meadow called Silver Park.

Nearly 5.5 miles from the trailhead, the Wheeler Trail merges with the four-wheel drive road. For the next 1 mile, the road heads downhill into the drainage of West Bellows Creek and ends at a fence where the Wheeler Trail continues for 0.5 mile to the base of the rock outcrops.

As the trail approaches the rock spires, there is a junction with the Wason Park Trail heading to the left (west) and the Halfmoon Pass Trail straight ahead (north). For some of the best views, follow the Wason Park

Erosion of volcanic ash layers has created a moonscape at Wheeler Geologic Area.

Trail for about 0.25 mile up to an overlook. It is possible to circumnavigate the Geologic Area by following either trail upslope to a connecting trail across the top of the area.

The bizarre rock sculptures of the Wheeler Geologic Area are eroded Rat Creek Tuff. The Rat Creek Tuff is rhyolite ash with dark volcanic rock fragments. Unlike the other rocks in the area, most of the Rat Creek Tuff is not welded. The rock is relatively soft and friable, permitting the beautiful artistry of erosion.

Notice the many channels and grooves worn into the rock by flowing water. A close look reveals that the surface of the rock appears powdery. Fragments of hard, dark volcanic rock stand out in relief where the surrounding white ash has eroded away.

The cliffs bordering the area show horizontal layering. Note the layer that forms the ledge and cliff above the "organ pipes." This layer appears to be welded to some degree, making it more resistant to erosion.

Although the Rat Creek Tuff was deposited widely, the reason these unusual rock outcrops occur in only this small area is a puzzle. Perhaps you are standing in what was once a valley where the ash flows that formed the tuff were protected from erosion.

Before returning to the trailhead by the route you came, be sure to explore the nooks and crannies. However, to preserve and protect the area, please do not climb around on the rocky spires and steep slopes. The rock is fragile, and loose pebbles slide like ball bearings underfoot.

SLUMGULLION LANDSLIDE

GEOLOGY IN ACTION

Hike to the top of the Slumgullion Landslide and observe the scarred landscape it has created.

DISTANCE ■ **3 miles round trip**

ELEVATION ■ **11,064 to 12,200 feet**

DIFFICULTY ■ **Moderate**

TOPOGRAPHIC MAPS ■ **USGS Slumgullion Pass and Cannibal Plateau; Trails Illustrated #141**

GEOLOGIC MAP ■ **23**

KEY REFERENCE ■ **27**

PRECAUTIONS ■ **Use extreme caution when exploring along the top of the slide. Avoid this hike during afternoon thunderstorms. This trail is open to horses, mountain bikes, motorcycles, and all-terrain vehicles.**

FOR INFORMATION ■ **Gunnison Ranger District**

About the Landscape: The Slumgullion Landslide is a path of destruction more than 4 miles long that formed about 700 years ago in a catastrophic avalanche of mud and earth. Movement continues on this long slope of rock and debris, now the product of numerous smaller landslide events since that time.

When explosive volcanic eruptions formed the Lake City Caldera about 22 million years ago, the rocks along the rim where the landslide eventually took place were altered by hot gases and fluids. Over time, weathering of these rocks produced abundant clay minerals, which can become very slippery and unstable, especially when wet. When a section of the *caldera* caved in about 700 years ago, rock and debris slid and flowed downslope, a type of mass movement known as an earthflow. The toe of the flow ultimately blocked the Lake Fork of the Gunnison River, creating Lake San Cristobal.

Since the time of the original landslide event, rock debris within the landside area has continued to flow downslope. Less than 400 years ago, a second major flow began, this one much slower but more long-lived than the first. This second flow started at the top of the original slide and stretched downslope some 2.5 miles.

A visit to the Slumgullion Landslide is a glimpse of present-day geology in action. Recent studies show that the Slumgullion Landslide is still creeping slowly downhill at rates that vary from about 3 to 20 feet per year.
Trail Guide: This hike follows an old two-track road to the top of the landslide area on Mesa Seco for a view straight down the slide toward Lake San Cristobal.

To reach the Cannibal Plateau Trailhead, drive 10 miles east from Lake City on Colorado Highway 149 (Silver Thread Scenic Byway) to Slumgullion Pass. As the highway climbs to the pass, there are several worthwhile stops for overlooks of Lake San Cristobal and the Slumgullion Landslide. Turn left (north) onto Forest Road 788 at the sign for Slumgullion Campground and drive 1 mile on this wide gravel road to the trailhead on the left.

From the trailhead, the trail climbs a moderate to steep grade and emerges above treeline after about 0.5 mile. The sharp drop-off to the left of the trail past the last stand of trees is the edge of the Slumgullion Landslide. A steep cut in the hillside, called a scarp, developed where the rock and debris pulled away. The trail continues to climb steeply uphill, roughly paralleling the scarp.

About 1.5 miles from the trailhead where the trail nears the crest of Mesa Seco, depart from the trail and walk to the left toward the scarp. Use extreme caution and avoid getting too close to the edge. You are now standing on the ancient rim of the Lake City Caldera at the head of the Slumgullion Landslide. Although the rest of the caldera rim has largely eroded, it was once about 9 miles across.

From this high vantage point, the Slumgullion Landslide stretches to the west toward Lake San Cristobal. The mountains beyond the lake are composed of volcanic ash deposits that once filled the caldera and domes of *igneous rock* that pushed up after the caldera's collapse. These mountains

The Slumgullion Landslide blocked the Lake Fork of the Gunnison River, creating Lake San Cristobal.

probably stand about where the middle of the Lake City Caldera once was.

The bright yellow cliffs below you are more than 700 feet high and form the bowl-like depression of the main scarp. Downslope, linear ridges and tilted trees in hummocky areas mark the more active parts of the slide. Numerous ponds have formed in closed depressions on the surface, suggesting that water continues to play an important role in the ongoing

Geology in action—tilted trees indicate the Slumgullion Landslide is still moving downhill.

movement. Quagmires of mud and clay are also part of the fabric of the slide. Use caution if you explore any of the active areas adjacent to the highway.

Once you have studied the features of this unique landform, return to the trailhead by the route you came.

WEST FORK SAN JUAN RIVER

SOAK IN A GEOTHERMAL POOL

A hike into the headwaters of the San Juan River brings you to a hot spring on the bank of the river.

DISTANCE ■ **9 miles round trip**

ELEVATION ■ **8,040 to 9,000 feet**

DIFFICULTY ■ **Moderate**

TOPOGRAPHIC MAPS ■ **USGS Saddle Mountain and South River Peak; Trails Illustrated #140**

GEOLOGIC MAP ■ **26**

KEY REFERENCE ■ **28**

PRECAUTIONS ■ **Please respect the private property at the start of the hike. When soaking in the hot spring, drink plenty of water and avoid alcohol. Camping is permitted only in designated sites.**

FOR INFORMATION ■ **Pagosa Ranger District**

About the Landscape: The headwaters of the San Juan River are in the high volcanic plateaus of the southeastern San Juan Mountains. This hike follows a well-worn trail up the San Juan River's West Fork to an area where hot geothermal waters seep to the surface along *faults* in the volcanic layers dissected by the river. A natural hot spring on the bank of the river is a perfect spa fueled, like the volcanic activity that once shaped its landscape, by heat generated deep in the earth.

Trail Guide: To reach the West Fork Trailhead, drive 14.5 miles east from Pagosa Springs on US Highway 160 to the West Fork Road (Forest Road 648). Turn left (north) at the sign for the West Fork Campground and drive 3 miles to the parking area at the end of the road (the trailhead is 0.9 mile past the campground).

The hike starts by following a gated access road through private land. Just past the cabins about 0.5 mile from the trailhead, a sign points to a trail on the right (Rainbow Trail Hot Springs 4 miles). Follow this trail as it winds through the forest. At about the 1-mile point, the trail enters the Weminuche Wilderness.

About 2 miles from the trailhead, the trail reaches a viewpoint above the river. The West Fork of the San Juan River cascades over volcanic boulders several hundred feet below. The sheer wall on the opposite side of the canyon reveals red and purple layers of volcanic *breccia* and *lava* cut by the river. High up on this cliff, the rock layers are tilted and fractured by faulting.

A short distance past the viewpoint, the trail passes a cliff of volcanic breccia on the left. Here is a close look at one of the many layers deposited by catastrophic flows of ash and rock debris from ancient volcanoes that spread across the San Juan region between about 35 and 30 million years ago. These gray *andesite* boulders, "floating" in a tan matrix of volcanic ash, are part of the Cornejos Formation, a stack of volcanic rock layers built during the first phase of volcanic activity in the San Juan Mountains.

A series of switchbacks brings the trail down to river level where it crosses a bridge that spans the river at about the 2.5-mile point. After about another 0.25 mile, the trail crosses another bridge, this one over the side drainage of Beaver Creek. As the trail climbs above the creek, it passes more outcrops of breccia capped by a lava flow of gray andesite to the left of the trail. After continuing to climb above river level, following switchbacks through the forest, the trail reaches the junction with the Beaver Creek Trail on the right, 4.5 miles from the trailhead. To continue toward the hot spring stay on the trail to the left.

After crossing a small side stream about 0.5 mile past the Beaver Creek

167

Soaking in a natural hot spring along the West Fork of the San Juan River

Trail junction, there is a fork in the trail. The short spur trail to the left leads to a number of well-worn camping areas in the forest above the river. To find the hot spring, continue on the main trail past the campsites and look for a trail to the left that leads to the river. A crudely constructed "pool" sits at the edge of the river. It's time to soak!

Colorado is known for its numerous hot springs which, as you might expect, are related to its geologic history. Hot springs occur where water, heated deep underground, emerges at the surface. The instigator of the volcanic activity that constructed the San Juan Mountains was a great pool of red-hot *magma,* called a *batholith,* that pushed toward the surface. Although the volcanoes are dormant today (and have been for more than 20 million years), groundwater is heated as it circulates near the hot rock that still lies beneath the mountains. Faults and *fractures* in the overlying rock layers create pathways for this hot water to make it to the surface as hot springs. Since rivers often follow along fault zones where the rock is more easily eroded, hot springs are often found along rivers—like here in the headwaters of the San Juan River. This means that magma deep within the earth is letting off a little steam into the waters that bubble up right where you sit.

Once you are sufficiently relaxed and "magmatized," simply retrace your steps back to the trailhead.

▶ *Sandstone-walled canyons and mesas define western Colorado's canyon country. Entrada Sandstone at Rattlesnake Canyon.*

Part 2
THE COLORADO PLATEAU

Chapter 10
COLORADO'S CANYON COUNTRY

Red rock cliffs, deep canyons, and scenic mesas make the Colorado Plateau one of the most visually stunning landscapes in the world. The Plateau is actually a spectrum of layers, subtly shaded by past geologic events. It is a large geologic province that dominates the western third of Colorado and spills across the Four Corners area into Utah, Arizona, and New Mexico. Within Colorado, the Colorado Plateau stretches north from Durango and Mesa Verde, past Grand Junction, to the canyonlands of Dinosaur National Monument.

The region was originally named the "Colorado Plateaus" by John Wesley Powell who, in 1869, led the first expedition down the Green and Colorado Rivers. At that time, he defined the "Plateaus" as that area drained by the Colorado River and its tributaries. It's true that the Colorado River and its tributaries sculpted western Colorado's layercake landscape into its kaleidoscope of landforms. But the rivers are relative newcomers to the region, etching and undercutting it "only" within the past 10 million years.

For much of its geologic history, the Colorado Plateau was swept by the same wildly fluctuating environments as the rest of Colorado. The landscape was repeatedly flooded by seas, crossed by raging rivers, submerged beneath lakes, and parched by wind-blown dunes. All of these events contributed layers of *sediment* that became the plateau's distinctly colorful *strata.*

The difference between the plateau and the unsettled Rocky Mountains to the east, where tumultuous upheavals have upset the rock record, is that the Colorado Plateau has remained relatively stable. As Colorado's Rockies were repeatedly uplifted and eroded, faulted and folded, seared by intrusions of boiling magma, and buried by explosive volcanic eruptions, the Plateau region was an island of relative geologic calm. Throughout these major events, the plateau's layers were gently warped but rarely broke.

There are exceptions, of course. One major interruption in the calm was the formation of the Uncompahgre Plateau, where 300 million years ago, the western range of the *Ancestral Rocky Mountains* vaulted up along the eastern edge of what is now the Colorado Plateau. Erosion of the Uncompahgre Highland stripped away its overlying sedimentary layers and

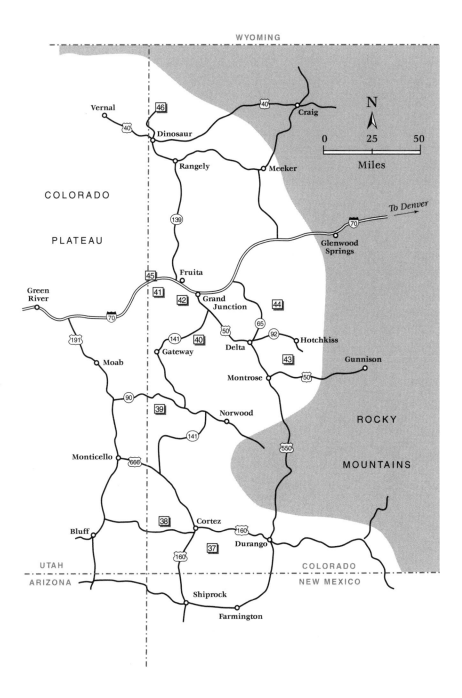

Colorado Plateau geology hikes

exposed the *basement rock* core that had pushed up to form the range. The sediment that washed from the mountains helped fill the Paradox Basin, a deep, fault-bounded trough that developed along the southwestern flank of the mountains.

During Mesozoic time, the eroded roots of this old highland were crossed by Triassic rivers, buried by Jurassic wind-blown sand dunes, and then submerged beneath the *Cretaceous Seaway*. Later, uplift during the *Laramide Orogeny* reactivated deep-seated *faults,* and the *basement rocks* were pushed skyward once again. The basement rocks are revealed now along the flanks and in deep canyons of the Uncompahgre Plateau and where the Gunnison River has cut its way down into Black Canyon. Their juxtaposition with the Mesozoic red *sedimentary rocks* has created the *Great Unconformity* where more than 1 billion years of layers are missing from the geologic record.

Despite the Colorado Plateau's wrinkled eastern edge, most of its landscape has only gradually uplifted and gently folded. As the Rocky Mountains surged upward during the Laramide Orogeny about 70 million years ago, the plateau region was corrugated by minor uplifts that warped and domed the rock layers, bending them along *monocline* stair steps. Even so, during all of the tumult, the layers were rarely shaken enough to break.

Broad downwarps in the folded rock layers were often inundated with water, such as at Lake Uinta which once covered the area where Colorado, Utah, and Wyoming now meet. Sediment washed from the Rockies into the lake, adding even more layers to the plateau's sedimentary pile. Thick layers of mud from the lake bottom became the Green River Shale, known today for its famous fish fossils and for oil *shale* deposits on the Roan Plateau north of Grand Junction.

Taken together, all of the plateau's sedimentary layers still stack like the layers of a birthday cake. Although some layers have eroded away or were deposited only in localized areas, the sequence of geologic events in the region can still largely be read from bottom to top.

This entire landscape was raised along with the rest of Colorado during the past 25 million years. About 10 million years ago, the rate of uplift accelerated, finally energizing the region's modern rivers, which swept down from the newly heightened Rockies, cutting deeply into the sedimentary pile. The force of water dissected the rocks, endowing the Plateau with its rich abundance of layered canyons, cliffs, and monuments. The artistry of weathering and erosion further shaped the exposed sedimentary layers into this landscape unlike any other place on earth.

172

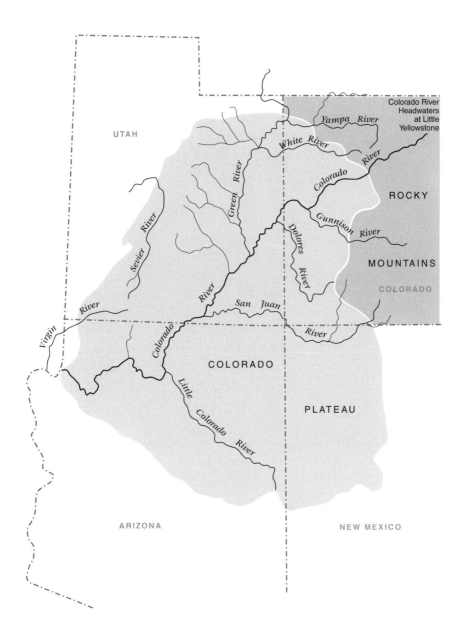

Colorado River and its tributaries

COLORADO'S GEOLOGIC LAYERCAKE

Although the *sedimentary rock* layers of the Colorado Plateau are often referred to as "layercake geology," as you might expect, in reality the relationships between layers is a bit more complicated. To rephrase the metaphor, the rock layers of the Colorado Plateau are like a sloppy layercake made by a messy (and hungry) baker, where some of the layers pinch and swell or ultimately disappear, while other layers interfinger, blending into one another. To make matters worse, some layers were partially "eaten" (that is, eroded) before the next layer was placed on top, or perhaps the baker forgot to spread certain layers at all.

The study of how rock layers, or *strata*, fit together is called *stratigraphy*. To describe the stratigraphy of the Colorado Plateau, geologists have subdivided the rocks into formations. Each formation has recognizable characteristics, making it distinguishable from adjacent rock layers. For example, in Colorado National Monument,

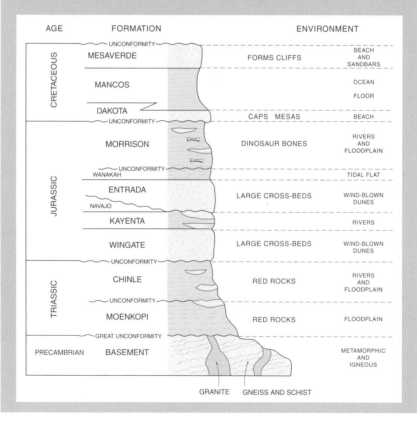

the cliff-forming Wingate Sandstone with its large, wind-blown *cross-beds,* appears much different than the ledges of thin, river-channel sandstones of the overlying Kayenta Formation.

The names of formations are typically derived from the place where the rocks are best exposed or where they were first described in detail. In cases where formations are similar or represent the same time period, they may be lumped into larger units, called groups, such as the various sandstones of the Mesaverde Group. In some cases, widespread layers may be named differently in different regions. For example, the Sawatch Quartzite in Colorado is called the Tapeats Sandstone in the Grand Canyon. This is like calling the same layer "custard" in one piece of layercake and "vanilla cream" in another.

Hike
37

KNIFE EDGE TRAIL

Mesa Verde National Park

Explore geologic clues that reveal the ancient shoreline where the mesa's defining sandstone cliffs formed.

DISTANCE ■ **2 miles round trip**

ELEVATION ■ **7,820 to 7,860 feet**

DIFFICULTY ■ **Easy**

TOPOGRAPHIC MAP ■ **USGS Point Lookout**

GEOLOGIC MAP ■ **27**

KEY REFERENCE ■ **29**

PRECAUTIONS ■ **Watch for rockfalls and stay away from crumbling ledges.**

FOR INFORMATION ■ **Mesa Verde National Park**

About the Landscape: This hike proves that a trail does not have to be long or difficult to be rewarding. A short walk over level terrain provides classic views of the rocks that form Mesa Verde's precipitous North Rim, a massive *sandstone* cliff or *escarpment.* Along the way, clues in the rocks hint that the North Rim was once a sandy shore.

Mesa Verde is a deeply dissected plateau of Cretaceous *sedimentary rock* that dominates the landscape in the Four Corners region of southwestern Colorado. It is a relic of a past landscape that was once connected to the lower reaches of the La Plata and San Juan Mountains. Erosion along Mesa Verde's North Rim has separated it from the mountains. Isolated, it stands

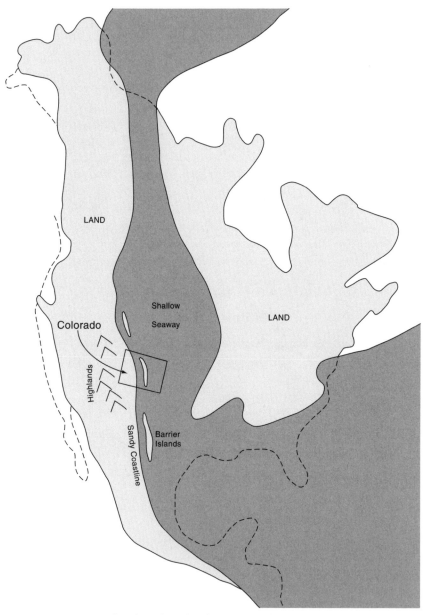

Cretaceous Seaway floods Colorado about 100 million years ago

more than 2,000 feet above Montezuma Valley to the north.

This plateau is most famous for housing the largest cliff dwellings in the southwest. Apart from the spectacular cliff dwellings, the most prominent feature of Mesa Verde is the resistant, massive sandstone cliff that

176

forms the northern edge of the plateau. This imposing cliff is made of the Cretaceous Mesaverde Group, a sedimentary sequence that records the retreat and readvance of a vast inland sea that extended from Texas and Mexico north to the Arctic Ocean. Between 100 and 70 million years ago, the *Cretaceous Seaway* repeatedly submerged all of Colorado, including the Colorado Plateau.

Trail Guide: To reach the Knife Edge Trailhead, drive 10 miles east from Cortez, or 8 miles west from Mancos, on US Highway 160 to the Mesa Verde National Park entrance. Follow the winding park road 4 miles to the Morefield Campground. The trailhead is located off the parking area at the extreme north end of the campground.

Follow the trail north through a meadow to the head of Morefield Canyon. A short distance after passing the junction with the Prater Ridge Trail, the Knife Edge Trail turns left (west) where it meets an old road. Here, only 0.3 mile from the trailhead, is one of Mesa Verde's classic views.

The massive cliffs of the North Rim stretch from east to west. The cliffs are composed of the Point Lookout Sandstone, an 80 million-year-old marine deposit from barrier beaches and sandbars near the shoreline of the retreating Cretaceous Seaway. Point Lookout, for which the sandstone formation is named, is the farthest promontory to the east. At the base of the cliff, the Mancos Shale Formation stretches out in barren slopes. The Mancos Shale is largely a deposit of mud and silt that settled in deep off-shore water. As the Cretaceous Seaway retreated (and thus got smaller), its shoreline receded seaward across the *shale,* juxtaposing barrier beaches and sandbars on top of the earlier deep-water shale deposits.

From here, the trail follows the old "Knife Edge" road which continues west below the cliff that forms Prater Ridge. A number of yellow, trunk-sized Point Lookout Sandstone boulders have fallen from the cliff above and scattered along the trail. Where the trail passes between two knee-high boulders, take a close look at the upper surface of the larger boulder on the left. Notice the network of marks that stand out in slight relief.

These features are the trackways and burrows of shrimplike crustaceans that inhabited the Cretaceous sea floor not far from shore. Called trace fossils, since they reveal only the traces of organisms and not their hard body parts, they indicate that the Point Lookout Sandstone was deposited in a marine environment. They are preserved along a bedding plane, a surface that once formed the bottom of the sea and remained undisturbed as the next layer of sand was deposited on top.

Continue on to an area where VW-sized Point Lookout Sandstone boulders are strewn along the trail. *Ripplemarks* are exposed on top of one of the boulders closest to the edge of the trail. These ripples were formed by

Trace fossils in Mesa Verde's Point Lookout Sandstone

currents washing back and forth across the sandy bottom of the Cretaceous Seaway. Some of the boulders display *cross-beds*. These thin, slanted lines in the rock are cross-sections of areas where many layers of sediment were deposited on the undulating surfaces of the sea floor.

At the end of the maintained trail, a sign reads, "Do not go beyond this point." Return to the trailhead by the same route, keeping an eye out for additional evidence of the ancient Cretaceous shorelines.

Hike 38

SAND CANYON

CLIFF DWELLINGS IN JURASSIC STRATA

Explore a colorful section of Jurassic sedimentary rocks that also harbors a number of ancient ruins.

DISTANCE ■ **5 miles round trip**

ELEVATION ■ **5,470 to 6,000 feet**

DIFFICULTY ■ **Easy**

TOPOGRAPHIC MAPS ■ **USGS Battle Rock and Woods Canyon**

GEOLOGIC MAP ■ **28**

KEY REFERENCE ■ **30**

PRECAUTIONS ■ **Avoid hot summer temperatures, drink lots of water, and beware of flash floods. Remember that archaeological sites are protected** by law. Please do not disturb the ruins or remove or displace artifacts. Please stay on the main trail. Off-trail travel can damage fragile soils.

FOR INFORMATION ■ San Juan Field Office or Anasazi Heritage Center

About the Landscape: The trail up Sand Canyon provides easy access to a classic Colorado Plateau landscape. Colorful layers of Jurassic *sedimentary* rocks line the canyon walls and well-preserved cliff dwellings perch in alcoves of eroded Jurassic Entrada Sandstone. Sand Canyon is found in the far southwestern corner of Colorado, tucked into the shadow of Sleeping Ute Mountain.

Trail Guide: To reach the Sand Canyon Trailhead, drive 3 miles south from Cortez on US Highway 160/666. Shortly after crossing McElmo Creek, turn right onto McElmo Canyon Road. Follow this winding paved road west for almost 13 miles. The trailhead is 0.5 mile after the bridge across McElmo Creek. Park directly on the *sandstone* surface near the information kiosk and trail register.

The trail begins by climbing up a gentle incline and crossing a white sandstone surface. The surface is composed of Navajo Sandstone, a major

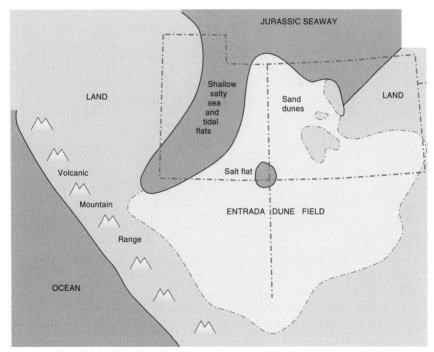

Extent of Entrada sand dunes during the Middle Jurassic, about 165 million years ago

179

wind-blown sand formation that stretches throughout much of the canyon country. The patterns in the surface are the eroded edges of *cross-beds* that formed as the crests of dunes edged forward in the wind. Numerous examples of cross-beds look like furrows in the rock along this trail.

After about 0.25 mile, the trail turns east, following below a prominent red and white sandstone cliff that will become very familiar during this hike. This is the wind-blown sandstone of the Jurassic Entrada Sandstone. The cliff-forming Entrada derives from an ancient desert landscape that dominated the Four Corners region during Middle Jurassic time, about 165 million years ago. The large dunes of the Entrada "sea of sand" left behind a thick pile of sand that was later buried by the stream, floodplain, and lake deposits of the Jurassic Morrison Formation.

Hugging the base of this red and white Entrada cliff, the trail turns north across a bench of white Navajo Sandstone. Just over a shallow rise, you come to the first of many picturesque sandstone promontories. Note that the color change in this outcrop, from white on top to red below, seems to occur without a change in the nature of the rock. Instead, it reflects a change in the chemical state of the iron-bearing minerals, typically hematite, within the rock. The red color is caused by oxidized iron, like rust, which occurs in interactions with groundwater after the sediment is deposited and buried.

Looking to the east, you can trace the red-white Entrada Sandstone cliff on the opposite side of the canyon. The sedimentary layers above this cliff are the colorful Jurassic sandstones and *shales* of the Wanakah Formation, Junction Creek Sandstone, and Morrison Formation. In the far distance, the Cretaceous sandstone cliff of Mesa Verde's North Rim peeks out through the notch cut by McElmo Canyon.

About 1 mile from the trailhead, you will see the first cliff dwelling clinging to the back wall of a smoothly sculpted rock overhang. The well-preserved square stone structure is one of many fragile cliff-based pueblos still hanging on in Sand Canyon. Most date back to the 1200s.

All the cliff dwellings in Sand Canyon are built in south- to southeast-facing alcoves formed by the differential erosion of the red-white Entrada cliff. In bend after bend, suitable rock overhangs house evidence of stone structures. Sharp eyes can also pick out ruins in alcoves along the east wall of the canyon.

Nearly 2.5 miles from the trailhead a sign reads, "The next mile is rocky and steep. Recommended for foot traffic only." This is a good point for turning back and retracing your steps.

▶ *Cliff dwellings in Sand Canyon*

The hike back to the trailhead is highlighted by the summit of Sleeping Ute Mountain framed against receding cliffs of Entrada Sandstone. Like many of the mountain ranges that pierce the Colorado Plateau, Sleeping Ute Mountain is a *laccolith.* This mushroom-shaped intrusive body domed up between 72 and 64 million years ago, carrying Cretaceous rocks of the Mancos Shale and Mesaverde Group upward with it. Through time, all the softer overlying sedimentary layers eroded away, exposing the resistant, mushroom-shaped igneous core.

DOLORES RIVER CANYON

SALT TECTONICS AND RED ROCK

This easy hike along the Dolores River leads through colorful sedimentary rocks upturned along the flank of Paradox Valley, a major salt-cored anticline.

DISTANCE ■ **6 miles round trip**
ELEVATION ■ **5,000 to 5,100 feet**
DIFFICULTY ■ **Easy**
TOPOGRAPHIC MAP ■ **USGS Paradox**
GEOLOGIC MAP ■ **29**
KEY REFERENCE ■ **31**
PRECAUTIONS ■ **Use caution where the trail crosses unconsolidated slopes or along ledges. Swift currents make swimming in the river dangerous.**
FOR INFORMATION ■ **Grand Junction Resource Area**

About the Landscape: A walk along the Dolores River Canyon beneath towering red rock cliffs is an encounter with Triassic and Jurassic sedimentary landscapes, now compacted into the colorful layers of the cliffs.

From its headwaters in the La Plata Mountains, the Dolores River cuts a meandering slice through a series of northwest–southeast trending ridges, valleys, and plateaus that were formed by an interesting process called salt tectonics. About 300 million years ago, during Pennsylvanian time, as much as 4,000 feet of *salt* accumulated by the evaporation of seawater in the Paradox Basin region of the Colorado Plateau. As the salt deposits were buried by sediments eroding from the rising *Ancestral Rockies,* the less dense salt oozed from below, pushing upward on overlying layers and arching them into elongate domes called salt *anticlines.* As the region slowly uplifted over the past 26 million years, along with the rest of Colorado, younger sedimentary layers eroded off the tops. Surface water eventually found its way inside these salt-cored anticlines and dissolved some of the salt. This caused the anticlines to collapse in on themselves. Continued erosion ultimately formed a series of elongate valleys with walls of Triassic and Jurassic sedimentary layers. The red rocks along the Dolores River lie along the flank of the Paradox Valley, a collapsed salt-cored anticline.

Trail Guide: To reach the Dolores River Canyon Trailhead, take Colorado Highway 141 west from Naturita for 2 miles to the junction with Colorado Highway 90. Turn left and drive 22 miles to the Bedrock General Store. Turn left just before the store onto the dirt road and drive 2 miles to where it is blocked by a sign.

Begin the hike beyond the sign, following the rapidly deteriorating road that eventually becomes the trail. As the trail winds along a slope above a bend in the Dolores River, notice how the river flows out of this canyon

Sandstone cliffs rise above the Dolores River.

and across the valley to the northeast, entering the steep-walled red rock canyon on the far side. This valley is called Paradox Valley because it is a "paradox" that the Dolores River cuts directly across it rather than flowing down its length to the west.

The river established its course while eroding through younger sedimentary layers that once covered the Paradox salt anticline. By the time it had eroded down to the level of the anticline, it had developed quite a rut. The Paradox Valley collapsed into its present shape too late to capture the flow of the river, which stayed in the rut you see today.

Rather than following the river along a wide meander, the trail leaves the river bank and crosses a bench below the cliffs before it meets the river again upstream. As the trail follows directly below the steep cliff of Jurassic Wingate Sandstone, look for *cross-beds* and *ripplemarks* on the face of the boulders at the base. On the cliff face above, cross-beds are etched out in relief, remnants of the wind-blown dunes that later became the Wingate Sandstone.

From here, the trail follows upstream, crossing several side drainages cut into Chinle Formation *sandstone* and *conglomerate* layers deposited by a Triassic stream system.

The trail reaches a vantage point looking down on the Dolores River from above. This is a good place to decipher the *stratigraphy* of the canyon walls. Start by picking out the wind-blown Wingate Sandstone, the lowest massive cliff on the opposite side of the canyon. Above the Wingate are the stepped sandstone ledges of the stream-deposited Kayenta Formation. Overlying the Kayenta is the Navajo Sandstone, also formed by wind-swept dunes.

Higher up, the upper part of the two-step cliff is the Entrada Sandstone, also of wind-blown origin. The Entrada forms the distinctive striped cliff along the canyon walls. Above the Entrada is the stepped slope of the Wanakah Formation, and finally, sandstones and *shales* of the Morrison Formation rise as a forested slope to the skyline.

The trail continues along the river and then crosses a side canyon cut into the Chinle Formation. Look along the trail for ripplemarks and layers of pebble conglomerate from this ancient stream system. Next, look for a group of large Wingate boulders off to the right of the trail. Etched into flat sufaces on many of these upright sandstone blocks are petroglyphs, carved by ancient native peoples.

As the trail approaches La Sal Creek, it cuts through an overhanging ledge of interbedded sandstone and shale in the Chinle Formation. The sandstone layers seem to cut across the shale layers, truncating them along the length of the exposure. These sands were deposited in channels cut into the mudbanks of an adjacent floodplain.

At La Sal Creek, the trail gets lost in a thicket of willows before it ends along the creek bank. This is a good place to cool off before turning back and retracing your steps to the trailhead.

UNAWEEP CANYON

Hike 40

AN ANCIENT RIVER CHANNEL AND THE GREAT UNCONFORMITY

The mysterious carving of Unaweep Canyon through 1,000 feet of solid basement rock took the force of a river far mightier than the two small streams that occupy it today.

DISTANCE ■ 1 mile round trip

ELEVATION ■ 6,780 to 6,840 feet

DIFFICULTY ■ Easy

TOPOGRAPHIC MAP ■ USGS Jacks Canyon

GEOLOGIC MAP ■ 30

KEY REFERENCE ■ 32

PRECAUTIONS ■ This hike does not follow a designated or maintained trail. Routes are easy to find. Walk on rock outcrops as much as possible to avoid crushing the fragile soil and beware of cliff edges.

FOR INFORMATION ■ Grand Junction Resource Area

About the Landscape: In the Ute language, Unaweep means "canyon with two mouths," and the origin of this unusual canyon still puzzles geologists. The canyon slices across the mid-section of the Uncompahgre Plateau, a 100-mile-long uplift located southwest of Grand Junction, Colorado. Today, only two small streams flowing in opposite directions (East and West Creeks) occupy the canyon. But it must have taken the erosive power of a much larger river over an extended time period to cut 1,000 feet into the resistant Precambrian igneous and metamorphic *basement rocks* of the uplifted Uncompahgre Plateau. Where is that river today?

Imagine a river flowing through the canyon, swollen with snowmelt, carving the canyon deeper and deeper. Geologists speculate that the Gunnison River, now located east of the Uncompahgre Plateau, may once have flowed westward through Unaweep Canyon, but the evidence is only circumstantial. Gravels of similar composition are found along the present-day

Gunnison and toward the west end of Unaweep Canyon near Gateway. It is possible that an ancestral channel of the Gunnison River slowly carved Unaweep Canyon over millions of years as the Uncompahgre Plateau uplifted.

At some point, uplift may have outpaced the river and the Gunnison may have begun to flow northward, joining with the Colorado River and abandoning its channel through the canyon. Or the Colorado River may have "captured" the flow of the Gunnison, forcing it to abandon its route through the canyon. This process, called "stream piracy," occurs when a river cuts a channel through soft rocks until it ultimately erodes headward into the course of another river nearby, thereby capturing its flow.

The competing theory of Unaweep Canyon's origin is that both the Colorado and Gunnison may have once carved the canyon together. Then the Colorado River was pirated away by a nearby stream and ultimately pirated the Gunnison away from the ancestral course.

Trail Guide: To reach the start of this hike, drive to Divide Road heading west 15 miles from Whitewater on Colorado Highway 141, or east 20 miles from Gateway. Turn onto Divide Road, a well-maintained gravel road, and drive 0.5 mile to the first switchback. Park on the short spur to the left, facing the red rock cliff.

This hike does not follow a designated or maintained trail. Start out from the parking area by finding your way through fallen boulders of red Wingate Sandstone. After about 50 yards, the route traverses over outcrops of dark Precambrian basement rock.

Traverse upslope over the basement outcrops until you reach a bench at the base of the red rock slope. You are now standing at about the level of the *Great Unconformity.* Below your feet is Precambrian basement rock and above is a slope of the Triassic Chinle Formation red rock, capped by a red cliff of the Jurassic Wingate Sandstone.

Missing between the Chinle Formation and the ancient basement of the Uncompahgre Plateau are thousands of feet of Precambrian and Paleozoic rocks that are present in other areas of the Colorado Plateau. This *unconformity* was formed nearly 300 million years ago during Pennsylvanian and Permian time when basement rocks pushed upward to form the western segment of the *Ancestral Rocky Mountains,* called the Uncompahgre Highland. Overlying sedimentary layers were stripped off by streams flowing off the mountains, beveling the uplift down to a nearly level plain. Later, during the Triassic, Chinle streams meandered across

◀ *The origin of Unaweep Canyon still puzzles geologists.*

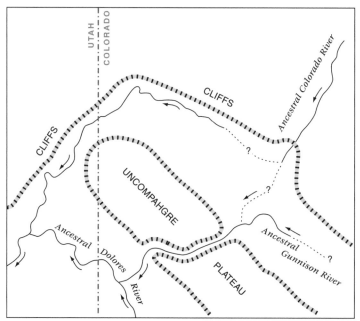

A. Before abandonment of Unaweep Canyon

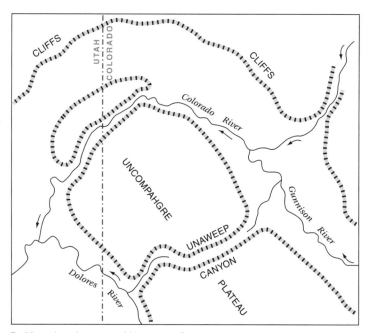

B. After abandonment of Unaweep Canyon

Possible cutting of Unaweep Canyon by ancestral channels of the Gunnison and Colorado Rivers the region, depositing sand and mud along their courses. Great Jurassic dunes of wind-blown sand then engulfed the area leaving behind a sand pile that would become the Wingate Sandstone. Together, the eroded basement rocks and the sedimentary layers covering them would later rise to become the Uncompahgre Plateau.

Today, the unconformity forms a bench all along the rim of Unaweep Canyon. Try to follow a route that contours, or stays level, along this bench. Look carefully for an outcrop of *conglomerate* that forms a 3-foot ledge in the Chinle slope with a shallow overhang underneath. You have found the actual surface of the Great Unconformity! The conglomerate at eye level was left behind about 200 million years ago by the Chinle streams. Under your feet are crystalline rocks more than 1.4 billion years old, a staggering gap in the rock record of over 1 billion years!

Continue downslope over basement outcrops until you reach a rock promontory with an excellent view to the west up Unaweep Canyon. Above you, a Wingate cliff forms a narrow sandstone fin. This landform was possibly carved by a meander in the ancestral river when it flowed through Unaweep Canyon eons ago.

After taking in the views of Unaweep Canyon and puzzling over its origin, return to your vehicle by retracing your steps.

Hike 41

RATTLESNAKE CANYON

SANDSTONE ARCHES

Rattlesnake Canyon is the second largest grouping of natural sandstone arches in the United States, after Utah's Arches National Park.

DISTANCE ■ **3 miles round trip**

ELEVATION ■ **5,860 to 5,400 feet**

DIFFICULTY ■ **Easy**

TOPOGRAPHIC MAP ■ USGS Mack

GEOLOGIC MAP ■ 31

KEY REFERENCE ■ 33

PRECAUTIONS ■ A four-wheel drive vehicle is needed to reach the trailhead. The Black Ridge access road is steep and rocky for the last 3 miles. It becomes impassable when wet due to the swelling clays in the Morrison Formation. Inquire about local conditions. Use caution exploring the cliffs above the arches.

FOR INFORMATION ■ Grand Junction Resource Area

Sandstone arch in Rattlesnake Canyon

About the Landscape: Along the uppermost rim of Rattlesnake Canyon, a short trail winds among brilliant salmon-colored cliffs. Here, many stages of natural *sandstone* arch development are displayed in the 165 million-year-old Jurassic Entrada Sandstone, the same rock formation from which Utah's Arches National Park is carved.

Rattlesnake Canyon dissects the remote northern edge of the Uncompahgre Plateau where dramatic cliffs of Triassic and Jurassic red rocks are upwarped along a major *monocline.*

Trail Guide: Getting to the Rattlesnake Canyon Trailhead requires a four-wheel drive vehicle. Follow the Rim Rock Road 11 miles from the west entrance of Colorado National Monument (near Fruita) and turn right onto Glade Park Road. Follow this wide gravel road 0.2 mile and turn right again onto Black Ridge Road. Follow the BLM public access markers, but be sure to bear left at the first fork where you see signs for both directions. Drive 9.3 miles on Black Ridge Road to the trailhead at the end of the road. Be warned that the last 3 miles are steep, rocky, and impassable when wet. For those without four-wheel drive, an alternate way to get to Rattlesnake Canyon is by hiking 6.8 miles up the Pollack Trail, beginning along the Colorado River west of Fruita.

From the trail register, the trail immediately steps down a sandstone ledge then follows an old road along a bench. It soon meets the junction with the Upper Arches Trail. Follow the sign for the Upper Trail, heading left along the top of the Entrada Sandstone cliff, past the arches on the left, to the end of the ridge for a panoramic view. To get down to the Lower Arches Trail, look for a cairn (rock pile) that marks the route down through the first arch to meet the trail below. Contour around the sandstone until you can step down through the arch. Just when it seems you are stuck, a hand or foothold appears in the rock. Once below the arch, the trail follows a bench at the base of the Entrada cliff.

Arches in every stage of development stretch out along the cliff. Look first for vertical *fractures* in the rock. Then look for an area where a chunk of sandstone has fallen out of a fracture. Water seeps into the fractures, expanding as it freezes and ultimately wedging the rock apart. The pull of gravity then dislodges the rock. This is the first stage in developing an alcove. Next, notice that there are alcoves of all different shapes and sizes, some further along in their development than others. Eventually, as the alcove wall thins, a block of sandstone will fall through the wall of an alcove, creating a window through to the sky. There are several of these "skylights" visible from the trail. Block by sandstone block, the windows open wider, transforming into arches. Ultimately, however, the arches come crashing down. Look for areas along the cliff where arches have collapsed.

In addition to the arches, excellent examples of large scale *cross-beds* stand out in relief on the face of the Entrada Sandstone cliff. These sweeping surfaces represent the advancing faces of wind-blown sand dunes. Notice how the angles of the cross-beds change direction in beds that overlie each other, as if the wind changed direction and the dunes started migrating in the opposite direction. This could well be the case. The sands of the Entrada blew in Jurassic winds over a vast dune field bordering an arm of a sea to the west. Coastlines are known for erratic winds.

In the distance, you can see several bends in the Colorado River's flow through Horse Thief Canyon. Notice the steeply inclined cliffs of Entrada Sandstone between the river and the edge of the Uncompahgre Plateau. These layers were tilted by the Plateau's uplift during the *Laramide Orogeny*. This structure is a monocline, a simple warp in the layers over a fault in the *basement rocks* below. This fold in the rocks is why it's possible to be looking at arches in the Entrada along the edge of the Uncompahgre Plateau and also see the Entrada at lower elevations in the canyons along the Colorado River.

The trail departs from the cliff face as it heads around the point, following the bench back to where it meets the Pollack Trail. Turn right at the junction and hike back to the top of the ridge to complete the loop. From there, the main trail leads back to the trailhead.

MONUMENT CANYON

SANDSTONE MONUMENTS AND THE GREAT UNCONFORMITY

The Wingate Sandstone is eroded into free-standing fins and spires along the Redlands monocline of the Uncompahgre Plateau.

DISTANCE ■ 6 miles round trip

ELEVATION ■ 6,260 to 5,350 feet

DIFFICULTY ■ Moderate

TOPOGRAPHIC MAPS ■ USGS Colorado National Monument; Trails Illustrated #208

GEOLOGIC MAP ■ 31

KEY REFERENCE ■ 33

PRECAUTIONS ■ Carry plenty of water, wear a hat, and avoid the extreme midday heat in summer.

FOR INFORMATION ■ Colorado National Monument

About the Landscape: Colorado National Monument is an area of colorful Triassic and Jurassic *sedimentary rocks* that were bent, faulted, and fractured as the Uncompahgre Plateau uplifted during the *Laramide Orogeny*. This hike follows a massive red rock cliff of Wingate Sandstone that has eroded into spectacular free-standing fins and spires along the edge of the Uncompahgre Plateau. The trail also leads into the heart of the *sandstone* canyons along the northeastern edge of the plateau and traverses the *Great Unconformity* where more than 1 billion years of rock layers are missing.

Trail Guide: To reach the Monument Canyon Trailhead from Grand Junction, enter the National Monument at the east entrance and follow Rim Rock Road to the Monument Canyon Trail parking area (just after Coke Oven Overlook). From the west entrance of the Monument at Fruita, follow Rim Rock Road past the Visitor Center to the trailhead.

The Monument Canyon Trail winds down to the base of the red rock cliffs and follows a side canyon that eventually leads to the head of Monument Canyon. After a few switchbacks, the trail follows a ledge in a salmon-colored cliff of Entrada Sandstone. Cross-bedding patterns in the rock formed as the faces of advancing sand dunes were buried by Jurassic winds about 175 million years ago.

After passing the junction with the Coke Ovens Trail on the right, you come to the trail register. At this point, the trail steps down through stream-deposited sandstone and *conglomerate* of the Kayenta Formation. Look for

192

ripplemarks and medium-scale, curved *cross-beds* produced by currents in Jurassic stream channels.

Below the Kayenta ledge, a series of tight switchbacks follow a *talus* slope down to the base of the towering Wingate Sandstone cliff. Large, sweeping cross-beds are evident along the cliff face. The Wingate is a pile of wind-blown sand that accumulated earlier in the Jurassic.

The character of the landscape changes as the trail meets the canyon bottom and winds its way over rounded, deeply weathered outcrops of Precambrian *basement rock.* These *metamorphic rocks* are banded *gneiss* and *schist* that formed by heat and pressure at great depths during mountain-building events about 1.7 billion years ago. Then about 1.4 billion years ago, *magma* squeezed into cracks in the rock and slowly cooled to form *pegmatite dikes* and irregular *granitic* bodies. Chunks of granitelike rock that contain large crystals of quartz, feldspar, and flakes of mica have weathered from the pegmatite dikes.

You have now reached the Great Unconformity, a gap in the rock record that spans more than 1 billion years. Thousands of feet of Precambrian and Paleozoic rocks, present in other areas of the Colorado Plateau, are missing between the brick red Chinle Formation, deposited by streams during

The trail through Monument Canyon brings you to the base of towering Independence Monument.

the Triassic about 225 million years ago, and the underlying basement core of the Uncompahgre Plateau. These missing rocks were stripped off by erosion during uplift and demise of the ancestral Uncompahgre Highland, the western arm of the *Ancestral Rocky Mountains* that vaulted skyward about 300 million years ago in roughly the same place where the present Uncompahgre Plateau is located.

As the trail swings around to the north, the canyon opens up and the first of many free-standing stone towers comes into view. From this vantage point, the vertical fractures that give the tower shape are clearly evident.

As the trail winds along the base of the cliff heading west, more sandstone pillars come into view, including the beloved Kissing Couple (you will know it when you see it!). The trail eventually leads to Independence Monument, where a short spur trail takes you up a saddle in the Chinle Formation to the base of this 450-foot-high fin of Wingate Sandstone. From here, it's easy to imagine a continuous rock wall joining the cliffs on either end of the monument. The orientation of the sandstone fin is determined by vertical fractures that cut through the rock. Erosion was more rapid along the fractures and, over time, has removed the surrounding rock on either side. Today, only a small resistant cap of Kayenta Sandstone protects the top of the monument. Once that caprock erodes away, Independence Monument will wither. This type of weathering is called *differential erosion.* The lower Kayenta Sandstone is cemented with *quartz* (silica), making it more durable and resistant to erosion. The Wingate Sandstone is held together by *calcite* which is softer and tends to dissolve when wet.

Although the Monument Canyon Trail continues for another 3 miles where it emerges to meet Colorado Highway 340, this is the turnaround point for this hike. Return to the trailhead by the route you came.

Hike 43

NORTH VISTA TRAIL

Black Canyon of the Gunnison

Stand 2,000 feet above the Gunnison River for a dramatic view at Exclamation Point.

DISTANCE ■ **3 miles round trip**
ELEVATION ■ **7,650 to 7,702 feet**
DIFFICULTY ■ **Easy**
TOPOGRAPHIC MAPS ■ **USGS Grizzly Ridge; Trails Illustrated #245**
GEOLOGIC MAP ■ **32**
KEY REFERENCE ■ **34**

PRECAUTIONS ■ Use extreme caution when exploring along the canyon rim. Avoid exposed areas during summer thunderstorms.

FOR INFORMATION ■ Black Canyon of the Gunnison National Park

About the Landscape: Few canyons in the world rival the Black Canyon of the Gunnison for its dramatically sheer depths.

The Black Canyon region was caught in both the *Ancestral Rocky Mountain* and *Laramide Orogeny* uplifts and was also a battleground for violent volcanic eruptions that built the West Elk and San Juan Mountains. But despite all this action, a river was born and established itself with a mind of its own, carving a deep chasm down the length of a Laramide-age uplift, called the Gunnison Uplift, cored by Colorado's 1.7 billion-year-old *basement rocks.*

The Black Canyon of the Gunnison River spans two worlds. Along its lower reaches, the tilted layers of colorful Mesozoic strata flanking the river belong in the realm of the Colorado Plateau. Upriver, remnants of once-widespread volcanic rocks overlie the dark Precambrian basement rocks of the canyon's inner gorge. Clearly, the Black Canyon lies at a crossroads between the Colorado Plateau and the Rocky Mountains.

Trail Guide: To reach the North Vista Trailhead on Black Canyon's north rim, drive 21 miles east from Delta on Colorado Highway 92 to Hotchkiss where the highway makes a jog to the south toward Crawford. About 3.3 miles past Crawford, turn right onto Black Canyon Road (just past Crawford Lake) and follow the signs 12 miles to Black Canyon of the Gunnison National Park. The trailhead is located at the North Rim Ranger Station.

From the Ranger Station, this easy trail follows the forested north rim of Black Canyon to Exclamation Point.

About 0.5 mile down the trail, a sign marks an overlook on the left. Here at the end of a short spur trail is the first good view into Black Canyon. The famous "Painted Wall" forms the steep cliff to the right (west). Rising almost 2,300 feet above the river, the Painted Wall is the tallest *escarpment* in Colorado. Under your feet at the edge of the overlook is the pink- to salmon-colored Entrada Sandstone. This colorful layer sits directly on top of 1.7 billion-year-old metamorphic basement rocks.

The Entrada dunes were deposited by Jurassic winds along what was left of the eroded western arm of the Ancestral Rocky Mountains called the Uncompahgre Highland. Millions of year's worth of Paleozoic sedimentary layers were stripped from the crest of the uplift, setting the stage for the *Great Unconformity.* During the early part of the Mesozoic, Triassic and Jurassic *sediments* were deposited up to but not over the exposed and beveled highland. About 165 million years ago, the Jurassic Entrada sands were deposited across the surface, leaving a gap in the record that spans

Colorado's basement rocks are exposed in the Black Canyon of the Gunnison River.

more that 1.5 billion years. Across the canyon, the Entrada has eroded, and the planed off highland now serves as the bench at rim level.

The trail continues through the forest until it forks about 1.25 miles from the trailhead. A sign marks a trail to the left that leads to Exclamation Point. Follow this trail until you can walk no more—you have reached the edge of the abyss! From this vantage point, there is a clear view upstream (east) into the narrows of the inner canyon. Downstream, the Painted Wall towers above the river.

The Gunnison River has carved this deep chasm into the Gunnison Uplift, a Laramide-age uplift that pushed upward about 60 million years ago along faults that date back to the Ancestral Rockies. The rim and walls of the canyon are carved from 1.7 billion-year-old igneous and metamorphic basement rocks with prominent veins of *pegmatite*. How did the Gunnison River entrench itself in some of the hardest rock in Colorado?

Long before dams were built upstream holding back floods of water and gritty sediment, the Gunnison River raged as a powerful torrent that entrained rocks and boulders like a great tumbler. Initially, the river flowed across a landscape of West Elk and San Juan *volcanic rocks* that smothered the Gunnison Uplift and the older sedimentary layers that covered it. As the volcanic piles grew, the area slowly warped downward into a *syncline* and the west-flowing drainage became channeled between the volcanic centers directly above the Gunnison Uplift.

Slowly, the river scoured deeper into its channel. Once entrenched, the river continued to follow its established course with complete disregard for the hard basement rocks that lay hidden below. As the area uplifted with the rest of Colorado, the river cut deeper and deeper during the past 10 million years, ultimately superimposing itself on the basement core.

In only the last 2 million years, the river has carved most of its path through the resistant basement rock, supercharged by floods of water and grit from melting *Ice Age glaciers*—just yesterday in geologic terms!

After taking in the view (but not stepping too close to the edge!), follow the trail back to the ranger station.

Hike
44

CRAG CREST

GRAND MESA'S BASALT BACKBONE

Explore the Crag Crest Trail as it traverses the lava flows that cap Grand Mesa.

DISTANCE ■ 6 miles round trip (or 10-mile loop)

ELEVATION ■ 10,152 to 11,189 feet

DIFFICULTY ■ Moderate

TOPOGRAPHIC MAPS ■ USGS Grand Mesa; Trails Illustrated #127

GEOLOGIC MAP ■ 16

KEY REFERENCE ■ 35

PRECAUTIONS ▪ Use extreme caution when crossing narrow, cliff-edge sections of trail. Watch for loose rocks underfoot. Avoid exposed areas during summer thunderstorms.

FOR INFORMATION ▪ Grand Junction Ranger District

About the Landscape: The Crag Crest Trail follows along the backbone of Grand Mesa, a high, forested plateau east of Grand Junction that looks out on sweeping views of the Colorado Plateau and the western Rocky Mountains.

Grand Mesa is formed by thick layers of *basalt lava* that flooded an ancient landscape. The *magma* welled up from cracks, or fissures, in the earth somewhere east of the mesa about 10 million years ago. Long after the lava flows cooled, erosion over millions of years striped away the softer rock that flanked the mesa, leaving the basalt-capped mesa to stand tall as a mountain.

Trail Guide: To reach the Crag Crest Trailhead, drive 17 miles east from Grand Junction on Interstate 70 to the exit for Colorado Highway 65. Drive south 34.5 miles to Forest Road 121 (sign for Crag Crest 4 miles). Turn left and follow this road 2.5 miles. Turn left again, onto a dirt road at the sign for Forest Road 121 and drive 0.9 mile to the parking area on the right along the shore of Eagleston Lake opposite the Crag Crest Campground. The trailhead is located across the road to the right (east) of the campground entrance.

The trail starts out by climbing a gentle grade along a boulder field of dark gray basalt. These boulders eroded from the 400-foot-thick layer of *volcanic rock* that caps Grand Mesa. Above the boulder field, the trail reaches a junction less than 0.25 mile from the trailhead. Continue straight ahead, following the Crag Crest Trail. It climbs gradually toward the earthen dam that forms Upper Eagleston Lake about 0.5 mile from the trailhead. At the 1-mile point, the trail passes another lake (Bullfinch Reservoir) on the right. About 1.5 miles from the trailhead, the route intersects the junction with the Butts Lake Trail off to the left.

Beyond the intersection, the Crag Crest Trail continues straight ahead and then climbs more steeply, paralleling a high basalt cliff to the left (north). *Faults* control the east–west orientation of the cliff, or *escarpment*, which formed as a *fault-block* dropped down along the east–west line. The trail follows the base of the cliff on this down-dropped fault-block.

The trail then switchbacks up the steep escarpment, crossing more boulder fields of basalt. The numerous small holes, or *vesicles*, in the basalt boulders were formed by gas bubbles trapped in the lava when it cooled. This rock is called vesicular basalt. In some boulders, elongate

Hiking Grand Mesa's Crag Crest Trail

vesicles formed when the gas bubbles were stretched as the lava continued to move during cooling.

The trail reaches the crest of the ridge, Grand Mesa's "backbone," about
2 miles from the trailhead. At the top, the Crag Crest Trail traverses westward
along the high, spinelike ridge where you are greeted with sweeping views.
To the north, the east–west-oriented boulder-filled valley immediately
below is a *graben,* or down-dropped fault-block. Beyond this valley to the
north is Battlement Mesa, another basalt-capped high plateau like Grand Mesa.

Small holes, called vesicles, in basalt that were stretched while hot lava continued to move as it cooled

For about the next 2 miles, the trail follows the crest of the narrow ridge past outcrops of vesicular basalt. Immediately below to the left (south) are a number of rock basins filled by lakes. Faulting and slumping of the basalt layers along the margin of the mesa formed this string of jeweled basins. Nearby, several lobes of boulders appear piled along the base of the cliffs. But these piles are actually moving—more slowly than your eye can see. They are *rock glaciers,* cored by ice and on the move.

Anywhere along this ridge is a good turnaround point for this hike. At one particular point along the trail, the ridge narrows to no more than 5 feet wide bounded by sheer cliffs on either side. Adventurous hikers may want to continue across the ridge to a forested plateau where the trail eventually meets Lower Crag Crest Trail and loops back to the trailhead (10 miles total).

Hike
45

TRAIL THROUGH TIME

DINOSAUR GRAVEYARD

Visit a dinosaur quarry and view fossil bones in the rocks.

DISTANCE ■ 1.5-mile loop
ELEVATION ■ 4,640 to 4,680 feet
DIFFICULTY ■ Easy
TOPOGRAPHIC MAP ■ USGS Bitter Creek Well

GEOLOGIC MAP ■ 31

KEY REFERENCE ■ 36

PRECAUTIONS ■ Please remember that collecting rocks, fossils, or plants is not permitted. Digging in the quarry is by special research permit only.

FOR INFORMATION ■ Grand Junction Resource Area

About the Landscape: Like an outdoor museum, this short, easy hike will transport you back in time to a period when dinosaurs ruled the earth. Let your imagination run wild as giant plant-eating sauropods, more fondly dubbed brontosaurs, graze along forested stream banks while predatory, meat-eating allosaurs stalk their next victim (or scavenge carcasses at a water hole). Located within 2 miles of the Utah border, the Trail Through Time traverses sedimentary layers in the Morrison Formation. Here, dinosaur bones remain encased in the rocks where they were entombed about 150 million years ago during the Jurassic.

Dinosaur bones remain encased in the rocks along the Trail Through Time near the Utah Border.

The Museum of Western Colorado in Grand Junction and the Dinosaur Discovery Museum in nearby Fruita are worthwhile stops before heading out to the trailhead. Both institutions sponsor continuing research and house displays from local discoveries. During the summer months, paleontologists actively dig in search of new fossils. It's possible to join the digs by contacting the Dinosaur Discovery Museum or the Museum of Western Colorado.

Trail Guide: To reach the Dinosaur Quarry Trailhead, drive 18 miles west from Fruita on Interstate 70 to Exit 2 (sign for Dinosaur Quarry Trail). Turn right (north) and drive 0.5 mile to the parking area and trailhead.

About 200 yards from the trailhead, an information kiosk at the dinosaur quarry introduces the variety of dinosaurs collected at the site and describes the geology of the area.

Since the first discovery of dinosaur bones at this site in 1981, fossils from at least seven different dinosaur species have been uncovered: allosaurs and ceratosaurs, the ferocious predators and scavengers with strong claws and sharp, saw-edged teeth; the gigantic sauropods Aptosaurus, Brachiosaurus, Camarasaurus, and Diplodocus, with long necks ideal for browsing on tall trees or low plants; and an armored nodosaur.

The place where you are standing was an ancient shallow lake bordering river channels that meandered across a vast floodplain located where parts of Colorado, Utah, and Wyoming are today. Several rivers flowed across the floodplain from volcanic mountains in western Utah. Dating of volcanic ash deposits on the floodplain indicates that the dinosaurs thrived here about 152 million years ago.

From the quarry, the trail heads to the right (north) contouring along the slope. From this point on, a series of well-placed interpretive signs identify fossil sites or point out aspects of the geology and surrounding landscape.

Only a short distance from the quarry, the first sign points out fossils of Camarasaurus. The fossil bones are preserved in a ledge of *sandstone* and *conglomerate.* These bones swept downstream in an ancient river until they were buried by sand and gravel, perhaps on a sandbar at a bend in the river. As the soft, fleshy parts of the animal decayed, the hollow spaces in the bones filled with silica-rich water that, over time, hardened into *quartz* and petrified the bone. Abundant volcanic ash in the Morrison Formation provides a rich source of silica that favors this preservation of fossils. Look closely to see how well this slow process preserved some of the fine detail in the structure of the bone material.

Beyond these first fossil bones, the trail climbs a gentle slope through boulders of sandstone and conglomerate. The next sign points to plant fossils in the rocks at your feet. These light-colored pieces of petrified wood are the fossilized remains of vegetation from the Cedar Mountain Formation, a 120 million-year-old Cretaceous rock layer that overlies the Morrison and caps the mesas along the trail. As you continue hiking, keep a sharp eye out for more plant fossils in rocks scattered along the trail.

At about the 0.5-mile point, the trail crosses a fence over wooden steps. It then winds downhill through soft, pastel-colored rock layers of *mudstone,* a fine-grained *sedimentary rock* from the floodplain crossed by streams ladened with dinosaur bones.

Toward the end of the loop, another sign points to dinosaur bones bound in a thin ledge of sandstone at your feet. Preserved here is a partial skeleton (vertebrae) of a juvenile Diplodocus. As a full-grown adult, this large sauropod would have reached 90 feet in length. This giant animal had long, rakelike teeth, perfect for stripping leaves off branches.

Beyond the last dinosaur fossils, the trail follows a wash, passes a few more interpretive signs, then intersects a gravel road that leads back to the parking area.

HARPERS CORNER

Hike 46

BIRD'S-EYE VIEW OF FAULTS AND FOLDS

The ripple effects of the Uinta Mountain uplift are revealed in the canyons of the Yampa and Green Rivers in Dinosaur National Monument.

DISTANCE ■ **2 miles round trip**

ELEVATION ■ **7,600 to 7,510 feet**

DIFFICULTY ■ **Easy**

TOPOGRAPHIC MAPS ■ **USGS Jones Hole; Trails Illustrated #220**

GEOLOGIC MAP ■ **33**

KEY REFERENCE ■ **37**

PRECAUTIONS ■ **Please remain on the trail and use extreme caution at the precipitous overlook. Avoid the overlook during approaching thunderstorms.**

FOR INFORMATION ■ **Dinosaur National Monument**

About the Landscape: If you have ever dreamed of a bird's-eye view of Colorado's geologic landscape, this trail is for you. The Harpers Corner Trail leads to a spectacular viewpoint rising more than 2,000 feet above Echo Park, where the Green and Yampa Rivers meet. From this high vantage point, three canyons are in view—Lodore and Yampa Canyons upstream and Whirlpool Canyon downstream. The Laramide Uinta Mountain Uplift ruffled the once flat-lying sedimentary layers now exposed in the canyons, dramatically upturning them along the Mitten Park *fault* and *monocline*.

Although Dinosaur National Monument is best known for its prolific dinosaur quarry in the Jurassic Morrison Formation, the landscape along the northern edge of the Colorado Plateau, dominated by these bent and broken rock layers in a twisting maze of canyons, is not to be missed.

Trail Guide: To reach the Harpers Corner Trailhead, drive 1.5 miles east on US Highway 40 to the sign for Dinosaur National Monument. Turn left (north) and follow the Harpers Corner scenic drive 32.5 miles to the parking area at the end of the road.

The Harpers Corner Trail traverses a narrow, forested ridge to a rock promontory high above Whirlpool Canyon and Echo Park. The trail starts out by making a couple of switchbacks down a gentle grade, then follows a well-worn trail all the way to the viewpoint. The boulders along the trail are from the Bishop Conglomerate, composed of rocks eroded from the crest of the Uinta Uplift. This widespread layer blanketed much of the area before canyon cutting began.

As the trail climbs a gentle incline to the viewpoint, the rocks beneath your feet become beds of solid gray *limestone*. Look closely to find fossils of the clamlike shells of *brachiopods,* disk-shaped segments of *crinoid* stems, and tiny, twiglike fossils called bryozoans. You are walking on an ancient sea floor from the Morgan Formation of Pennsylvanian age.

From the viewpoint, the Green River in Whirlpool Canyon lies to the west (left) and Echo Park to the east (right). The confluence between the Green and Yampa at Echo Park is obscured by Steamboat Rock, a long ridge of light-colored *sandstone.* This light-colored *strata* is the Weber Sandstone, a thick layer of wind-blown sand that accumulated in this area about 300 million years ago during Pennsylvanian time. Although in view at river level, the Morgan Formation that you stand upon is the rock layer that lies just below the white sandstones of the Weber.

But how can you be standing on these limestone layers so high, when the Weber Sandstone forms the walls of the canyons far below?

The answer involves the disruption of the rock layers along the Mitten Park fault and monocline. The fault is visible across the river on the right side (east) of the viewpoint. At river level, the rock layers that extend to the left from Steamboat Rock are bent sharply upward at the fault zone against horizontal layers on the left. This fault shifted older rocks, left of the fault, upward relative to the younger rocks on the right of the fault. The dark red Precambrian sandstones raised to river level to the left of

Sedimentary layers are bent and broken along the Mitten Park fault and monocline.

the fault are 1 billion-year-old Uinta Mountain Group sedimentary *basement rocks.*

Motion along the fault caused the layers on top of the fault to be folded into a steep monocline, although the top step in the monocline has eroded away. Look far to the right (south) of the river to see where the white Weber

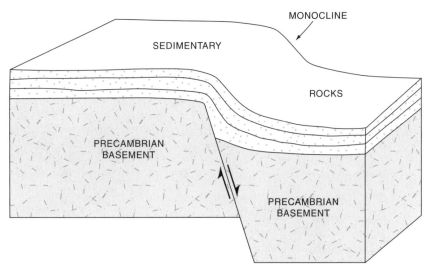

Sedimentary rock layers draped over a fault in the Precambrian basement

Sandstone steps upward twice more along monoclines draped over the Yampa fault.

This bending and breaking of the rocks took place as the Uinta Mountains pushed skyward during the *Laramide Orogeny* about 70 million years ago. The motion warped these sedimentary layers along the northern edge of the Colorado Plateau. Renewed uplift over the past 25 million years further disrupted these once flat-lying strata.

A curious feature of the scene before you is that the rivers cut directly across the faults and folds rather than taking the easy way around. This is because the rivers established their courses when the faults and folds in the rocks were buried beneath a younger veneer of sediments eroded from the nearby mountains (including the Bishop Conglomerate). The rivers first established themselves as they carved a lazy, sinuous course through the flat-lying layers. With renewed uplift of the region, the rivers entrenched themselves in their own meanders. As they eroded more deeply, they eventually reached the older folded and faulted layers. By this time, however, they were set in their ways and continued to follow their courses despite the faults, folds, and resistant rock layers they encountered.

After taking in this spectacular view of the geologic landscapes before you, simply retrace your steps back to the trailhead.

▶ *Gently rolling grasslands dominate Colorado's High Plains.*

Part 3
THE HIGH PLAINS

Chapter 11
COLORADO'S HIGH PLAINS

The High Plains are anything but plain. Although cast in the shadow of the Rocky Mountains, the High Plains have an unexpected wealth of geologic history. Beneath gentle hills and swales, this vast grassland protects a relatively undisturbed geologic record of Colorado's past mountain, sea, and desert landscapes.

As the western part of the more expansive Great Plains, the High Plains form an undulating plateau that is distinguished from the Great Plains by the Ogallala Formation, a *sandstone* and *conglomerate* jumble that washed down onto the plains from the Rockies. The Ogallala was once a continuous layer that extended eastward from the mountain front out across all the plains. Erosion has whittled this layer down to the remaining resistant Ogallala caprock which defines the High Plains by extending southward from Nebraska across eastern Colorado to the panhandle of Texas.

Close to the mountains, the South Platte and Arkansas Rivers have excavated the eastern edge of the High Plains plateau, stripping away the Ogallala caprock and creating a broad, gentle valley along the mountain front called the Colorado Piedmont. For the purposes of this book, the Colorado Piedmont is considered part of the High Plains.

The High Plains remained a place of relative geologic calm while faults to the west chaotically raised the landscape during Colorado's great mountain-building upheavals. Unlike the mountains, where much of the geologic record has eroded away and swept downstream, the High Plains are the receptacle for much of this sedimentary record. Layers of mountain rubble carried by rivers are interspersed with layers that mark advances of ancient seaways and crossings of desert dunes. The result is a stacked sequence on the High Plains that, from bottom to top, reads like a textbook of Colorado history.

With the most recent pulse of Rocky Mountain uplift, starting 10 million years ago, the South Platte, Arkansas, and Purgatoire Rivers were unleashed onto the plains. As was so often true in the past, today's vast expanse of land and sky is broken by these rivers that are slowly carrying the modern Rockies toward the plains. As the High Plains also slowly uplifted and tilted with the mountains, these rivers etched away at their

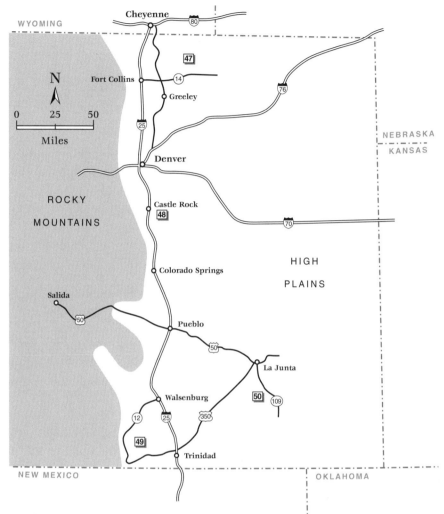

High Plains geology hikes

landscape, giving form to the horizon and exposing the older rock layers hidden beneath the younger veneer. It is within these riverine canyons and valleys that cross-sections of Colorado's history can be explored.

Like the mountains, the foundation of the High Plains is 1.7 billion-year-old Precambrian igneous and metamorphic *basement rock* that formed during repeated collisions along the North American Plate about where Wyoming is today. In the mountains, these basement rocks have ridden up and down in a series of mountain-building events. Since the plains were placid amid the chaos to the west, the basement of the High Plains still lies in the basement!

During Cambrian time, about 500 million years ago, the horizontal platform that underlies the plains was laid when a series of Paleozoic seas flooded Colorado, covering the basement rocks with layers of *sediment* each time the seas advanced and withdrew.

When these Paleozoic marine cycles were interrupted by uplift of the *Ancestral Rocky Mountains* about 300 million years ago during Pennsylvanian time, the High Plains remained part of the stable interior. As the mountains began to wear away, sand and gravel were piled by rivers in *alluvial fans* at the mouths of canyons. Along the mountain front, which was located about where the Front Range is today, winds whipped the sands into dunes. The riverborne alluvial fans became the Fountain Formation, and the wind-blown dunes became the Lyons Sandstone. Both layers underlie the extreme western edge of the plains, their upturned edges exposed like fringe in the *flatirons*.

When dinosaurs trod all across Colorado during the Mesozoic, rivers meandered across broad, swampy floodplains. Tracks and bones of dinosaurs are preserved within sedimentary layers, the most famous of which is the 150 million-year-old Jurassic Morrison Formation. The *shales* of the Morrison Formation vanished in erosion from the newly emerged Rockies, but they are well-preserved on the High Plains (and the Colorado Plateau). Dinosaur tracks are plentiful at the surface now because the Purgatoire River uncovered these older layers in the Picket Wire Canyonlands on the High Plains.

About 100 million years ago during the Cretaceous, Colorado's ancient landscape was again flooded by an ancient inland sea, called the *Cretaceous Seaway,* that stretched from the Arctic to the Gulf of Mexico. The plains became a beach, known today as the Dakota sandstone. As the coastline advanced and retreated across the region, this thick blanket of sandstone and shale accumulated on top of the older rock layers, adding to the stack.

Then about 75 million years ago, the sea slowly withdrew just before parts of Colorado began to rise. Mountain building of the *Laramide Orogeny* ensued, and the basement rocks of Colorado's Rockies began to push skyward.

Adjacent to the Laramide mountain building, parts of the High Plains were gently warped. Closest to the mountain front, a major downwarp called the Denver Basin filled with a thick pile of sediment shed from the rising Rockies. These eroded shards of mountains are preserved in the *arkose sandstone* and conglomerate of the Dawson Formation beneath Denver and exposed around Castle Rock. As the mountains continued to rise, the eroding streams carved into the basement rocks that core the mountains, dumping even more sediment into the flanking basin. In its deepest part, the Denver Basin is filled with more than 13,000 feet (nearly 2.5 miles) of sediment.

As the mountains continued to erode, streams also spread a veneer of sand and gravel across the plains as far as Kansas and Nebraska. One of the larger stream systems deposited the Castle Rock Conglomerate, a distinctive caprock exposed southeast of Denver. Then around 25 million years ago, the modern Rockies began their rise, elevating the High Plains and the Colorado Plateau on their shoulders.

The High Plains became grazing land for the first time as camels, rhinoceroses, horses, and tapirs plied the grasslands. Fossils of these animals, along with a strange beast with long horns called Titanotheres, are found in Colorado today in the Oligocene White River Formation exposed in such places as Pawnee Buttes.

Over the past 10 million years, the final pulse of uplift in the Rockies carried the High Plains to their present elevation. As the plains slowly uplifted and tilted to the east, the rivers widened their channels, cutting terraces and eroding deeper canyons through the rising mountains. It was during this time that the sand and gravel of the Ogallala Formation spread over the entire plains from Canada to Texas.

As uplift continued, the rivers flowed more forcefully, depositing less sediment and, instead, eroding the High Plains landscape. A flood of water from melting *Ice Age glaciers* over the past 2 million years contributed to the sculpting power of the rivers and their tributaries. They dissected the Plains, stripping away the younger sedimentary layers and uncovering the secrets of Colorado's past.

PAWNEE BUTTES

Hike 47

SEDIMENTARY BUTTES RISE ABOVE THE HIGH PLAINS

Hike across the plains to the base of the Pawnee Buttes, famous landmarks on the High Plains.

DISTANCE ■ **3 miles round trip**
ELEVATION ■ **5,400 to 5,150 feet**
DIFFICULTY ■ **Easy**
TOPOGRAPHIC MAPS ■ **USGS Pawnee Buttes and Grover SE**
GEOLOGIC MAP ■ **None**
KEY REFERENCE ■ **38**

PRECAUTIONS ■ To protect nesting birds of prey, from March 1 to June 30 please stay on the main trail and do not climb the escarpment. Collecting fossils is prohibited.

FOR INFORMATION ■ Pawnee National Grassland

About the Landscape: The Pawnee Buttes provide a little relief on the High Plains. They are famous landmarks that stand nearly 300 feet above the generally smooth plains on the Pawnee National Grassland.

The buttes are capped by resistant beds of Ogallala Formation *sandstone* and *conglomerate* that shield the sedimentary layers beneath from erosion. With the uplift of the plains beginning about 10 million years ago, streams cut down into and excavated parts of the Ogallala and the softer *sediments* of the Oligocene White River Formation beneath. The easily eroded layers of the White River Formation are preserved in the buttes only because they are capped by particularly resistant segments of the Ogallala.

Trail Guide: To reach the Pawnee Buttes Trailhead, drive east from Fort Collins 42 miles on Colorado Highway 14 to the town of Briggsdale. Following the signs for the Pawnee Trail Scenic Byway, turn left onto County Road 77 and drive 15.4 miles to County Road 120 (sign for Grover 6 miles). Turn right and follow this road 6.8 miles, being cautious of the sharp bends. At the T junction, turn right onto County Road 390 which immediately turns to gravel. Drive 5.9 miles then turn left onto County Road 112. After driving another 6.7 miles, turn right at the next T junction and follow signs for the Pawnee Buttes for another 3.3 miles to the trailhead.

The trail begins by heading east on a well-worn path along a shallow drainage. Immediately after passing through a gate, the trail forks. Take the right fork which winds up onto the ridge that extends eastward toward the Pawnee Buttes. During the bird of prey nesting period from March 1 to June 30, take the left fork instead.

The top of the ridge is capped by the resistant sandstones and conglomerates of the Ogallala Formation. As you cross the ridge toward the buttes, note the well-preserved *cross-beds* along the edge of the cliff or *escarpment*. The Ogallala sediments, which at one time spread over the entire Great Plains from Texas to Canada, were deposited by streams draining the eastern slope of the Rocky Mountains 10 to 5 million years ago during the Miocene. Look closely at the conglomerate to see pieces of *quartz* and *feldspar* that eroded from the Precambrian core of the Rocky Mountains.

Up until the end of Ogallala deposition, the High Plains sloped gently eastward. Then a change occurred from deposition of the Ogallala to downcutting by streams which disrupted this surface. The Ogallala has eroded in places, such as along the edge of this escarpment and around

212

The Pawnee Buttes are protected from erosion by the caprock of the Ogallala Formation.

the buttes. Once the Ogallala cap is removed by erosion, the soft underlying *mudstone* and *siltstone* layers of the White River Formation erode easily. Badlands often form, such as those that decorate the base of this escarpment, but eventually, most of this soft sediment washes downstream.

As you crest the ridge, a faint trail leads off to the right along the Ogallala escarpment. After enjoying the panoramic view to the right, return to the junction and take the left trail, stepping down through a series of Ogallala rock ledges to a drainage between receding escarpments.

About 1 mile from the trailhead, the two trails join to follow a common route to the base of West Pawnee Butte. As you look closely at the buff-colored White River Formation that makes up most of the butte, consider that within it are trapped the remnants of an ancient landscape. Paleontologists have uncovered fossils from more than 100 species of Oligocene vertebrates in this rock layer. Where you stand, camels once meandered on the skyline, wild horses galloped through wind-swept grasses, and tapirs and rhinoceroses drank at watering holes.

The trail rounds the south side of West Pawnee Butte, then joins an old road. About 0.25 mile down the road, a sign indicating private land marks the turnaround point for this hike. Follow the same route back to the trailhead or complete the short loop on the way back to your vehicle.

CASTLEWOOD CANYON

A CONGLOMERATION OF CASTLE ROCK CONGLOMERATE

Stream gravel washed by an ancient river system from the Rocky Mountains rims a canyon on the High Plains.

DISTANCE ■ 3.6-mile loop

ELEVATION ■ 6,560 to 6,160 feet

DIFFICULTY ■ Moderate

TOPOGRAPHIC MAP ■ USGS Castle Rock South

GEOLOGIC MAP ■ 34

KEY REFERENCE ■ 38

PRECAUTIONS ■ Beware of flash floods in the canyon bottom following summer thunderstorms. Use caution when exploring the conglomerate along the rim. Watch for poison ivy along forested sections of the trail.

FOR INFORMATION ■ Castlewood Canyon State Park

About the Landscape: The Castle Rock Conglomerate is found only in a limited area on the High Plains southeast of Denver. At Castlewood State Park, it forms the rim rock along a scenic canyon carved by Cherry Creek.

The Castle Rock Conglomerate is a grab bag of sand and gravel from the Rocky Mountains that flooded through an ancient river system onto the High Plains about 34 million years ago during the Oligocene. The Thirty-nine Mile volcanic field in South Park to the west spewed volcanic material into the mix and ultimately became cemented into the *conglomerate.*

Trail Guide: To reach the Westside Trailhead in Castlewood State Park, drive 6.5 miles east from Castle Rock on Colorado Highway 86. Turn right onto Castlewood Canyon Road and drive 2.1 miles on this road to the state park entrance station. Trailhead parking is located at the picnic area 1 mile past the entrance station.

This hike begins by following the Creek Bottom Trail upstream (south). From the trailhead in the picnic area, bear left at the first fork, then right at the next junction and follow the trail downslope into the canyon. The

Castle Rock Conglomerate up close

trail winds through the forest past large boulders of Castle Rock Conglomerate that have tumbled down from the rim.

The conglomerate boulders are a glued together assortment of sand, gravel, and boulders that washed down onto the High Plains about 34 million years ago. At that time, the Rockies were reduced to low, rounded mountains by the erosion that followed the Laramide uplift. The coarse sediment of the Castle Rock Conglomerate implies that this debris tumbled from slopes very nearby. This is somewhat of a mystery considering the subdued geologic conditions of the time. It may represent a short pulse of localized uplift that supplied a great quantity of sediment to this ancient river system, forming a sloping apron at the front of the uplift called an *alluvial fan.*

The trail reaches a fenced cliff along the canyon about 0.3 mile from the trailhead. Here is a good view across the canyon at the conglomerate cliffs that define the east rim. In the canyon bottom, Cherry Creek continues to shape the canyon by carving through the softer conglomeratic sandstone layers of the Dawson Formation that underlie the Castle Rock Conglomerate.

The Creek Bottom Trail continues down the canyon to the banks of Cherry Creek near the waterfall about 0.5 mile from the trailhead. Here you can explore an amazing array of boulders. Take time to look at the variety of rounded cobbles and boulders cemented into the rocks surrounding the trail. See if you can find some of the bowling ball–sized boulders of brown and pink *rhyolite* within the conglomerate. Imagine the great floods of an ancient river that transported these rocks from the Thirtynine Mile volcanic field in South Park.

The trail follows Cherry Creek for about another 0.5 mile past the signed junction with the Historic Dam Trail and then past the ruins of the dam itself above the trail on the right. After crossing the footbridge just past the dam, the trail becomes the Rim Rock Trail which climbs steeply over stone steps for about the next 0.25 mile up to the east rim of the canyon.

On top, the Rim Rock Trail follows north over a conglomerate pavement for about 1.5 miles along the rim of the canyon. At the edge of the rim, sets of *fractures* meeting at roughly right angles indicate how the rim retreats. As the conglomerate is undermined by erosion of the softer *sandstone* below, seasonal water seeps into the fractures and expands as it freezes, widening the fractures and eventually wedging rectangular blocks of conglomerate down from the rim.

As it reaches its northern end, the Rim Rock Trail winds down through the forest to the bottom of the canyon. As it descends from the rim, look for *cross-beds* in the tilted blocks of conglomerate along the trail. These cross-beds represent the inclined faces of gravel bars advancing in swift currents in the ancient river channel.

Ultimately, the trail crosses another footbridge over Cherry Creek where it meets the north end of the Creek Bottom Trail. Take the Creek Bottom Trail as it winds away from the creek and heads back to the Westside

Trailhead. About 100 yards from the creek, bear left at the junction with the Homestead Trail (no sign). To complete the loop, continue through the forest back to the trailhead.

WEST SPANISH PEAK

IGNEOUS ROCKS PIERCE THE HIGH PLAINS

Walk along a ridge or climb to the summit of West Spanish Peak, an igneous intrusion exhumed by uplift and erosion.

DISTANCE ▪ **5.5 miles round trip**

ELEVATION ▪ **11,248 to 13,626 feet**

DIFFICULTY ▪ **Easy hike along ridge; strenuous climb to summit**

TOPOGRAPHIC MAPS ▪ **USGS Cucharas Pass, Spanish Peaks, and Herlick Canyon**

GEOLOGIC MAPS ▪ **35, 36**

KEY REFERENCE ▪ **39**

PRECAUTIONS ▪ **Lightning storms are a serious concern during summer months. Be sure to get an early start for the summit. The last .75 mile climbs 2,000 feet—watch every step.**

FOR INFORMATION ▪ **San Carlos Ranger District**

About the Landscape: The Spanish Peaks are majestic mountains of *igneous rock* located on the High Plains near Colorado's southern border. Despite their almost perfect cone shape, these mountains did not form as volcanoes. They were the center for a cluster of igneous intrusions that cooled at depth about 25 million years ago and now are revealed at the surface by uplift and erosion.

East and West Spanish Peaks (12,683 and 13,626 feet) are unique for their network of igneous *dikes* that radiate out for miles like spokes on a wheel. Dikes are formed when *magma* cools within vertical *fractures* in rock. Over time, uplift and *differential erosion* of the less resistant *sedimentary rock* that surrounds the Spanish Peaks has exposed this internal "plumbing system." The dikes look like walls rising through the forest and extending out across the valley.

The strenuous hike to the summit of West Spanish Peak climaxes with a commanding 360-degree view, but an easy walk along the ridge offers many equally spectacular views of the area's geology.

Trail Guide: To reach the West Peak Trailhead, drive south from the small town of La Veta past the golf course on Colorado Highway 12. The road eventually climbs to Cucharas Pass (well past the ski resort) 16 miles from

Walls of igneous rock, called dikes, radiate out from the Spanish Peaks.

La Veta. At Cucharas Pass, turn left onto Forest Road 46 and drive 6 miles to the marked trailhead at Cordova Pass (formerly Apishapa Pass).

The hike begins by heading northwest through a stand of spruce trees that obscures West Spanish Peak from view. As you emerge from the trees into a small meadow, you get the first view of the peak.

The trail follows a mostly gentle grade along a ridge connected to the shoulder of West Spanish Peak. It cuts through swatches of forest and crosses several meadows where the rocks along the trail are mostly rounded cobbles and boulders of Precambrian *granite, gneiss,* and white *quartz.* These Precambrian rocks are from the Cordova Pass *conglomerate* in the Cucharas Formation, part of the thick pile of Eocene sedimentary rocks through which the Spanish Peaks intruded. They are remnants of a block of Precambrian basement that uplifted during the Laramide, eroded downstream, and then accumulated as an *alluvial fan* along the front of the Sangre de Cristo Range.

A short distance beyond the first outcrops of igneous rocks near the trail, you will see a scenic turnout on the left. Here you can survey the surrounding landscape while standing on a massive outcrop that is part of a dike. You might be tempted to call the rock you are standing on a true granite, but take a close look and convince yourself that quartz (typically clear or translucent) is not present. The large crystals, called phenocrysts, are *feldspar* minerals which are surrounded by black peppery flakes of *hornblende.* This rock is called syenite, a quartz-poor *granitic* rock that makes up much of West Spanish Peak.

In the distance, a number of other dikes pierce the maroon sedimentary rocks of the Cucharas Formation, rising above the forest and extending out into Cucharas Valley to the north. The prominant white ridge is a *hogback* of Cretaceous Dakota Sandstone that extends for miles along the lower slopes of the Culebra Range. Goemmer Butte, a circular plug of *volcanic rock,* is the isolated mass of rock in the valley.

Eventually, the trail works its way down the side of the dike through an Aspen grove. After reaching a saddle, the trail takes its first major bend and starts to climb. At the bend, the rock on the hillside changes abruptly to the maroon *sandstone* of the Cucharas Formation which forms the side of the mountain almost all the way to the summit.

At the next switchback, you reach the junction with the Apishapa Trail. Here, turn left and climb the switchbacks through bristlecone pine trees. As the trail climbs more steeply, you come to a switchback to the right, just below treeline. Above, on the bare mountainside, are the welded remains of the Cucharas sedimentary layers "cooked" by the igneous intrusion of West Spanish Peak. In places you can see how dark igneous rocks have squeezed up through the sedimentary layers.

Continue climbing until you are standing above treeline. Now it's decision time. There is no longer a beaten trail before you. The route from here climbs 0.75 mile up the steep, rocky face of the peak. It's a safe climb if you watch every step.

The view from the top puts you at the center of the igneous *stock* and its many radiating dikes. To the east is the domed summit of East Spanish Peak, a slightly younger sister igneous intrusion.

The descent off the mountain is a bit of a scramble; be careful in areas of loose rock. Once back down to the trail, simply retrace your footsteps back to the trailhead.

 Hike 50

DINOSAUR LAKE

DINOSAUR TRACKS IN PICKET WIRE CANYONLANDS

Hike to a dinosaur crossroads at a Jurassic watering hole in the Morrison Formation.

DISTANCE ■ **10.6 miles round trip**
ELEVATION ■ **4,660 to 4,350 feet**
DIFFICULTY ■ **Moderate**
TOPOGRAPHIC MAPS ■ **USGS Riley Canyon and Beaty Canyon**
GEOLOGIC MAP ■ **36**

KEY REFERENCE ■ **40**

PRECAUTIONS ■ Camping is not allowed in Picket Wire Canyonlands. Use caution crossing the river to the tracksite.

FOR INFORMATION ■ Picket Wire Canyonlands

About the Landscape: A walk into the canyons along the Purgatoire River is a walk back in time that brings you to North America's largest dinosaur tracksite. Picket Wire Canyon is sliced into a slight uplift of the High Plains by the Purgatoire River, revealing the older rock layers that underlie the plains as well as footprints of the reptiles that once traversed them.

Giant plant-eating brontosaurs, along with smaller meat-eating allosaurs, approached a one-time watering hole by tracking through soft, limey mud during the Jurassic about 150 million years ago. Today, their tracks, along with traces of more than 100 other animals, are preserved in *limestone* layers that are now part of the Morrison Formation. Picket Wire Canyonlands is one of the most accessible sites for viewing this formation along the shoreline of ancient "Dinosaur Lake."

Trail Guide: To reach the Picket Wire Canyonlands Trailhead, drive 13 miles south from La Junta on Colorado Highway 109. Turn right (west) onto County Road 802 at the sign for Vogel and Picket Wire Canyons and follow signs to Picket Wire Canyon. After 8.1 miles, turn left (south) at another sign and continue for 6.2 miles to yet another sign and bulletin board. If it has rained recently, the road to the trailhead may be closed. (It is possible to park here and walk to the trailhead, but this adds 7 miles round trip to the hike.) Turn left at the sign again and follow Forest Service Road 500A for 3.5 miles to the trailhead at the end of the road.

From the trail register, the trail follows an old road that drops steeply below a ledge of ripplemarked Dakota Sandstone into Withers Canyon, a tributary of Picket Wire Canyon. In the canyon bottom, a well-worn trail leads to the main drainage of the Purgatoire River. About 1 mile from the trailhead, turn right at the sign pointing toward the dinosaur tracks.

About 2.5 miles from the trailhead, the trail begins to climb above a bend in the Purgatoire River. This is the best view of the river from the trail. For about the next 0.5 mile, the trail winds among large boulders of 100 million-year-old Dakota Sandstone that have tumbled down from the cliffs above. At the crest of the first rise, look for a large broken boulder above the trail on the right. Petroglyphs are etched into the *sandstone* inside the split where the boulder is broken on its west face.

The trail passes an 1890s cemetery and the crumbling remains of the Dolores Mission about 3.7 miles from the trailhead.

About 1 mile before reaching the dinosaur tracks, the trail passes

Dinosaur tracks preserved in the rocks spark the imagination.

between some low hills capped by brown sandstone. Below the sandstone is the gray-green and maroon *shale* of the Morrison Formation. The soft pastel-colored shale exposed here on these hills represents muddy *sediment* deposited on the floodplain of a river during the Jurassic. The Morrison Formation is famous for its dinosaur fossils, including the trackways here in Picket Wire Canyon.

After about 5 miles, the road forks. A sign points to the left toward the dinosaur tracks. The tracks are located along the river below a parking area.

Which dinosaur tracks are visible depends on recent flooding which can cover some tracks and expose others. Three-toed tracks of carnivorous allosaurs ply the ground near the sign describing the site area. The main brontosaur tracksite is located on the opposite side of the river, upstream from the sign. Use caution when crossing the river, especially during high flows after recent rains.

Once on the opposite side, walk along the top of the gray limestone rocks above river level. This limestone layer is also in the Morrison Formation. Look for shallow depressions leading across these rocks. The depressions are tracks of giant brontosaurs that trod here about 150 million years ago during the Jurassic.

Look closely at the rock to see minute circles called ooids. Ooids are small grains of calcium carbonate sand that form tiny balls when washed back and forth by waves and currents. You are standing on the shore of a lake that was a watering hole where dinosaurs came to drink and forage on vegetation. The landscape surrounding you was probably not unlike the semi-arid plains of East Africa today.

The brontosaur tracks found at this site were the first ever recorded in the world. The parallel orientation of the many tracks indicates that a group of animals were traveling together in the same direction. This suggests social behavior never before suspected in dinosaurs. In all, more than 1,300 tracks have been found along the river at this site, making it the largest dinosaur trackway found in North America, and perhaps the world.

When you have filled your imagination with the dinosaurs that walked before you, simply follow your steps back to the trailhead.

Roadsign from a vanished era

Glossary

alluvial fan—a large fan-shaped accumulation of sediment deposited by streams where they emerge at the front of a mountain range

Ancestral Rocky Mountains—ancient mountains (the Uncompahgre and Front Range Highlands) that rose 300 million years ago near where the Front Range and Uncompahgre Plateau are today

andesite—fine-grained, medium gray volcanic rock of intermediate composition between rhyolite and basalt

anticline—upward fold in rock layers that creates an arched or domelike uplift of sedimentary layers

arkose sandstone—a type of sandstone containing more than 25 percent feldspar

basalt—fine-grained, dark-colored volcanic rock rich in iron-bearing minerals

basement rock—in Colorado, the oldest rocks of Precambrian age, generally composed of gneiss, schist, and granitic rocks over 1 billion years old

batholith—a large body of igneous rock that cooled underground, greater in size than 60 square miles

brachiopod—ancient clamlike sea animals, commonly found as fossil shells in Paleozoic limestones

breccia—conglomerate-like rock made up of angular pieces of volcanic rock usually bound in volcanic ash; also called volcanic breccia

calcite—light-colored mineral composed of calcium carbonate ($CaCO_3$) that often fills veins in igneous rocks and forms the sedimentary rock limestone

caldera—large circular depression formed by explosion or collapse of a volcano; sometimes called a crater

Central Colorado Trough—elongate down-dropped basin area located between uplifts of the Ancestral Rocky Mountains that existed about 300 to 245 million years ago

cirque—bowl-like depression carved into a mountaintop by ice at the head of a glacier

composite volcano—volcano built from layers of pyroclastics (ash and rock debris) alternating with solidified lava flows; also called stratovolcano

conglomerate—sedimentary rock composed of rounded gravel (pebbles, cobbles, and boulders) cemented together, usually found with sandstone

continental accretion—growth or increase in size of a continent by collision of tectonic plates that then become part of the continental mass; often results in mountain building and intense metamorphism

Cretaceous Seaway—shallow inland sea that stretched from the arctic to the Gulf of Mexico and flooded Colorado about 100 million years ago

crinoid—ancient stalked marine animal, commonly found as small, disk-shaped fossils from the segmented stems in Paleozoic limestones

cross-bed—pattern of slanting parallel lines common in sedimentary rocks (typically sandstone) that marks advancing crests of wind-blown dunes or water-transported sediment

differential erosion—varying rates of weathering, most common in sedimentary rocks, where some areas or layers of rock are more resistant than others

dike—narrow igneous intrusion along vertical fractures cut through surrounding rock

end moraine—ridge of sediment piled at the front edge of a glacier; also called terminal moraine

erratic—boulder transported by a glacier and left behind when the ice melted

escarpment—cliff or steep slope edging higher land

exfoliation—process of weathering and erosion common in granitic rocks in which concentric slabs of rock break off from the larger rock mass; forms a large, rounded landform called an exfoliation dome

extrusive igneous rock—molten rock that cools at the earth's surface (volcanic)

fault—break in rocks along which movement has occurred

fault-block—uplifted section of rock bounded on both sides by faults; also called a **horst**

feldspar—group of light-colored minerals often found as crystals in intrusive igneous rocks; the most common rock-forming mineral

flatirons—triangular-shaped landforms along mountain ranges formed by erosion of steeply inclined rock layers or hogbacks

fracture—crack or break in rocks along which no movement has occurred; also called a **joint**

glacier—thick mass of ice moving under the influence of gravity that forms by compaction and recrystallization of old snow; also called ice sheet

gneiss—metamorphic rock that displays distinct banding of light and dark mineral layers (pronounced "nice")

graben—down-dropped block of rock bounded on both sides by faults

granite—light-colored, coarse-grained intrusive igneous rock with quartz and feldspar as dominant minerals and typically peppered with mica and hornblende

granitic—general term for all light-colored, granitelike igneous rocks

granodiorite—coarse-grained intrusive igneous rock with less quartz and more feldspar than true granite and typically darker

Great Unconformity—*see* **unconformity**

hand lens—small magnifying glass used to examine rocks up close

hanging valley—valley whose floor is high above a main valley, usually formed where a small side glacier once met a large glacier

hogback—ridge formed by erosion of resistant, steeply inclined sedimentary layers, such as the Dakota hogback

hornblende—black bladelike mineral common in igneous and metamorphic rocks

hornfels—fine-grained, gray-green metamorphic rock produced by "baking" of sedimentary rocks by an igneous intrusion in which sedimentary features may still be preserved

horst—uplifted section of rock, or fault-block, bounded on both sides by faults

hydrothermal—describes rocks and minerals formed or altered by hot water generated deep underground; associated with mineral deposits and hot springs

Ice Age—general term for repeated glacial episodes during the Pleistocene (1.8 million to 8,000 years ago)

igneous rock—rock that forms from the solidification of molten rock or magma

intrusive igneous rock—molten rock emplaced within preexisting rock that cools and hardens below the surface

laccolith—igneous intrusion that squeezes between sedimentary layers and domes the overlying layers

Laramide Orogeny—major Rocky Mountain uplift event between 70 and 45 million years ago when huge blocks of basement rocks pushed up from below, warping overlying sedimentary layers into broad anticlines

lateral moraine—ridgelike pile of sediment along the side of a glacier

lava—fluid, molten igneous rock erupted on the earth's surface

limestone—sedimentary rock composed mostly of the mineral calcite and often containing marine fossils

Little Ice Age—recent but minor glacial period between 700 and 200 years ago when many of North America's glaciers advanced

magma—molten or fluid rock material from which igneous rock is derived

mantle—a thick layer of rock deep within the earth that separates the earth's crust above from the earth's core below

marble—metamorphic rock formed by the "baking" and recrystallization of limestone

metamorphic rock—a rock formed from a preexisting rock that is altered ("baked") by high temperatures and pressures, causing minerals to recrystallize but not melt

mica—group of minerals that form thin, platy flakes, typically with shiny surfaces, especially common in metamorphic rocks

migmatite—rock composed of a complex mixture of metamorphic rock and igneous granitic rock

monocline—bend or steplike fold in rock layers where all strata are inclined in the same direction

mudstone—fine-grained sedimentary rock formed from hardened clay and silt that lacks the thin layers typical of shale

Pangea—an ancient supercontinent that began breaking apart about 200 million years ago to form the present-day continents

pegmatite—very coarse-grained intrusive igneous rock of granitic composition that typically fills fractures to form veins

plate—large, mobile slab of crustal rock making up large sections of the earth's surface; also called tectonic plate

plate tectonics—theory that the earth's surface is divided into huge slabs of rock (tectonic plates) that move relative to one another causing earthquakes, mountain building, and other geologic events

pluton—intrusive igneous body that cools deep underground, such as a batholith

pyroclastic—ash mixed with larger igneous rock fragments produced by explosive volcanic eruptions

quartz—very hard, clear or translucent mineral composed of silica (SiO_2)

quartzite— metamorphic rock composed of sand-sized quartz grains that have fused together by heat and pressure; also a hard, well-cemented quartz-rich sandstone, such as the Sawatch Quartzite

rhyolite—light-colored volcanic igneous rock that is the extrusive equivalent of granite

rifting—process whereby the earth's crust is stretched and thinned, usually where two plates or sections of plates are pulling apart, such as in the Rio Grande Rift

Rio Grande Rift—A network of deep, down-faulted valleys or grabens that extend from the upper Arkansas Valley near Leadville, and continue south through the San Luis Valley and into New Mexico along the Rio Grande River

ripplemarks—small ridges preserved on sedimentary rock surfaces formed by moving wind or water when the sediment was deposited

rock—naturally formed, consolidated material composed of grains of one or more minerals

rock glacier—glacierlike tongue of boulders or broken rock moving slowly downhill that is usually cored with water or ice

Rocky Mountain Surface—flattened Eocene-age land surface formed by erosion of Laramide Orogeny uplifts

salt—general term for sediment formed by evaporation of seawater; includes the minerals halite (table salt) and gypsum (calcium sulfate)

sandstone—sedimentary rock composed of sand-sized grains (usually quartz) cemented together

schist—metamorphic rock composed of platy mica minerals aligned in the same direction

sediment—collection of loose, solid particles usually weathered and eroded from preexisting rocks, but can also be crystallized from water (such as salt) or secreted by organisms (such as fossil shells)

sedimentary rock—rock resulting from the consolidation of loose eroded sediment, remains of organisms, or crystals forming directly from water

shale—fine-grained sedimentary rock formed from hardened clay and silt that typically splits into thin layers

sill—sheetlike intrusive igneous rock intruded between horizontal layers of sedimentary rock (compare to **dike**)

siltstone—fine-grained sedimentary rock composed mainly of silt-sized particles

slate—fine-grained metamorphic rock formed by "baking" and recrystallizing shale or mudstone and which splits easily along flat, parallel planes

stock—medium-sized igneous intrusion smaller than a batholith, not greater in size than 60 square miles

strata—distinct layers of stratified rock

stratigraphy—study or description of layered or stratified rocks

striation—scratch or groove in bedrock caused by rocks within a glacier grinding the earth's surface as the glacier moves

subduction—process whereby one tectonic plate descends beneath another

syncline—troughlike downward sag or fold in rock layers (opposite of an anticline)

talus—accumulation of broken rocks or boulders at the base of a cliff

thrust fault—special kind of "reverse" fault in which older rock layers are pushed up and over younger layers; movement takes place along a low-angle or almost horizontal surface

tuff—igneous rock formed from hardened volcanic ash

unconformity—surface that represents a break or gap in the geologic record where rock layers were eroded or never deposited, such as the Great Unconformity which separates younger sedimentary layers above from much older basement rocks below

vesicles—tiny holes in volcanic rock caused by gas bubbles trapped in lava when it cooled (vesicular)

volcanic rock—rock that forms from the solidification of molten rock or magma at the earth's surface (extrusive igneous rock)

Appendix A
Recommended Reading

The American Alps: The San Juan Mountains of Southwest Colorado. D.L. Baars. Albuquerque: University of New Mexico Press, 1992.

Calderas of the San Juan volcanic field, southwestern Colorado. T.A. Stevens and P.W. Lipman. USGS Professional Paper 958, 1976.

Cenozoic History of the Southern Rocky Mountains. B.F. Curtis (ed.). Boulder: Geological Society of America, Memoir 144, 1975.

The Colorado. F. Waters. Athens, Ohio: Swallow Press, 1985.

Colorado Geology. H.C. Kent and K.W. Porter (eds.). Denver: Rocky Mountain Association of Geologists, 1980.

Colorado's Dinosaurs. J.T. Jenkins and J.L. Jenkins. Denver: Colorado Geological Survey, 1993.

Colorado: The Place of Nature, the Nature of Place. T.P. Huber. Niwot, Colorado: University Press of Colorado, 1993.

Colorado West: Land of Geology and Wildflowers. R.G. Young and J.W. Young. Grand Junction: Robert G. Young, 1984.

The Field Guide to Geology. D. Lambert. New York: Facts on File, 1988.

Geologic Highway Map. Colorado Geological Survey, 1991. 1:1,000,000.

Geologic History of the Colorado Front Range. D.W. Boyland and S.A. Sonnenberg. Denver: The Rocky Mountain Association of Geologists, 1997.

Geologic Map of Colorado. O. Tweto. USGS, 1979. 1:500,000.

The Geologic Story of the Great Plains. D.E. Trimble. Theodore Roosevelt Nature and History Association, 1990.

Geology of Colorado Illustrated. D.R. Fouts. Grand Junction: Your Geologist, 1994.

Guide to the Colorado Mountains. R.M. Ormes. Boulder, Colorado: Johnson Books, 1992.

The Historical Atlas of the Earth. R. Osborne and D. Tarling. New York: Henry Holt and Company, 1996.

Pages of Stone—Geology of Western National Parks and Monuments. Number 1: Rocky Mountains and Western Great Plains. H. Chronic. Seattle: The Mountaineers, 1988.

Pages of Stone—Geology of Western National Parks and Monuments. Number 4: Grand Canyon and the Plateau Country. H. Chronic. Seattle: The Mountaineers, 1988.

Physical Geology. C.C. Plummer and D. McGeary. Dubuque, Iowa: William C. Brown, 1996.

The Practical Geologist. D. Dixon and R.L. Bernor (eds.). New York:
   Simon and Schuster, 1992.
Prairie, Peak, and Plateau. J. Chronic and H. Chronic. Denver, Colorado:
   Geological Survey Bulletin 32, 1972.
Radiant Days—Writings by Enos Mills. J. Dotson (ed.). Salt Lake City:
   University of Utah Press, 1994.
Rising from the Plains. J. McPhee. New York: Farrar, Straus, Giroux, 1986.
Roadside Geology of Colorado. H. Chronic. Missoula, Montana: Mountain
   Press Publishing Company, 1980.
The Southern Rockies: A Sierra Club Naturalist's Guide. A.D. Benedict. San
   Francisco: Sierra Club Books, 1991.
The Southern Rocky Mountains. P. Larkin et al. K/H Field Guide Series.
   Dubuque, Iowa: Kendall/Hunt, 1980.

Another fan of Colorado's rocks—a marmot relaxing on a talus pile

Appendix B
Key References

1. Late Cenozoic history of the Northern Colorado Front Range. D.W. Boyland. In: Boyland, D.W. and Sonnenberg, S.A. (eds.). *Geologic History of the Colorado Front Range.* Rocky Mountain Association of Geologists, 1997, p. 125-133.
2. The geology and structure of the Mt. Richthofen–Iron Mt. region, north central Colorado. M.K. Corbett. *The Mountain Geologist,* v. 3, no. 1, 1964, p. 3-21.
3. *Time, Rocks, and the Rockies: A Geologic Guide to Roads and Trails of Rocky Mountain National Park.* H.A. Chronic. Missoula, Montana, Mountain Press Pub. Co., 1984.
4. *Mineral Resources of the Indian Peaks Study Area, Boulder and Grand Counties, Colorado.* R.C. Pearson. USGS Bulletin 1463, 1980, 109p.
5. The Mount Evans batholith in the Colorado Front Range: Revision and reinterpretation of its structure. J.N. Aleinikoff et al. *Geological Society of America Bulletin,* v. 105, 1993, p. 791-806.
6. Granite-tectonics of the Pikes Peak intrusive center of Pikes Peak composite batholith, Colorado. R.M. Hutchinson. In: Beus, S.S. (ed.). *Centennial Field Guide.* Geological Society of America, Rocky Mountain Section, v. 2, 1987, p. 331-334.
7. Florissant Fossil Beds National Monument: Preservation of an Ancient Ecosystem. H.W. Meyer and L. Weber. *Rocks and Minerals,* v. 70, 1995, p. 232-239.
8. Petrology and structure of the southern Wet Mountains, Colorado. R.E. Boyer. *Geological Society of America Bulletin,* v. 73, no. 9, 1962, p. 1047-1070.
9. *A Field Guide to Dinosaur Ridge.* M. Lockley and L. Marquard. Friends of Dinosaur Ridge and University of Colorado at Denver Dinosaur Trackers Research Group, 1995, 32p.
10. Bedrock geology of the Kassler quadrangle, Colorado. G.R. Scott. *USGS Professional Paper 421-B,* 1963, 125p.
11. *A Guide to the Geological History of the Pikes Peak Region.* J.B. Noblett. Colorado College, 1994, 43p.

12. General geology of the Hahns Peak and Farewell Mountains quadrangles, Routt County, Colorado. K. Sagerstrom and E.J. Young. *USGS Bulletin,* v. 1349, 1972, 63p.

13. Geology of the southwestern North Park and vicinity, Colorado. W.J. Hail, Jr. *USGS Bulletin,* v. 1257, 119p.

14. Mineral Resources of the Gore Range–Eagles Nest Primitive Area and Vicinity, Summit and Eagle Counties, Colorado. O. Tweto et al. *USGS Bulletin,* v. 1319-C, 1970, 127p.

15. *Aspen High Country—The Geology.* D. Laing and N. Lampiris. Aspen, Colorado, Thunder River Press, 1980, p. 38-40.

16. Geology of the southern Mosquito Range, Colorado. J. Chronic. *Mountain Geologist,* v. 1, no. 3, 1964, p. 103-113.

17. Extensive zeolitization associated with hot springs in central Colorado. W.N. Sharp. *USGS Professional Paper 700-B,* 1970, p. B14-B20.

18. The Great Sand Dunes of Southern Colorado. R.B. Johnson. *USGS Professional Paper 575-C,* 1967, p. C177-C183.

19. Laramide and Neogene structure of the northern Sangre de Cristo Range, south-central Colorado. D.A. Lindsey et al. In: Lowell, J.D. (ed.). *Rocky Mountain Foreland Basins and Uplifts.* Rocky Mountain Association of Geologists, 1983, p. 219-228.

20. Mineral resources of the Flat Tops primitive area, Colorado. W.W. Mallory et al. *USGS Bulletin,* v. 1230-C, 1966, 30p.

21. The Geologic Story of the Aspen Region. B. Bryant. *USGS Bulletin,* v. 1603, 1988, 53p.

22. West Elk volcanic field, Gunnison and Delta Counties, Colorado. D.L. Gaskill et al. In: Epis, R.C. (ed.). *Western Slope Colorado.* New Mexico Geological Society, 32nd Field Conference Guidebook, 1981, p. 305-316.

23. Grenadier fault block, Coalbank to Molas Passes, southwest Colorado. D.L. Baars et al. In: Beus, S.S. (ed.). *Centennial Field Guide.* Geological Society of America, Rocky Mountain Section, v. 2, 1987, p. 343-348.

24. Mineral resources of study areas contiguous to the Uncompahgre Primitive Area, San Juan Mountains, southwestern Colorado. T.A. Steven et al. *USGS Bulletin,* v. 1391-C, 1977, 126p.

25. *The American Alps: The San Juan Mountains of Southwest Colorado.* D.L. Baars. University of New Mexico Press, 1992, p. 143-144.

26. Mineral resources of the La Garita Wilderness, San Juan Mountains, southwestern Colorado. T.A. Stevens and C.L. Bienwiski. *USGS Bulletin,* v. 1420, 1977, 65p.

27. The Slumgullion Earth Flow: A Large Scale Natural Laboratory. D.J. Varnes and W.Z. Savage (eds.). *USGS Bulletin,* v. 2130, 1996, 95p.

28. Evolution of the Platoro caldera complex and related volcanic rocks, southeastern San Juan Mountains, Colorado. P.W. Lipman. *USGS Professional Paper 852,* 1975, 128p.

29. *Guide to the geology of Mesa Verde National Park.* M.O. Griffitts. Mesa Verde Museum Association, 1990, 88p.

30. The Jurassic section along McElmo Canyon in southwestern Colorado. R.O. O'Sullivan. In: *Mesozoic Geology and Paleontology of the Four Corners Region.* New Mexico Geological Guidebook, 48th Field Conference, 1997, p. 109-114.

31. Paradox Valley, Colorado; A collapsed salt anticline. W.L. Chenowith. In: Beus, S.S. (ed.). *Centennial Field Guide.* Geological Society of America, Rocky Mountain Section, v. 2, 1987, p. 339-342.

32. Ancient drainage changes in and south of Unaweep Canyon, southwestern Colorado. S.W. Lohman. In: Epis, R.C. (ed.). *Western Slope Colorado.* New Mexico Geological Society, 32nd Field Conference Guidebook, 1981, p. 137-143.

33. The geologic story of Colorado National Monument. S.W. Lohman. *USGS Bulletin,* v. 1508, 1981, 142p.

34. *The Black Canyon of the Gunnison: In Depth.* W.R. Hansen. Southwest Parks and Monuments Association, 1987, 57p.

35. *Colorado West: Land of Geology and Wildflowers.* R.G. Young and J.W. Young. Grand Junction, Colorado, Robert G. Young, 1984, 46p.

36. *Colorado's Dinosaurs.* J.T. Jenkins and J.L. Jenkins. Colorado Geological Survey, 1993, 74p.

37. Neogene tectonics and geomorphology of the eastern Uinta Mountains in Utah, Colorado, and Wyoming. W.R. Hansen. *USGS Professional Paper 1356,* 1986, 78p.

38. *The Geologic Story of the Great Plains.* D.E. Trimble. Theodore Roosevelt Nature and History Association, 1990, 54p.

39. Geology of the igneous rocks of the Spanish Peaks region, Colorado. R.B. Johnson. *USGS Professional Paper 594-G,* 1968, p. G1-G47.

40. *Dinosaur Lake: The Story of the Purgatoire Valley Dinosaur Tracksite Area.* M.G. Lockley et al. Colorado Geological Survey Special Publication 40, 1997, 64p.

Appendix C
Geologic Maps

1. Geologic map of the Poudre Park quadrangle, Larimer County, Colorado. W. A. Braddock et al., *USGS Map GQ-1620,* 1988. 1:24,000.
2. Geologic map of the Mount Richthofen quadrangle and the western part of Fall River Pass quadrangle, Grand and Jackson Counties, Colorado. J.M., O'Neil, *USGS Misc. Investigations Series Map I-1291,* 1981. 1:24,000.
3. Geologic map of Rocky Mountain National Park and vicinity, Colorado. W.A. Braddock and C.C. Cole, *USGS Misc. Investigations Series Map I-1973,* 1990. 1:50,000.
4. Mineral resources of the Indian Peaks study area, Boulder and Grand Counties, Colorado. R.C. Pearson, *USGS Bulletin,* v. 1463, 1980.
5. Geologic map of the Denver 1-degree x 2-degree quadrangle, north-central Colorado. B. Bryant et al., *USGS Misc. Investigations Series Map I-1163,* 1981. 1:250,000.
6. Geologic map of the Pueblo 1-degree x 2-degree quadrangle, south-central Colorado. G.R. Scott et al., *USGS Misc. Investigations Series Map I-1022,* 1978. 1:250,000.
7. Geologic map of the Florissant 15-minute quadrangle, Park and Teller Counties, Colorado. R.A. Wobus and R.C. Epis, *USGS Misc. Investigations Series Map I-1044,* 1978. 1:62,500.
8. Geologic map of the Trinidad quadrangle, south-central Colorado. R.B. Johnson, *USGS Misc. Investigations Series Map I-558,* 1969. 1:250,000.
9. Geologic map of Morrison quadrangle, Jefferson County, Colorado. G.R. Scott, *USGS Misc. Investigations Series Map I-790-A,* 1972. 1:24,000.
10. Bedrock geology of the Kassler quadrangle, Jefferson County, Colorado. G.R. Scott, *USGS Professional Paper 421-B,* 1963. 1:24,000.
11. Geologic map of the Colorado Springs–Castle Rock area, Front Range Urban Corridor, Colorado. D.E. Trimble and M.N. Machette, *USGS Misc. Investigations Series Map I-857-F,* 1979. 1:100,000.

12. General geology of the Hahns Peak and Farewell Mountains quadrangles, Routt County, Colorado. K. Sagerstrom and E.J. Young, *USGS Bulletin,* v. 1349, 1972.
13. Geologic map of the Craig 1-degree x 2-degree quadrangle, northwestern Colorado. O. Tweto, *USGS Misc. Investigations Series Map 1-972,* 1976. 1:250,000.
14. Geology of the southwestern North Park and vicinity, Colorado. W.J. Hail, Jr., *USGS Bulletin,* v. 1257. 1:24,000.
15. Mineral Resources of the Gore Range-Eagles Nest Primitive Area and Vicinity, Summit and Eagle Counties, Colorado. O. Tweto et al., *USGS Bulletin,* v. 1319-C, 1970. 1:48,000.
16. Geologic map of the Leadville 1-degree x 2-degree quadrangle, northwestern Colorado. O. Tweto et al., *USGS Misc. Investigations Series Map I-999,* 1978. 1:250,000.
17. Preliminary geologic map of the Montrose 1-degree x 2-degree quadrangle, southwestern Colorado. O. Tweto et al., *USGS Map MF-761,* 1976. 1:250,000.
18. Geologic map of the Trinidad quadrangle, south-central Colorado. R.B. Johnson, *USGS Misc. Geol. Investigations Map I-558,* 1969. 1:250,000.
19. Reconnaissance geologic map of the Sangre de Cristo Wilderness study area, south-central Colorado. R.B. Johnson et al., *USGS Misc. Field Studies Map MF-1635-B,* 1987. 1:62,500.
20. Reconnaissance geologic map of parts of the Twin Peaks and Blanca Peaks quadrangles, Alamosa, Costilla, and Huerfano Counties, Colorado. B.R. Johnson and R.M. Bruce, *USGS Misc. Field Investigations Map MF-2169,* 1991. 1:24,000.
21. Geologic Map of Maroon Bells quadrangle, Pitkin and Gunnison Counties, Colorado. B. Bryant, *USGS Map GQ-788,* 1979. 1:24,000.
22. Geologic Map of the Hayden Peak quadrangle. B. Bryant, *USGS Map GQ-863,* 1970. 1:24,000.
23. Geologic map of the Lake City Caldera area, western San Juan Mountains, southwestern Colorado. P.W. Lipman, *USGS Misc. Investigations Series Map I-962,* 1976. 1:48,000.
24. Geologic map of the Telluride quadrangle, southwestern Colorado. W.S. Burbank and R.G. Luedke, *USGS Map GQ-504,* 1966. 1:24,000.
25. Geologic map of the Ouray quadrangle. R.G. Luedke and W.S. Burbank, *USGS Map GQ-152,* 1962. 1:24,000.
26. Geologic map of the Durango quadrangle, southwestern Colorado. T.A. Stevens et al., *USGS Misc. Investigations Series Map I-764,* 1974. 1:250,000.

27. Geologic map of the Mesa Verde area, Montezuma County, Colorado. A.A. Wanek, *USGS Oil and Gas Investigations Map OM-152,* 1954. 1:63,360.

28. Geology, structure, and uranium deposits of the Cortez quadrangle, Colorado and Utah. D.D. Haynes et al., *USGS Misc. Geol. Investigations Map I-629,* 1972. 1:250,000.

29. Geology of the salt anticline region of southwestern Colorado. F.W. Carter, *USGS Professional Paper 637,* 1970. 1:62,000.

30. Geology, structure, and uranium deposits of the Moab quadrangle, Colorado and Utah. P.L. Williams, *USGS Misc. Geol. Investigations Map I-360,* 1964. 1:250,000.

31. Geology and structure of Grand Junction quadrangle, Colorado and Utah. P.L. Williams, *USGS Misc. Geol. Investigations Map I-736,* 1973. 1:250,000.

32. Geologic Map of the Black Canyon of the Gunnison River and vicinity, western Colorado. W.R. Hansen, *USGS Misc. Geol. Investigations Map I-584,* 1971. 1:31,680.

33. Geologic map of Dinosaur National Monument and vicinity, Utah and Colorado. W.R. Hansen et al., *USGS Misc. Investigations Series Map I-1407,* 1983. 1:50,000.

34. Geologic map of the Denver 1-degree x 2-degree quadrangle, north-central Colorado. B. Bryant et al., *USGS Misc. Investigations Series Map I-1163,* 1981. 1:250,000.

35. Reconnaissance geologic map of the Cucharas Pass quadrangle, Huerfano and Las Animas Counties, Colorado. D.A. Lindsey, *USGS Misc. Field Studies Map MF-2294,* 1996. 1:24,000.

36. Geologic and structure contour map of the La Junta Quadrangle, Colorado and Kansas. G.R. Scott, *USGS Misc. Geol. Investigations Map I-560,* 1968. 1:250,000.

Appendix D
Addresses and Contact Information

Anasazi Heritage Center, Bureau of Land Management, 27501 Colorado Highway 184, Dolores, CO 81323; (970) 882-4811

Aspen Ranger District, White River National Forest, 806 West Hallam, Aspen, CO 81611; (970) 925-3445

Black Canyon of the Gunnison National Park, 102 Elk Creek, Gunnison, CO 81230; (970) 641-2337

Boulder Ranger District, Roosevelt National Forest, 2995 Baseline Road, Rm. 110, Boulder, CO 80303; (303) 444-6600

Box Canyon City Park, P.O. Box 468, Ouray, CO 81427; (970) 325-4464

Castlewood Canyon State Park, 2989 S. Highway 83, Franktown, CO 80116; (303) 688-5242

Clear Creek Ranger District, Arapaho National Forest, P.O. Box 3307, Idaho Springs, CO 80452; (303) 567-3000

Colorado National Monument, Fruita, CO 81521-9530; (970) 858-3617

Colorado State Forest, 2746 Jackson County Road 41, Walden, CO 80480; (970) 723-8366

Columbine Ranger District, San Juan National Forest, Box 439, 367 S. Pearl, Bayfield, CO 81122; (970) 884-2512

Dinosaur National Monument, 4545 East Highway 40, Dinosaur, CO 81610; (970) 374-3000

Dinosaur Ridge Visitors Center, 16831 W. Alameda Parkway, Morrison, CO 80465-9703; (303) 697-3466

Eagle Ranger District, White River NF, P.O. Box 720, 120 W. 5th, Eagle, CO 81631; (970) 328-6388

Estes-Poudre Ranger District, Roosevelt National Forest, 1311 South College, Fort Collins, CO 80524; (970) 498-2775

Florissant Fossil Beds National Monument, P.O. Box 185, Florissant, CO 80816; (719) 748-3253

Garden of the Gods Visitor Center, 30th and Gateway Road, Colorado Springs, CO 80904; (719) 634-6666

Grand Junction Ranger District, Grand Mesa National Forest, 2777 Crossroads Blvd., Grand Junction, CO 81501; (970) 242-8211

Grand Junction Resource Area, Bureau of Land Management, 2815 H Road, Grand Junction, CO 81506; (970) 244-3000

Great San Dunes National Monument, 11999 Highway 150, Mosca, CO 81146-9798; (719) 378-2312

Gunnison Ranger District, Gunnison National Forest, 216 North Colorado, Gunnison, CO; (970) 641-0471

Hahns Peak Ranger District, Routt National Forest, 57 Tenth Street, Steamboat Springs, CO 80487; (970) 879-1870

Holy Cross Ranger District, White River National Forest, P.O. Box 190, Minturn, CO 81645; (970) 827-5715

Leadville Ranger District, San Isabel National Forest, 2015 North Poplar, Leadville, CO 80461; (719) 486-0749

Mesa Verde National Park, P.O. Box 8, Mesa Verde, CO 81330-0008; (970) 529-4465

Ouray Ranger District, Uncompahgre National Forest, 2505 South Townsend, Montrose, CO 81401; (303) 249-3111

Pagosa Ranger District, San Juan National Forest, P.O. Box 310, Pagosa Springs, CO 81147; (970) 264-2268

Pawnee National Grassland, USDA Forest Service, 660 O Street, Greely, CO 80631; (970) 353-5004

Picket Wire Canyonlands, Comanche National Grasslands, 1420 East 3rd Street, La Junta, CO 81050; (719) 384-2181

Pikes Peak Ranger District, Pikes Peak National Forest, 601 South Weber, Colorado Springs, CO 80903; (719) 636-1602

Rocky Mountain National Park, Estes Park, CO 80517; (970) 586-1206

Roxborough State Park, 4751 N. Roxborough Drive, Littleton, CO 80125; (303) 973-3959

Saguache Ranger District, Rio Grande National Forest, 46525 Highway 114, Saguache, CO 81149; (719) 255-2553

Salida Ranger District, San Isabel National Forest, 325 West Rainbow Boulevard, Salida, CO 81201; (719) 539-3591

San Carlos Ranger District, San Isabel National Forest, 3170 Main Street, Cannon City, CO 81212; (719) 269-8500

San Juan Field Office, Bureau of Land Management, 15 Burnett Court, Durango, CO 81301; (970) 247-4874

South Park Ranger District, Pike National Forest, P.O. Box 219, Fairplay, CO 80440; (719) 836-2031

Yampa Ranger District, Routt National Forest, 300 Roselawn, Yampa, CO 80483; (970) 638-4516

Index

238

239

About the Authors

Ralph and Lindy Hopkins have a passion for hiking and interpreting the landscape. Ralph's interests in geology and photography led him to do his master's thesis in geology at Northern Arizona University where he studied and photographed rocks along the rim of the Grand Canyon. Lindy's fascination with nature led her to study the natural sciences at Stanford and the University of Washington. Ralph and Lindy both lecture on nature topics aboard expedition vessels in the world's wild destinations with Lindblad Expeditions. Ralph's photos from their travels have appeared in numerous books, calendars, and magazines, including *National Geographic*, *Geo*, and *Outside*. To view Ralph's online photographic portfolio visit *www.wilderlandimages.com*.

THE MOUNTAINEERS, founded in 1906, is a nonprofit outdoor activity and conservation club with 15,000 members, whose mission is "to explore, study, preserve, and enjoy the natural beauty of the outdoors. . . ." The club sponsors many classes and year-round outdoor activities in the Pacific Northwest, and supports environmental causes through educational activities, sponsoring legislation and presenting educational programs. The Mountaineers Books supports the club's mission by publishing travel and natural history guides, instructional texts, and works on conservation and history.

Send or call for our catalog of more than 450 outdoor titles

The Mountaineers Books
1001 SW Klickitat Way, Suite 201
Seattle, WA 98134
800-553-4453
mbooks@mountaineers.org
www.mountaineersbooks.org